Blue Ginger

EAST MEETS WEST COOKING WITH MING TSAI

Blue Ginger

by Ming Tsai and Arthur Boehm

Photographs by Alan Richardson

Foreword by Ken Hom

Clarkson Potter/Publishers
New York

Some recipes have previously appeared on Food Network's website.

Copyright © 1999 by Ming Tsai
Photographs copyright © 1999 by Alan Richardson

Published by Clarkson Potter/Publishers, New York, New York. Member of the Crown Publishing Group.

Random House, Inc.   New York, Toronto, London, Sydney, Auckland
www.randomhouse.com

CLARKSON N. POTTER is a trademark and POTTER and colophon are registered trademarks of Random House, Inc.

Printed in the United States of America

Design by Subtitle

Library of Congress Cataloging-in-Publication Data

Tsai, Ming, (Ming-Hao)
   Blue Ginger : East meets West cooking with Ming Tsai / by Ming
Tsai and Arthur Boehm.
   Includes index.
   1. Cookery, Asian.   I. Boehm, Arthur.   II. Title.
TX724.5.A1T777   1999
641.595–dc21   99-36393

ISBN 0-609-60530-5

10 9 8 7 6 5

To Polly, my wife, partner, lover, boss,
and, most importantly, best friend.
—M.T.

And for Mildred Boehm in memory, and with love.
—A.B.

Contents

Foreword   viii

Introduction   x

East Meets West Pantry   1

1 Soups   10

2 Dim Sum   36

3 Rice and Noodles   70

4 Seafood   96

5 Birds   122

6 Meat   140

7 Over the Top   164

8 Sides   202

9 Oils, Dips, and Seasonings   224

10 Desserts   242

Mail Order Sources   266

Afterword   267

Acknowledgments   268

Index   269

Foreword

Ethnic cuisines—Chinese, Thai, Vietnamese, Japanese—have long been popular in America, yet, somewhat paradoxically, few of us who cook and enjoy good food have exploited the diversity of food, seasonings, and ingredients from these major cuisines.

This is only somewhat paradoxical. Food preferences are so deeply rooted psychologically and culturally that reluctance to try new foods and flavors is the norm. Surrounded by new and exotic foods, it is natural to cling to the familiar.

Yet we do change, adapt, adopt, and accept. What a food writer calls "the collision of food worlds over the past generation" has resulted in a "permanent cross-fertilization." Our initial reluctance to sample the new is rapidly being overcome, and our cooking is being revitalized by an uncharacteristic openness to foreign ingredients and techniques.

These changes are far more noticeable now than they were when I wrote my first cookbook over twenty years ago. The number and variety of restaurants featuring "immigrant" cuisines have grown impressively. This melding of the familiar and exotic is part of a growing trend toward what I called "East-West Cuisines" in 1980, a cooking style blending compatible ingredients and techniques that were formerly isolated within Asian or European kitchens. Its increasing acceptance is no doubt related to the influence of la nouvelle cuisine, an approach that consciously draws upon foreign foods, flavors, and techniques, and to the increasing internationalization of so many aspects of modern life: pizzas in Hong Kong, sushi bars in Paris, and blue jeans everywhere.

The increasing acceptance of Asian influences on American cooking, however, is perhaps due to a long-established tradition of Chinese restaurants. This association has been given richer meaning since the opening of China to the West, the emergence of Japan and other Southeast Asian countries as economic powerhouses, and a renewed interest manifest in many films and books. In regard to the nations of the "Pacific Rim," there has been a surge of American involvement, trade, and tourism. And, at home, the influx of Asian immigrants of all nationalities over the past forty years has increased remarkably.

These new arrivals brought with them their traditional tastes in foods, spices, and flavorings. Many opened specialty food shops catering to their traditional cuisines; many others opened restaurants offering native dishes and menus. The result has been to expand the culinary horizons of all of us.

Familiarity does not necessarily breed contempt; rather, it often allows for a relaxed and respectful approach to what was once strange. American cuisine is now receiving an education of the palate. These immigrant cuisines are covered in cookbooks, magazines, newspapers, and television series, including that of Ming Tsai. Today even traditional supermarkets stock fresh ginger, coriander, chiles, and other ingredients once found only in encyclopedias. Along with roasting and boiling, we now use our woks and know how to stir-fry vegetables and steam whole fish. Along with boiled corn, we now know and enjoy pita bread, tofu, soy sauce, and sushi.

Ming Tsai's book takes these culinary developments in what I think is a new, exciting direction. The direction is a very personal one; the collision of food worlds directly parallels his own history. Born in America to Chinese parents, Ming Tsai, who was raised in Ohio, is much traveled and has worked in Asia as well as Europe, especially in France. He represents both East and West. He has adopted and blended their better aspects. As a chef and television personality, he is ideally suited to assist in the amalgamation of these different culinary traditions.

Blue Ginger arose out of his efforts to blend the cuisines of Asia, America, and Europe. I believe, however, the results are pertinent for cooks everywhere. I know you will agree with me that the richness to be discovered in Ming's book of blending East and West cuisines more than compensates for any perceived losses in our traditional ways. The message of his cuisine is delight in human creativity and discovery, and the enjoyment of simple pleasures. I wish you a happy voyage on this culinary adventure with Ming Tsai as your guide.

Ken Hom
Catus, France

Introduction

When people ask me to define my cooking, I'm happy to oblige. It's a subject close to my heart.

I begin with the obvious: my food is based on the ingredients and cooking techniques of both East and West. Too often, however, so-called fusion cooking (*con-fusion* cooking, some of us call it) produces chaos on the plate and in the mouth. This results from not respecting a culture's ingredients and the traditional techniques that turn them into wonderful eating.

Successful East-West cooking, the kind I strive to prepare, finds just the right, harmonious way to combine distinct culinary approaches. My Savory Braised Oxtail with Preserved Lemon Polenta, for example, joins the immediacy and bold flavors of an Eastern braise with Western cornmeal-preparation techniques to produce completely satisfying food. When a dish is not just new but better—when I can find a superior way to celebrate oxtail's earthiness, say, or the deep sour tang of preserved lemons, and then join the two—that's real East-West cooking.

It took me a while to "discover" this cuisine. Unlike other Western chefs who blend culinary traditions, I began by "cooking East." My parents were born in Beijing, so I grew up steeped in the joys of the Chinese table. I watched my mom, dad, and grandparents cook and later joined them at the stove at home and at the Mandarin Kitchen, a Chinese restaurant they owned in my hometown of Dayton, Ohio.

Though I studied to be a mechanical engineer, my thoughts kept returning to food and the pleasure of making it. My first trip to Paris helped convince me that food was my career, and I established French cuisine as my second major culinary influence. Intrigued by French dessert and bread making, so unlike anything done in the Asian kitchen, I enrolled at the Cordon Bleu and worked at the famed food emporium Fauchon with master pastry chef Pierre Hermé. I then became the sous chef at the restaurant Natacha in Paris. When one of my first sauces there, a black bean beurre rouge, was a hit, I knew I'd found a real way to combine French and Chinese cooking traditions.

I refined my approach at Silks in San Francisco working with Asian cooking expert Ken Hom, a founding father of East-West cuisine. From there I went to Japan to master sushi rice and reveled in the pure taste and artful economy of Japanese food presentation.

When I returned home, I opened a Southeast Asian restaurant in Palo Alto, California, then became an executive chef in Santa Fe, where I did East Meets Southwest cuisine, experimenting with such local ingredients as corn, avocados, and chiles.

When I opened Blue Ginger with Polly Talbott Tsai, my wife and partner, I made a vow to use only the best ingredients, perfectly prepared, to produce true East-West dishes—food that would excite diners through its balance of flavors, contrasting ingredient textures, colors, and temperatures, and that reflected a happy mingling of Chinese, Southeast Asian, Japanese, French, and American culinary traditions.

I think I've succeeded. The positive response I got to Blue Ginger's food made me very happy. At the same time, I began my Food Network show *East Meets West with Ming Tsai*, which was also well received. Demonstrating my dishes on TV, I became reacquainted with my love of teaching, of showing people how to have real success in the kitchen.

This book was born of that love. I created it to show you what I do in the kitchen and how you can get the same delicious results I do every day, to demystify Asian cooking techniques and ingredients, and to help you have a great time in the kitchen and at the table.

To that end, I've provided a full range of my East-West dishes for all occasions, starting with fabulous soups, like Corn Lemongrass Soup with Lobster Salad, or mouthwatering dim sum, such as Crab and Fennel Wontons with Mango-Lime Puree. For entrees, there are rice and noodle dishes—you must try Sweet and Spicy Beef Noodles—bird and meat dishes, and savory seafood specialties, including my signature Blue Ginger Sea Bass with Soba Noodle Sushi. For special times, when you really want to flex your cooking muscles, there's a whole chapter devoted to blow-out dishes like Foie Gras and Morel Shu Mai with Caramelized Sauternes-Shallot Broth and Truffled Edamame Puree—even a game plan for a complete Chinese Fire Pot feast. To bring your meals to a spectacular close, I include fabulous desserts such as Lemongrass Parfait with Pineapple Salsa. And I don't forget wine, a natural partner of good food. You'll find recommendations for wine styles and personal wine favorites that I know you'll like.

Cooking is so joyful! As a chef, I get to please people in so many ways. I want to pass my passion on to you in dishes that reflect so much pleasurable eating over time, but which are also excitingly new. When we sat down at table, the Tsais would often say *qing-chi*—please dine! Let me also add *bon appétit,* peace, and good eating!

—Ming Tsai

East Meets West Pantry

Oils and Vinegars

Canola oil. Lower in saturated fat (it contains about 6 percent) than any other vegetable oil, canola oil is expressed from rapeseed, from which we get broccoli rape (or rabe). It also contains omega-3 fatty acids, the polyunsaturated fat said to lower blood levels of cholesterol and triglycerides. I prefer it not only for health reasons but because of its clean, "neutral" flavor.

Chinese black vinegar. Used traditionally in braises and sauces, this dark vinegar with a rich but mild taste is made from rice, wheat, millet, or sorghum. Like balsamic vinegar, which it somewhat resembles, Chinese black vinegar can have, if well aged and produced, a striking complexity of flavor and aroma. I prefer Chinkiang black vinegars, which are named for the Chinese province of their production and made from glutinous rice and malt. They have a pleasing mild sweetness.

Peanut oil. This golden oil has long been used as an everyday cooking oil in China because of its relatively mild taste and high smoke point. I prefer cold-pressed and semi-refined peanut oils, which have a definite though not overwhelming peanut flavor. Look for Chinese or Hong Kong brands—my favorite is Lion & Globe—which are usually available in Asian markets.

Rice wine vinegar. This white to golden vinegar with a light clean taste adds a mild acidity to foods. Popular brands include the Japanese Marukan and the Chinese Narcissus. Avoid, in any case, seasoned white wine vinegars, which are commonly available.

Toasted sesame oil. Made from toasted sesame seeds, this thick, rich oil is golden to dark brown in color and marvelously aromatic. Unlike lighter, almost flavorless sesame oils, which can be used in cooking, the toasted variety is used as a seasoning only.

Wrappers

Banana leaves. These natural wrappers, long used in Mexico, the Caribbean, and Southeast Asia to enclose food for steaming, are most widely available in Latin American markets. They come fresh or frozen—fresh are best. Rinse and dry fresh leaves before using them, and cut away their fibrous stems. Already-cut 1-pound packages of frozen leaves are convenient; defrost these at room temperature, unfold them carefully, and cut them to size. Wipe all banana leaves gently with a damp cloth before using them.

Dumpling skins. Available fresh and frozen in several shapes and thicknesses, these come most often in 1-pound packages. Labels usually indicate the kind of dumpling—potstickers, boiled dumplings, and so on—for which the skins are intended. Most of these are round and about $3\frac{1}{2}$ inches in diameter, but thickness varies from about $\frac{1}{32}$ to $\frac{1}{16}$ inch thick. When substituting these wrappers for the homemade versions in the book, use wrappers designed for the dumplings you're making. All dumpling wrappers keep well for up to a week in the fridge, or for one to two months, frozen. Defrost frozen wrappers overnight in the refrigerator before using them.

Lotus leaves. Taken from the lotus plant, which grows throughout Asia, these large leaves (11 to 14 inches in diameter) add both flavor and a subtle perfume to foods they're added to (when fresh) or enclose (when dried). They're available in Asian markets and will keep indefinitely if stored in a cool, dry place.

Lumpia/Menlo wrappers. Sometimes called Shanghai-style egg roll wrappers, these skins are used typically to prepare lumpia, savory Filipino egg rolls. The wrappers are made from flour and water, or cornstarch, eggs, and water, and are sold frozen in 1-pound packages of about thirty-two wrappers. Although they can be eaten as is, they deep-fry to a delicate crispness I really enjoy.

Rice paper. An essential ingredient in Vietnamese and other Southeast Asian cuisines, rice paper is used to make spring and summer rolls, and other savory tidbits. The wrappers, which are prepared from rice flour, water, and salt, are sold in packages of 50 to 100 and must be softened in warm water before use to make them pliable. You'll need 8- to 10-inch round sheets for the recipes in this book.

Wonton wrappers. These skins, made from flour, eggs, and salt, come packaged in a variety of forms—round and square, thick and thin. I use square wrappers for the recipes in this book and prefer the thinnest available—usually labeled "extra thin." The skins can be used to make shu mai and ravioli and will last refrigerated for about a week, or frozen for up to two months.

Dried Seaweeds

Hijiki. Brittle and black, hijiki comes in $1/2$- to 1-inch strands. It has a mild aniselike flavor and is high in calcium. I use hijiki in salads and soups. It must be rehydrated in warm water for about twenty minutes to be usable.

Konbu. Available in pliable sheets, konbu or kelp tastes delightfully of the sea. The Japa-nese use it primarily to make dashi, the mother stock of their cooking, from which miso soup is prepared. Konbu sheets are packaged in various sizes; I use the smaller sheets (roughly 6 by 7 inches).

Nori. Used preeminently as a maki sushi wrapper, nori comes in thin sheets of iridescent black, dark green, or purplish seaweed. Buy toasted nori (labeled yakinori), which is usually sold flat in packages. The sheets measure 7 to 8 inches square. Nori, which has a sweet ocean taste, is extremely rich in protein, vitamins, calcium, iron, and other minerals. Unused nori should be wrapped in plastic and stored in a cool, dark place.

Wakame. Bright green when reconstituted, this strandlike seaweed has a lovely ocean taste and pleasing slippery texture. It is also extremely nutritious. Soak wakame in warm water for twenty minutes to soften it.

Noodles and Rice

Bean threads. I'm a great fan of these slithery noodles, which are sometimes called cellophane noodles or soybean vermicelli. Made from mung bean flour, these thin, translucent noodles are sold dried in packages from 1 ounce to 1 pound. They are never cooked to soften them, but soaked in warm water (or in hot soup) until tender.

Lo mein. These delicious egg and wheat flour noodles are one of the most commonly used in Chinese noodle cookery. They're available dried in cellophane bags or fresh in the refrigerator sections of many Asian markets and come in various widths or diameters, flat and round. I recommend the flat noodles for savory dishes and the round for brothy preparations. Fresh noodles can be stored in the refrigerator for up to four days or frozen up to three months. There is no need to defrost frozen noodles before using them.

Rice stick noodles. Like bean threads, though starchier, these mildly flavored rice-flour noodles are never cooked to soften them, but soaked in warm water instead. Rice stick noodles come in a variety of thicknesses; I recommend the flat kind that are about $\frac{1}{4}$ inch thick.

Shanghai noodles. Not a traditional noodle type, these $\frac{1}{8}$-inch-thick egg noodles labeled "Shanghai" are wonderfully appealing. They're usually packaged by the pound in plastic bags and freeze well. If you can't find them, substitute any thick fresh or dried spaghetti.

Soba noodles. Made with buckwheat flour, this earthy Japanese noodle is traditionally served cold with a dashi-soy dipping sauce; it is also used in broths. My favorite soba, called cha soba, is flavored and colored with green tea. It can be used interchangeably with regular soba noodles.

Udon noodles. Simple but delicious, these are the most commonly available Japanese noodles. You'll find udon, which are made with wheat flour, in various thicknesses, both flat and round, fresh and dried. The fresh are preferable.

Wonton noodles. A very thin Chinese egg noodle, these are the equivalent of Western angel hair pasta. Available fresh and dried, wonton noodles were used traditionally in soups containing the dumplings from which they took their name.

Glutinous rice. Not to be confused with the short-, medium-, or long-grain rices eaten by most Asians daily, glutinous or sweet rice is reserved for dishes in which the rice's stickiness is preferred. These include snacks and desserts. Most often sold as "sweet rice," glutinous rice must be rinsed thoroughly and soaked overnight before steaming.

Sushi rice. This short-grain rice, which is moderately sticky when cooked, is perfect for preparing rolled and hand-shaped sushi. Domestically grown sushi rice is now available and marketed under brand names including Calrose and Kokuho Rose. Labeling for this rice is often inconsistent and nondescriptive; look for the phrases "new rice," "new variety rice," or "Japanese rice" on the package.

Seasonings, Condiments, and Aromatics

Curry powder. There is no such thing as curry powder in Indian cooking, as most cooks know. Tinned or bottled curry powders are in fact convenient versions of the spice mixtures that Indian cooks compose daily. Curry powders can be excellent, however, depending on their maker and the product's freshness. My preferred blend is referred to as and often labeled Madras curry powder, a mixture favored in the southern Indian state of the same name. Most often a blend of curry leaves, turmeric, coriander, cumin, cinnamon, cloves, chili pepper, bay leaves, fenugreek, allspice, and black pepper, it has a mellow balance and is neither too hot nor too mild. Look for brands in which bits of bay leaf are visible, which I find the most flavorful. Like all curry powders, however, it must be used when fresh.

Fermented black beans. This pungent ingredient is an ancient Chinese cooking staple. To prepare it, soy beans are partially decomposed, then dried and sometimes salted. Store the beans, which are usually sold in bags, away from light in a cool place; they will last indefinitely. Always rinse fermented black beans well before using them to remove excess salt.

Fish sauce. Called *nam pla* in Thailand and *nuoc mam* in Vietnam, this Southeast Asian staple is a product of salted and fermented anchovies and is used there as the Chinese use soy sauce. I prefer the Thai Three Crab Brand, which has a fresh sea taste and slight sweetness. Though fish sauce will keep on the shelf, it is best stored in the fridge once opened.

Five-spice powder. This tantalizing spice blend, which consists usually of star anise, Szechwan peppercorns, clove, fennel, and cinnamon, has been used in China since ancient times. Because the number five is significant in Chinese belief, the five-spice blend is said to be beneficial to health. True or not, the mixture is a wonderful addition to a wide range of dishes. As with all spices, buy small quantities, store tightly in a cool, dry place, and check periodically to make sure the blend is still aromatic.

Galangal. A relative of ginger, this root (actually an underground stem) is a staple of Southeast Asian cooking. Galangal, which is also called blue ginger, is more sour-peppery than ginger and can be distinguished from it by its pink shoots and brown skin. Shred or slice galangal finely and use it to complement dishes that would otherwise benefit from a ginger-like seasoning. Wrapped well, it will remain fresh in the fridge for up to three weeks.

Hoisin sauce. A soy bean derivative, this reddish brown sauce is both sweet and spicy. Its composition varies from brand to brand but almost always consists of some combination of soybean paste, sugar, garlic, and vinegar. The Chinese use hoisin sauce as a condiment and glaze for roasted meats, most commonly with Peking duck. I use it often in marinades and with grilled dishes. When adding it to dishes, always cook hoisin in oil for a few minutes to rid it of its raw bean flavor.

Kechap manis. Indonesia's traditional soy sauce, this flavoring ingredient is thicker and sweeter than its Chinese or Japanese cousins. It excels as a marinade ingredient and may be used in place of Soy Syrup (see page 236).

Mirin. Referred to sometimes as Japanese sweet sake, mirin is rice wine with added sugar. Mirin is an essential ingredient in Japanese cooking and adds a subtle sweetness to many dishes; it is also used, traditionally, to glaze foods. Try to buy hon-mirin, which is naturally brewed and contains natural sugars, as opposed to aji-mirin, which can contain sweeteners.

Miso. A savory fermented soybean paste and seasoning, miso is the primary ingredient in the Japanese soup for which it's named. There are four main types: white miso (shiro-miso), made with rice (I use this in my signature Blue Ginger Sea Bass); yellow miso (shinshū-miso), tart, fairly salty, and the most commonly available rice type; red miso, made with barley, deeply flavored, and available in sweet and salty versions; and the dark brown bean miso, which is robust, very rich and salty. For the recipes in this book, I specify the lighter misos. Available in cans, jars, and plastic tubs, miso should be stored tightly covered in the fridge, where it will last up to three months.

Oyster sauce. This Cantonese ingredient and condiment is made from oysters, water, and salt (and sometimes cornstarch). Misuse and inferior brands have given the sauce a poor reputation, but it can be a delicious addition to a wide range of dishes. Sold usually in bottles, the best brands have more rich oyster flavor and less cornstarch. Look for oyster sauce that does not contain MSG or other additives—I recommend Amoy or Lee Kum Kee brands. Stored in the fridge, oyster sauce will last indefinitely.

Ponzu. A much-favored Japanese dipping sauce, made with a blend of citrus juices and, usually, rice vinegar and soy sauce, among other ingredients. It can be purchased in Japanese markets or you may substitute a blend of equal quantities of lime and lemon juices.

Rock sugar. The Chinese have used sugar in savory dishes since ancient times and have developed a repertoire of this sweetener. Among these is rock (or yellow) sugar, which adds subtle, mellow flavor, as well as a translucent finish, to Chinese braised or "red roasted" dishes. For savory cooking I prefer rock sugar to its white, granulated counterpart and urge you to buy this large-crystal sweetener.

Salt. I'm often told that salt is salt—not true! Unless specified otherwise, all of my recipes call for Kosher salt, which is coarser than table salt. Some specify sea salt, which is available in fine or coarse grains (the very large-grain variety, known commonly as gros sel, requires a table mill) and has a clean tastiness other salts lack. Its relatively large flakes also make it a pleasure to use. Of all sea salts, the French fleur de sel is considered the finest. Taken from the crust of salt-pond evaporation, it is delicate but also intensely flavored.

Shaoxing wine. This drinking and cooking staple originated in the Zhejiang province. Known also as Chinese rice wine, it is aged eighteen months to one hundred years—these venerable bottles are much prized. Shaoxing, which is made with millet and yeast in addition to rice and water, has a flavor similar to dry sherry, which is a suitable substitute for it. Avoid bottles labeled "Shaoxing cooking wine." Don't mistake Shaoxing for Chinese rice wine vinegar.

Soy sauce. Sometimes referred to as light or thin soy sauce to distinguish it from dark and mushroom-flavored varieties, this essential Asian cooking ingredient has been used for more than three thousand years. Soy sauce is made from a soybean, flour, and water mixture that is naturally fermented and allowed to age. Soy sauces vary in richness of flavor, saltiness, and viscosity depending on the place of their manufacture and the care with which they're produced. I prefer Japanese Kikkoman Soy Sauce, Chinese Pearl River Bridge Superior Soy Sauce (not to be confused with "soy superior sauce," a descriptive term for some dark soy sauce, see below), or Koon Chun's Thin Soy Sauce.

Soy sauce, dark. Aged for much longer periods than regular or light soy sauce, and sometimes containing molasses for flavor depth, dark soy sauce is used in dishes (never as a condiment) for hearty flavor. It is actually less salty than light soy sauce. This sauce is often labeled "black soy sauce" or "soy superior sauce." Brands I prefer include Koon Chun Black Soy Sauce and Amoy's.

Szechwan (Sichuan) peppercorns. The berries of a shrub from the prickly ash family, these budlike peppercorns have been favored by Szechwan cooks for millennia. Before trying them, people expect the peppercorns to have a pungent taste, but their flavor is subtle—clean, somewhat woody and slightly numbing to the tongue. Often combined with salt or other peppers for seasoning, the peppercorns should always be toasted before grinding them in a pepper mill, clean coffee grinder, or with a mortar and pestle.

To toast the peppercorns (or sesame seeds), heat a wok or heavy skillet over medium heat. Add the peppercorns in a single layer and toast them, stirring, until they're fragrant and on the point of smoking, about 3 minutes. Remove from the pan and cool before grinding.

Chiles and Chili Ingredients

Achiote, compressed and achiote powder. Sometimes called annatto, these brick-red seeds, taken from a tropical tree, have long been used to color foods. As a seasoning these provide a pleasingly musty flavor. Buy achiote, if you can, in compressed form. Available in Mexican and Latin American markets, this is actually a mixture of the seeds of other spices, garlic, and vinegar. If not available, use powdered achiote.

Ancho chile powder. Based on ground dried ancho chile, this spicy blend can also contain such ingredients as dried oregano and cumin. I prefer ancho chile powder to other kinds because of its deep flavor and attractive color.

Chipotle in adobo sauce. This canned condiment consists of dried, smoked jalapeños in a tomato, onion, paprika, and vinegar marinade. I like to puree the mixture and use it as a smoky-spicy ingredient in soups, dumplings, and sauces. Chipotle in adobo comes in 2- to 3-ounce cans. It's wise to puree an entire can (see page 51), use what you need, and store the rest for future cooking or use as an accompaniment to burgers, ribs, or similar dishes. The puree will last for months.

Jalapeño chiles. The most commonly used chile in Mexican cooking, jalapeños are on average 2 inches long and about 1 inch in diameter. Dark green in color, they range in heat from hot to very hot. Fresh jalapeños are widely available.

Sambal oelek. There are many hot chile pepper pastes used as table condiments in China and Southeast Asia; sambal oelek is the most common and most popular. Containing chiles, salt, vinegar, and sometimes garlic and tamarind, the fiery paste gives food a powerful flavor boost. Store sambal oelek in the refrigerator, where it will last indefinitely.

Serrano chiles. These slender green chiles, about 1 1/2 inches long, are a staple of Mexican cooking. They have a pronounced heat and fresh chile taste. Greenish yellow or red varieties are sometimes available.

Sriracha. A smooth, spicy, garlicky Vietnamese chile puree.

Thai bird chiles. Also called bird's eye chiles and bird peppers, these are especially fiery, tiny Thai peppers used both fresh and dried. Their name derives from the belief that they were harvested originally by birds who were said to enjoy them! Red or green and bullet-shaped, the peppers should be used with care.

Other ingredients

Bonito flakes. Used primarily in the preparation of dashi, the Japanese cooking stock, these pinkish flakes come from dried bonito. Buy them in bags or boxes in stores with a rapid turnover, because the flakes are perishable. Store in airtight containers.

Bok choy. Also called Chinese white cabbage, this staple of the Chinese kitchen is a lovely, all-purpose vegetable. Of its many varieties, the most frequently available kind has long white stems and large green corrugated leaves. Very small heads will be labeled baby bok choy. To prepare bok choy, separate the stems and rinse the vegetable well, or cut the cabbage as your recipe directs, wash and drain it well. Store bok choy well wrapped in paper towels in your refrigerator's vegetable crisper.

Choy sum. Sometimes called flowering cabbage for its relatively slender stalks and tiny yellow blooms, this Chinese cabbage has a particularly delicate taste. Wash the leaves well and prepare choy sum as you would bok choy.

Shanghai cabbage. This delectable Chinese cabbage is characterized by its curved, concave stems and smooth petal-like leaves. Small plants (about 6 inches long) are the most readily available in our markets. Prepare and store them as you would other bok choy varieties.

Napa cabbage. Known also as Peking cabbage, this barrel-shaped vegetable has a mild, nonmustardy taste. Its crinkly, tightly packed leaves are delightfully crisp. Buy firm, light-colored heads. Well wrapped, the cabbage should last in the fridge for up to one month.

Chinese chives. Flat-leaved and with a garlicky pungency, green Chinese chives are widely available in Asian markets. They are sold in large bunches and are 10 to 14 inches long. They will last, well wrapped in paper towels and placed in a plastic bag, in the fridge for about two days. Do not confuse Chinese green chives with the yellow or hollow flowering variety (which are the stems of the same plant) or with garlic chives, the flowering stalks of the garlic plant, although any of these would be a good substitute for the regular kind.

Chinese long beans. Growing up to three feet in length, these beans are a long-favored Chinese vegetable. They lack sweetness, but have a subtle taste and pleasing crunchiness that make them a good addition to numerous dishes. Buy thin firm beans that are without dark discolorations, taking into account that the tips of the beans are usually black.

Chinese dried black mushrooms. Harvested from fallen trees, these highly esteemed fungi are never actually black, but light to dark brown in color. Their succulent texture and smoky flavor make them welcome in many savory dishes.

In the market, you'll find many dried black mushroom grades; the most popular (and expensive) are the large, light brown ones with cracked surfaces. Buy these, if your pocketbook permits—but moderately priced varieties are good, too. All grades need to be rinsed and then soaked, covered in warm water for approximately 20 minutes to rehydrate them. Once softened, remove their tough stems and use the caps only. Save the soaking water for other cooking.

Store dried mushrooms in a cool, dry place in an airtight container—or freeze them, if you don't use the mushrooms often.

Coconut milk. An extraction made by seeping freshly grated coconut in boiling water or milk, coconut milk is available in Asian markets and many supermarkets. The milk is used in Southeast Asian rice desserts, curries, and shellfish recipes. Because coconut milk spoils quickly, it is wise to freeze any unused portion. Don't confuse coconut milk with the liquid found inside the coconut, which is insufficiently rich for most recipes that call for the milk. My favorite brand is Chaokoh from Thailand.

Daikon sprouts. Shoots of the long white radish that is probably Japan's most fundamental vegetable, these are a popular garnish and salad ingredient. I like their tender freshness and spiciness and use them similarly. Buy the sprouts—sometimes labeled radish sprouts—in 4-ounce hinged plastic containers, alive in a growing medium.

Dried scallops. Before refrigeration and other modern methods of preservation, fish and shellfish in China were commonly dried. Among these, scallops became an esteemed ingredient, sold in fine shops for high fees. Dried scallops (the species used is the sea scallop-like conpoy) are still in demand as a flavoring for soups, sauces, and other dishes, and are still relatively costly. A small quantity, however, goes a long way, because the scallops, once rehydrated, are shredded and used in small quantities. Buy dried scallops in a market that sells enough of them to ensure their "freshness," and store them in a covered jar on the shelf. If the scallops aren't available, you can substitute dried shrimp for them in most "dried scallop" recipes.

Edamames. Why haven't people yet discovered these young soybeans in their fuzzy green pods? Available fresh in Asian markets, usually from June through October, the beans, taken straight from the pods, are great for munching, and much better for you than chips or other snack foods. I like them best, however, cooked as you would fava beans to make luscious purees. When buying edamames (the name means "branch beans" in Japanese) look for firm, green pods. Frozen edamames are also available, and work well in purees.

Foie gras. One of the world's great eating experiences, foie gras is the fattened liver of ducks and geese. Fresh domestic foie gras, taken from ducks only, is now available and it is excellent. Most of us will have to order our foie gras (see Mail Order Sources, page 266), though specialty butchers often have it on hand or can get it for you. Packed in cryovac, the liver is usually sold whole, though now you can get it portioned or in thick slices. This luxurious treat is always expensive, but several grades are available, designated A, B, and C in descending order of quality. For the recipes in this book in which the liver is pureed to flavor and enrich sauces or stuffings, B and C grades are recommended. (See Tip, page 193, for foie gras handling information.)

Ginger. Most of us are familiar with this fresh root (actually a rhizome), which is one of the primary and indispensable flavorings of Chinese cooking. Available in large "hands," or in smaller portions, fresh ginger should be firm and glossy-skinned, without wrinkles or fibrousness where the knobs have been broken. Store the root, wrapped in paper towels and within plastic bags, in the vegetable crisper of your fridge. Unless otherwise specified, the ginger called for in this book should always be peeled before using. Baby or young ginger, if available, is also excellent; it has a little less bite than the older variety.

Kaffir lime leaves. The leaves of the kaffir lime tree, this Thai seasoning has a delightfully pungent limelike scent. Available fresh, frozen, or dried, in the order of desirability, the leaves are a welcome addition to a wide range of dishes. Remove the center rib if the leaf will be eaten.

La chang. The Chinese have made these dry, hard, definitely sweet sausages for millennia.

Sold in strings of two, with each measuring about six inches long, la chang must be steamed or otherwise cooked to be palatable. Most la chang are made with pork and pork fat and this is the variety I have in mind for the recipes calling for this ingredient in the book. La chang will last in the fridge for weeks or, well wrapped, for months in the freezer.

Lemongrass. Yellow green in color and resembling large scallions, lemongrass is a preeminent flavoring ingredient in Thai cuisine. I rely on its aromatic citrus taste in a wide range of dishes, from soups to desserts. Store fresh lemongrass in moist paper towels in the fridge, where it will keep for up to two weeks. In cooking, only the portion of the stalk from the base to the point at which the leaves branch is used.

Lychee honey. This amber-colored honey has the perfume of a lychee and a rich, deep honey flavor that's particularly pleasing. Buy it in Asian markets; if unavailable, you may use any mildly flavored honey in its place.

Mizuna. Feathery leaved and green in color, this delightfully flavored, slightly tart lettuce is Asian in origin. If you can't find it in your market, substitute baby mustard greens or mâche.

Panko. These buttery bread crumbs are used in Japanese cooking to coat foods for frying. Panko is available in cellophane packages, in which it lasts indefinitely if the packages are unopened. Once opened, freeze unused portions.

Rock shrimp. I call for rock shrimp often in my cooking. Firm in texture and with a delicious lobsterlike flavor, these small shrimp are caught in Florida and then shipped nationwide. They arrive in the market headless and peeled because their shells are hard to remove. They work very well chopped or pureed to make shrimp toast and other hors d'oeuvres, or whole in noodle dishes.

Shiso leaves. A member of the mint family and resembling basil in taste and aroma, these leaves come in green and red varieties. The green is the most widely available and also the most fragrant. Shiso leaves are available stacked in packages and make a lovely garnish. Green shiso is also used in sushi.

Tatsoi. A spicy lettuce with a mustardy taste, tatsoi has rounded leaves that are green rimmed. Its pungent flavor has made it a longtime Asian favorite. If unavailable, substitute baby spinach leaves or watercress.

Tea leaves: Oolong, jasmine, and black lychee. Tea, which is made from the leaves of an evergreen shrub, has been drunk for pleasure since the fifth or sixth century A.D.

Oolong tea leaves are partially fermented; this results in a tea that has the color, flavor, and aroma of fermented black tea and the green freshness of unfermented tea. Oolong tea leaves are widely available.

Jasmine tea leaves, which are green, are steamed and then scented with jasmine flowers. The tea made from them is delicately aromatic and makes a lovely dessert flavoring.

Black lychee tea leaves, which are fermented, produce a brisk tea with an inherent sweetness. It's worth searching out this tea, particularly for summer enjoyment—it's incredibly good iced. Look for black lychee tea in Asian markets.

Tofu. An ancient Chinese and Japanese product, tofu is made from curdled soy bean milk. Depending on how much liquid remains after the curds are pressed into cakes, the resulting tofu can be custardlike or chewy, and may be labeled soft, medium, or firm. "Silken" tofu is the most delicate kind, even if labeled "firm." Tofu is a nutritional powerhouse, protein-rich and also low in fat and cholesterol. It is sold packaged in water, vacuum-packed, and in bulk, and used in a wide variety of dishes, including stir-frys, salads, and soups. Tofu is extremely perishable. Refrigerate unused tofu promptly in its tub or pouch, or transfer it to water. Change the water daily.

Togarashi. Small Japanese red chiles, these are available fresh or dried. The dried variety is also sold ground, which is the form of togarashi I generally use. Bottled ground togarashi is available in Japanese specialty markets and other Asian food stores.

Truffles. One of the world's great culinary luxuries, truffles, both black and white, have been prized since ancient times. All truffles are fungi that grow underground in symbiosis with the roots of certain trees; black truffles, which I use in my recipes, are harvested primarily in France, where they are traditionally sniffed out by pigs and dogs. Fresh black truffles are expensive—if you are going to make the investment, buy them only in season (December through March) and from a reputable source (see Mail Order Sources, page 266). Look for truffles that are firm to the touch and highly aromatic. Use them within three days of purchasing, and store them well wrapped in the fridge.

Truffle oil. I'm a great fan of this product, which consists of black or white truffle-infused olive oil. Available typically in two- or four-ounce bottles at specialty markets or by mail (see Mail Order Sources, page 266), the oils are a fine way to get truffle aroma and taste at a reasonable price. For the recipes in this book, I call for white truffle oil.

Wasabi tobiko. Prepared with flying fish roe, which is crunchy and has a definite but pleasing fish taste, this caviar is seasoned with wasabi. It has a nice kick and makes a piquant garnishing ingredient.

Chapter 1

Soups

SOUP AND I GO WAY BACK. AS A CHUNKY LITTLE KID, I'D DEVOUR TWO OR THREE BOWLS AT A TIME, SO I WOULDN'T EAT TOO MUCH OF THE MORE FATTENING STUFF TO FOLLOW. IT WASN'T A HARDSHIP; THE STEAMING NOODLE SOUPS AND WONTON-FILLED BROTHS WERE DEEPLY SATISFYING DISHES.

Later, as an adult and chef, I indulged my love of soup in other ways. Staying close to my Asian culinary roots, but also exploring the joys of the European and American tables, I'd devise richly garnished soups with layers of flavor. And I learned how exciting it could be to contrast ingredient textures and temperatures in a single bowl. The Corn Lemongrass Soup with Lobster Salad and Ming's Pho, for example, counterpoint hot and cold, chewy and crunchy. Similarly, Miso Broth with Tatsoi-Enoki Salad presents a soothing broth enlivened by a crisp salad garnish. I love these soup and salad combos, which can stand on their own as perfect light dinners.

As sous chef at Silks in San Francisco, I made a different soup daily. Not every one was great, of course, but I did learn soup. And one of the most important lessons I learned was to begin soup making with a good stock. That's basic.

Stock is easily made, cooks unattended, and can be stored conveniently for later use. With a rich chicken stock like the one on page 14 on hand, your success with homemade soup is almost assured.

Because of its inherent ability to warm and comfort or cool and refresh, soup is particularly seasonal. Roasted Garlic and Celeriac Soup with Wild Mushroom Ragout, an earthy, deep-flavored brew, is perfect winter fare. Asian Gazpacho with Cilantro-Jicama Cream, with its touch of light richness, is, of course, great summer eating.

At Blue Ginger, we sometimes present soup as an *amuse bouche,* providing small portions in espresso cups to excite the appetite. Follow our example, with, say, the Thai-Spiced Mussel Soup with Leeks and Carrot Spaghetti, a light but spicy brew, and see how happily guests respond. The first thing that people eat when they sit down at a table is very important. Start with a great soup in small quantities for a VIP dinner and you're really in business.

Remember, when serving hot soup, to heat your soup bowls. Unlike other kinds of food that can be served after some cooling off, these soups demand to be eaten hot. Also, the more steam, the more aroma. This doesn't mean, however, that soup has to be prepared right before you serve it. Most soups freeze beautifully. Make double the quantity of a puree or broth, freeze it in well-sealed containers, and defrost it overnight in the fridge. With soup on hand, ready for family or guests, or for yourself, there's pleasure and comfort ahead.

Chicken Stock

Good chicken stock—light but deeply flavored—makes a huge difference to your cooking. Preparing it is no big deal; once you assemble the ingredients, the actual cooking involves little attention on your part. Make as large a quantity of stock at one time as you can manage and freeze it in 1-quart containers; it will last for up to three months.

Note that I don't call for salt in my stock recipes. This makes these stocks particularly versatile, as they add no saltiness of their own to dishes in which they're used.

MAKES 4 TO 6 QUARTS

5 to 6 pounds chicken backs, necks, wings, and reserved trimmings
3 large carrots, washed but unpeeled, roughly chopped
2 large onions, roughly chopped
3 celery stalks, roughly chopped
1 head garlic, halved
3 sprigs fresh thyme or 1 tablespoon dried
$1\frac{1}{2}$ teaspoons black peppercorns
$\frac{1}{2}$ bunch flat-leaf parsley
2 bay leaves

1. Rinse the chicken parts under cold water. Place the parts in a large pot, add cold water to cover (about 2 gallons), and bring to a boil. Reduce the heat and simmer. Using a skimmer, remove surface scum as it forms. Continue to simmer for 30 to 45 minutes.

2. Add the carrots, onions, celery, garlic, thyme, peppercorns, parsley, and bay leaves. If necessary add more water to keep the solids covered. Simmer, uncovered, occasionally skimming off fat, until the stock is richly flavored, about 3 hours.

3. Fill the sink with water and add ice. Strain the stock into another pot, discarding the solids, then submerge the pot in the cold water. When cooled, refrigerate to chill completely. Remove any remaining solidified fat with a large spoon. Use the stock within 3 days, or freeze.

MING'S TIP: TO MAKE A DARK CHICKEN STOCK, USEFUL IN DISHES THAT
REQUIRE A RICHER STOCK FLAVOR, PLACE THE WASHED CHICKEN
PARTS, CARROTS, ONIONS, CELERY, AND GARLIC IN A ROASTING PAN
THAT JUST ACCOMMODATES THEM AND ROAST IN A PREHEATED 350° F.
OVEN UNTIL WELL-COLORED, ABOUT 45 MINUTES. TRANSFER TO A
LARGE POT AND PROCEED AS ABOVE.

Vegetable Stock

Quickly made, vegetable stock is also great to have on hand and, like chicken stock, can be frozen. People who don't eat meat will embrace this stock, as it can be used whenever chicken or fish stocks are called for. I like this recipe for its sweet flavor notes, provided by apples and dates. The stock will keep, refrigerated, for one week or three months frozen.

MAKES 4 TO 6 QUARTS

3 large onions, roughly chopped
1 large fennel bulb, roughly chopped
4 large carrots, washed but unpeeled, roughly chopped
3 celery stalks, roughly chopped
1 Red Delicious apple
1/2 cup dates or raisins
3 sprigs fresh thyme or 1 tablespoon dried
1/2 bunch flat-leaf parsley
2 bay leaves
1 1/2 teaspoons black peppercorns

1. In a large pot combine the onions, fennel, carrots, celery, apple, dates, thyme, parsley, bay leaves, and peppercorns. Add cold water to cover (about 2 gallons) and bring to a boil. Reduce the heat and simmer, uncovered, until the vegetables are completely softened, about 2 hours.

2. Strain the stock and discard the solids. Allow to cool, then refrigerate or freeze.

Ming's Pho

This delicious dish is my version of *pho,* the humble yet elegant Vietnamese rice noodle soup. I first had *pho* in San Francisco's Chinatown, where it was served with small dishes of Thai basil and bean sprouts, hoisin sauce, and the chile puree seasoning called *sriracha*. It made an immediate impression.

I use translucent rice stick noodles for this fragrant version, which also features thinly sliced beef that cooks in the soup, and I've combined the traditional vegetable accompaniments into a salad garnish. The dish contrasts hot and cold, crunchy and smooth in a totally alluring way.

BEVERAGE TIP: LAGER (TSINGTAO, SHANGHAI, SINGHA)

SERVES 4

SALAD
2 cups mung bean sprouts
1 cup Thai or sweet basil leaves
Juice of 2 limes
1/2 tablespoon Thai fish sauce *(nam pla)*

SOUP
2 tablespoons canola oil
1 tablespoon finely chopped fresh ginger
2 serrano chiles, stemmed and finely chopped
4 leeks, white parts only, well washed and julienned
1 large carrot, peeled and julienned
Salt and freshly ground black pepper
1 tablespoon dark soy sauce
8 cups Chicken Stock (page 14) or low-sodium canned broth
3 star anise
1 8-ounce piece beef tenderloin, trimmed of all visible fat and sinew and chilled
   in the freezer until firm (see Tip)
1 8-ounce package rice stick noodles, soaked in warm water to cover until soft,
   about 20 minutes
1 teaspoon toasted sesame oil

1. To prepare the salad, combine the bean sprouts and basil leaves in a medium bowl and mix. In a small bowl, combine the lime juice and fish sauce and stir to mix. Reserve separately.

2. To make the soup, heat a medium saucepan over medium heat. Add the oil and swirl to coat the bottom of the pan. Add the ginger and chiles and sauté, stirring, until soft, about 3 minutes. Add the leeks and carrot and season with salt and pepper to taste. Add the soy sauce, chicken stock, and star anise. Bring the mixture to a simmer and allow to cook until reduced by one-fourth, about 15 minutes.

3. Meanwhile, using a very sharp knife or electric slicer, slice the beef as thin as possible. Cover. Refrigerate until ready to serve.

4. Just before serving, remove the star anise from the soup and discard. Add the drained rice stick noodles and simmer until heated through, about 5 minutes. Combine the salad with the reserved dressing and toss to coat. Ladle the soup into 4 bowls and lay 4 to 5 beef slices lightly on top of each portion. Drizzle with the sesame oil, garnish with the salad, and serve.

MING'S TIP: IN ORDER TO COOK QUICKLY, THE BEEF MUST BE SLICED QUITE THIN, THOUGH IT NEED NOT BE PAPER-THIN. IT'S MUCH EASIER TO CUT THE BEEF THIS THIN WHEN IT'S BEEN FROZEN TO FIRMNESS (NOT HARDNESS), 3 TO 4 HOURS. THE OTHER REQUIREMENT IS A THIN, VERY SHARP KNIFE—A CERAMIC BLADED KNIFE OR SUSHI KNIFE WOULD BE IDEAL.

S
O
U
P
S

Miso Broth
with Tatsoi-Enoki Salad

This is my interpretation of miso soup—that fundamental Japanese brew—partnered here with a crisp tatsoi salad and garnished with silky tofu.

Miso soup is made with dashi, Japan's ubiquitous stock. The stock is prepared with konbu, a nutritious seaweed, and flakes of dried bonito, a fish that's long been a staple of the Japanese diet. Making the stock and the soup is easy to do, but if you're pressed for time you can use dashi powder to prepare the stock. Look for brands that contain no MSG.

This makes a lovely light meal—welcome any time you need a simple but satisfying pick-me-up.

BEVERAGE TIP: MEDIUM-DRY, CHILLED SAKE (PREFERABLY A JI-SAKE OR GEKKEIKAN'S "HAIKU")

SERVES 4

DASHI
1 piece (about 5 × 6 inches) konbu
1 cup bonito flakes

1/4 cup yellow miso *(shinshū-miso)*
2 1/4-inch-thick slices fresh ginger
1/2 tablespoon wasabi powder
1 tablespoon rice wine vinegar
1/2 tablespoon soy sauce
2 tablespoons scallions, green parts only, cut into 1/8-inch slices
1/2 teaspoon sugar
Salt and freshly ground black pepper
1 2- to 3-ounce package enoki mushrooms
2 cups tatsoi leaves (or watercress or baby spinach)
1 cake soft tofu (about 3 × 3 × 2 inches), cut horizontally into 4 1/4-inch-thick slices

1. To make the dashi, clean the konbu by wiping it with a damp cloth. Place the konbu in a stockpot with 5 cups of cold water and heat over medium heat. Just before the water boils, remove the pot from the heat. Watch carefully; you do not want the water to boil or the dashi will become too strongly flavored. Allow to stand 5 minutes, remove the konbu, and return the pot to medium heat. When the stock once again nears the boiling point, remove the pot from the heat and add the bonito flakes. When the flakes sink to the bottom of the pot, strain the dashi through cheesecloth or a fine-mesh strainer. Measure 4 cups of dashi into the stockpot, reserving the rest for another use.

2. Add the miso and ginger to the dashi and bring to a simmer over medium heat. Simmer for 5 minutes and remove the ginger.

3. Meanwhile, in a small bowl, combine the wasabi and vinegar and stir to blend. Whisk in the soy sauce, scallions, and sugar, and season to taste with the salt and pepper. In a medium bowl, combine the enoki and tatsoi; add the wasabi vinaigrette and toss to coat.

4. Carefully place 1 slice of the tofu in each of 4 soup bowls. Ladle the broth on top, place a small mound of the salad on each of the tofu portions, and serve.

MING'S TIP: THIS RECIPE YIELDS ABOUT 5 CUPS OF DASHI. EXTRA DASHI CAN BE STORED IN THE REFRIGERATOR FOR UP TO 2 WEEKS OR FROZEN FOR UP TO 1 MONTH.

Asian Gazpacho
with Cilantro-Jicama Cream

Gazpacho is, of course, the refreshing raw vegetable soup of Spain. My East-West version honors the traditional use of tomatoes and cucumbers—what would gazpacho be without them?—but also includes Asian aromatics and seasonings. The cilantro cream accompaniment adds a nice richness and amplifies the soup's herbaceous flavor.

Like all gazpachos, this is best prepared in summer when tomatoes are at their peak, and tastes even better the next day.

BEVERAGE TIP: CRISP, ROUND VIOGNIER (ALBAN, HORTON)

SERVES 8

2 large cucumbers, peeled, seeded, and roughly chopped
2 large, very ripe tomatoes, roughly chopped
1 small red onion, roughly chopped
2 serrano chiles, stemmed
4 garlic cloves
1 tablespoon finely chopped fresh ginger
$\frac{1}{2}$ cup rice wine vinegar
Juice of 2 lemons
$\frac{1}{2}$ cup soy sauce
$\frac{1}{4}$ cup Worcestershire sauce
2 tablespoons sambal oelek
1 cup extra-virgin olive oil
Salt and freshly ground black pepper
1 cup Thai or sweet basil leaves
$\frac{1}{2}$ cup cilantro leaves
$\frac{1}{2}$ cup mint leaves

CILANTRO CREAM

$\frac{1}{2}$ cup cilantro leaves
1 cup sour cream (may substitute plain yogurt)
Juice of 1 lemon
$1\frac{1}{2}$ teaspoons sambal oelek
Salt and freshly ground black pepper
1 small jicama, peeled and cut into $\frac{1}{8}$-inch dice (about $\frac{3}{4}$ cup, see Tip)

1. In a food processor, combine the cucumbers, tomatoes, and onion and puree, working in batches if necessary. Add the chiles, garlic, and ginger and puree. Add the vinegar, lemon juice, soy sauce, Worcestershire sauce, sambal oelek, and olive oil and pulse to puree. Season to taste with the salt and pepper. Add the basil, cilantro, and mint and pulse just to incorporate and chop the herbs finely. Correct the seasonings, transfer to a medium bowl, and store, refrigerated, at least 4 hours and preferably overnight to allow the flavors to blend.

2. To make the cream, in a small bowl combine the cilantro, sour cream, lemon juice, and sambal oelek. Season to taste with the salt and pepper. Just before serving, fold in the jicama cubes.

3. Divide the soup among 8 chilled bowls. Top each with a dollop of the cream and serve.

MING'S TIP: THE JICAMA FOR THIS MUST BE CUT INTO SMALL DICE. THE EASIEST WAY TO DO THIS IS TO CUT THE JICAMA INTO $\frac{1}{8}$-INCH-THICK SLICES USING A MANDOLINE. STACK THE SLICES IN BATCHES AND THEN CUT INTO $\frac{1}{8}$-INCH STRIPS. CUT ACROSS THE STRIPS FOR $\frac{1}{8}$-INCH DICE.

Chipotle Sweet Potato Soup
with Bell Pepper–Bacon Salsa

I created this spicy, robust soup with one of my sous chefs, Tom Berry. We were aiming for a Southwestern-style dish that was just sweet enough and had some zing, and this bacon-flavored sweet potato mélange was the very tasty result. Served with a red pepper–based salsa that reinforces the soup's bacon flavor, this dish will satisfy but not overburden cold-weather appetites.

BEVERAGE TIP: FLOWERY GEWÜRZTRAMINER (ALSATIAN TRIMBACH, DELOACH)

SERVES 6

SALSA
4 slices bacon
1 small red onion, cut into $\frac{1}{4}$-inch dice
1 red bell pepper, cored, seeded, and cut
    into $\frac{1}{4}$-inch dice
Salt and freshly ground black pepper
Juice of 1 lime

5 garlic cloves, smashed
$\frac{1}{2}$ teaspoon finely chopped fresh ginger
2 small white or yellow onions, roughly
    chopped
2 tablespoons dark brown sugar
Salt and freshly ground black pepper
1 teaspoon pureed chipotles in adobo (see Tip, page 51)
$\frac{3}{4}$ cup dry white wine
3 large sweet potatoes, peeled and cut into $\frac{1}{2}$-inch dice
6 cups Chicken Stock (page 14) or low-sodium canned broth
6 tablespoons butter, chilled and roughly chopped
Juice of $\frac{1}{2}$ lime

1. To make the salsa, cook the bacon in a large, heavy skillet over medium heat, turning once, until crisp, about 10 minutes. Crumble the bacon and reserve. Pour most of the bacon fat into a heatproof container, leaving only enough to coat the pan lightly, and reserve.

2. Add the onion and red pepper to the pan in which the bacon cooked and sauté over medium heat, stirring, until brown, about 6 minutes. Season to taste with the salt and pepper. Add the reserved bacon and the lime juice. Correct the seasonings, transfer to a small bowl, and set aside at room temperature.

3. To make the soup, return the reserved bacon fat to the same pan and place over medium heat. Add the garlic, ginger, onions, and brown sugar, season with the salt and pepper to taste, and sauté, stirring, until the vegetables are brown, about 6 minutes. Stir in the chipotle puree and wine, and cook over medium heat until the mixture is reduced by about three-fourths, approximately 6 minutes. Add the sweet potatoes and stock and simmer until the potatoes are very soft, 20 to 25 minutes.

4. Using a hand blender or food processor, puree the soup mixture. Add the butter one piece at a time, blending again after each addition, to thicken the soup slightly. Stir in the lime juice and correct the seasonings. Immediately ladle into bowls, spoon a portion of the salsa onto each, and serve.

MING'S TIP: YOU CAN MAKE A VEGETARIAN VERSION BY OMITTING THE BACON AND USING VEGETABLE STOCK IN PLACE OF THE CHICKEN STOCK. SUBSTITUTE CANOLA OIL FOR THE RENDERED BACON FAT.

Thai Hot and Sour Soup
with Shrimp Toast

If you've been disappointed by the hot and sour soups you've tried, this Thai-inspired version is for you. Fragrant with lemongrass and Thai basil, it's also touched with ginger and chile (which extends the ginger's heat intriguingly). And unlike Chinese hot and sour soups, it's unthickened.

I serve it accompanied by real shrimp toast. This much-loved Chinese hors d'oeuvre, which makes a great party nibble, is traditionally made with water chestnuts. Though delicious, the fresh ones are difficult to find and the canned ones taste tinny to me, so I substitute jicama. It provides just the right sweetness and crunch.

BEVERAGE TIP: FRUITY RIESLING, NOT BONE DRY (AUSTRALIAN GROSSET, ALSATIAN TRIMBACH)

SERVES 6

4 tablespoons canola oil
2 cups fresh shiitake mushroom caps sliced $\frac{1}{8}$ inch thick
Salt
$\frac{1}{2}$ cup finely julienned fresh ginger
1 large onion, roughly chopped
4 stemmed Thai bird chiles
3 lemongrass stalks, white parts only, thinly sliced
$\frac{1}{4}$ cup Thai fish sauce *(nam pla)*
8 cups Chicken Stock (page 14) or low-sodium canned broth
6 kaffir lime leaves
1 star anise
1 cup enoki mushrooms
$\frac{3}{4}$ cup rice wine vinegar
$\frac{1}{2}$ cup Thai or sweet basil leaves
1 teaspoon freshly ground white pepper

MING'S TIP: USE A BOWL SET IN ICE WHEN PREPARING RAW SHRIMP AND OTHER RAW PROTEIN MIXTURES. THESE FOODS ARE MOST VULNERABLE TO AIRBORNE CONTAMINANTS AND NEED TO BE KEPT COOL TO PREVENT SPOILAGE.

TOAST

1 pound rock shrimp or regular shrimp, peeled and deveined

2 cups shredded napa cabbage

1 tablespoon finely chopped fresh ginger

1 tablespoon toasted sesame oil

1 egg

Salt and freshly ground white pepper

5 scallions, white and green parts, sliced $\frac{1}{8}$ inch thick and reserved separately

$\frac{1}{4}$ cup chopped fresh cilantro

$\frac{1}{2}$ cup finely diced jicama

Canola oil, for deep-frying

6 slices of sandwich-style bread, crusts removed

$\frac{1}{4}$ cup white sesame seeds

1. Heat a large skillet over medium heat. Add 2 tablespoons of the oil and swirl to coat the pan. When the oil shimmers, add the shiitake mushrooms and sauté, stirring, until soft, about 6 minutes. Season with the salt to taste, remove, and set aside.

2. Return the same skillet to the stove over medium heat. Add the remaining 2 table-spoons of oil and swirl to coat the pan. When the oil shimmers, add the ginger, onion, chiles, and lemongrass and sauté, stirring occasionally, until soft, about 6 minutes.

3. Stir in the fish sauce, then add the chicken stock, lime leaves, and star anise. Cook over medium heat until the liquid is reduced by one-fourth, about 20 minutes. Strain, return to the skillet, and add the reserved shiitakes, the enoki mushrooms, vinegar, basil, and white pepper. Taste and correct the seasonings. Keep hot.

4. To make the toast, combine the shrimp, cabbage, ginger, sesame oil, and egg in a food processor. Process to a puree and season with the salt and pepper. Transfer the mixture to a chilled bowl and fold in the white scallion slices, the cilantro, and jicama.

5. Fill a fryer or heavy, medium stockpot one-third full with the oil and heat to 375°F over high heat. Spread the shrimp mixture on the bread slices, sprinkle with the sesame seeds, and fry shrimp side down until golden brown, about 3 minutes. Flip and fry the second side until brown, about 2 minutes, remove with a large-mesh spoon, and drain on paper towels. Halve each slice diagonally.

6. Ladle the soup into 6 soup plates. Garnish with 2 toasts per serving, sprinkle with the scallion greens, and serve.

Roasted Garlic and Celeriac Soup
with Wild Mushroom Ragout

My chef-friend Ken Oringer and I came up with this earthy puree while at the restaurant Silks in San Francisco.

The idea of a root vegetable soup had been knocking around my head for a while; I've loved celeriac ever since I first had it in France with *sauce rémoulade,* a classic pairing. Celeriac's special celery-parsley taste is ideal for soup, especially when combined with roasted garlic for its mellow pungency and with celery (a favorite Chinese vegetable) for its fresh flavor note. Finished with crisp celeriac chips for great textural interest, this soup pleases everyone.

BEVERAGE TIP: BERRY-LIKE PINOT NOIR (ROBERT SINSKEY, LITTORAI "HIRSCH")

SERVES 8 TO 10

8 whole heads garlic

Extra-virgin olive oil

Salt and freshly ground black pepper

2 tablespoons canola oil, plus additional for deep-frying

3 large onions, roughly chopped

6 cups chopped celeriac (about 5 peeled heads) plus 20 paper-thin slices

1 cup chopped tender celery (the pale inner stalks from 1 large head)

10 cups Chicken Stock (page 14) or low-sodium canned broth

6 tablespoons butter

1 cup Wild Mushroom Ragout (page 211)

¼ cup Scallion Oil (page 229)

1. Preheat the oven to 375°F. Slice the tops off the garlic heads and fit the heads into a baking dish just large enough to hold them. Drizzle lightly with the olive oil and season with salt and pepper to taste. Cover tightly with foil and roast until the garlic is golden brown, about 45 minutes. Allow to cool, then squeeze the softened cloves into a small bowl. Reserve.

2. Heat a soup pot over high heat. Add the 2 tablespoons of canola oil and swirl to coat the bottom of the pot. When the oil shimmers, add the onions and sauté, stirring, until very brown, about 10 minutes. Add the roasted garlic, the chopped celeriac, and celery and sauté over medium heat, stirring, until starting to soften, about 8 minutes.

3. Add the chicken stock and season with the salt and pepper to taste. When the stock boils, reduce the heat and simmer uncovered for 30 minutes or until the celeriac is very soft. Transfer the soup to a food processor and puree in batches, adding the butter gradually by tablespoons through the feed tube. Correct the seasonings and keep hot.

4. Fill a small fryer or heavy, medium pot one-third full with canola oil and bring to 300°F over high heat. Add the celeriac slices and fry, turning once, until golden brown, about 4 minutes. Drain on paper towels and season immediately with salt to taste.

5. Ladle the soup into soup plates. Garnish each serving with a heaping tablespoon of wild mushroom ragout and a celeriac chip, drizzle with a teaspoon or so of scallion oil, and serve.

MING'S TIPS: THE CELERIAC CHIP GARNISH ADDS CHARACTER TO THE SOUP, BUT CAN BE OMITTED. INSTEAD, OFFER A CRUNCHY GARNISH OF CELERY SLICED THINLY ON THE BIAS, TOSSED WITH OLIVE OIL AND VINEGAR, AND SEASONED WITH SALT AND PEPPER. MOUND A PORTION OF THE SALAD ON TOP OF THE MUSHROOMS.

THIS RECIPE MAKES A GENEROUS QUANTITY OF SOUP. FREEZE ANY LEFTOVERS, OR STORE THEM, REFRIGERATED, FOR UP TO 3 DAYS.

Corn Lemongrass Soup
with Lobster Salad

I based this dish on velvet corn soup, a traditional Chinese favorite, which is often made with crabmeat. My version is prepared with fresh corn kernels and their cobs, so it exudes pure corn flavor. The only thickening is a light liaison provided by the cobs. And instead of crab, the soup features a fresh lobster salad with more crunchy corn. All in all, a memorable start to any meal. Leftover soup can be stored in the fridge for up to three days.

BEVERAGE TIP: BUTTERY, VANILLAN CHARDONNAY (TALBOTT, KISTLER)

SERVES 8 TO 10

2 tablespoons canola oil
3 cups roughly chopped yellow onions
2 tablespoons finely chopped ginger
2 cups chopped lemongrass, white parts only
8 cups corn kernels, preferably fresh, cobs
    reserved if using fresh (8 to 10 ears)
8 cups Chicken Stock (14) or low-sodium canned
    broth
Salt and freshly ground black pepper

SALAD
1 baguette, cut diagonally into long $\frac{1}{4}$-inch slices
    (8 to 10 slices)
1 cup corn kernels, preferably fresh
$\frac{1}{2}$ pound cooked lobster meat (1 large lobster tail,
    boiled, cooled, and shelled)
$\frac{1}{2}$ cup fennel cut into $\frac{1}{8}$-inch dice
$\frac{1}{4}$ cup chives cut into $\frac{1}{2}$-inch lengths
Juice of 1 lemon
1 tablespoon canola oil
1 tablespoon extra-virgin olive oil
Salt and freshly ground black pepper
8 teaspoons Chile Oil (page 230)

1. Heat a soup pot over medium heat. Add the oil and swirl to coat the bottom of the pot. When the oil shimmers, add the onions, ginger, and lemongrass and sauté, stirring, until soft, about 8 minutes. Add the corn kernels and cobs, if using, and the stock. Season with the salt and pepper to taste and cook until the corn is very soft, about 35 to 45 minutes. Discard the cobs, if used, transfer the soup to a food processor, and puree. Strain the soup and correct the seasonings.

2. Meanwhile, make croutons for the salad. Preheat the oven to 275°F. Place the bread on a baking sheet and allow to dry in the oven, about 20 minutes.

3. Bring a large pot of salted water to a boil. Fill a small bowl with water and add ice. Add the corn to the boiling water and cook until just tender, about 3 minutes for fresh, 15 seconds for frozen. Remove the corn with a fine-mesh spoon and transfer to the ice water. When cool, drain the corn well.

4. In a medium bowl, combine the lobster, corn, fennel, chives, lemon juice, and oils. Season to taste with the salt and pepper and toss to mix thoroughly.

5. Divide the soup among 8 large soup bowls. Add a crouton to each portion and top with the salad. Drizzle each with about 1 teaspoon of chile oil and serve.

MING'S TIP: TO HONOR TRADITION, YOU CAN SUBSTITUTE 1 POUND OF LUMP CRABMEAT, PICKED OVER, FOR THE LOBSTER. THE CRAB'S SWEETNESS WILL COMPLEMENT THE CORN'S, AND VICE VERSA.

Carrot Garlic Soup
with Curry Potato Hash

Carrots are among the sweetest of all vegetables—and one of the most neglected. It's a shame. Used most often as a flavoring ingredient, they really shine when brought center stage. I've done just that for this suave, creamy soup, which also celebrates garlic. I can't live without that fragrant bulb, and if you share my passion (or even if your garlic appreciation is more tempered), you'll love its mellow presence in this soup. Offered with a curried potato hash, the soup has just the right match of textures and flavors. Serve it as a first course or with a side salad as a simple supper.

BEVERAGE TIP: SEMILLON WITH SLIGHT SWEETNESS OR SEMILLON BLEND (CARMENET, LYNCH BAGES BLANC)

SERVES 4

2 tablespoons canola oil
2 large red onions, roughly chopped
½ cup whole, peeled garlic cloves (about 4 heads)
1 tablespoon packed brown sugar
1 teaspoon freshly ground white pepper
1 cup roughly chopped celery
4 cups roughly chopped carrots
Salt
5 cups Chicken Stock (page 14) or low-sodium canned broth
1 tablespoon butter

POTATOES
2 cups Curry Oil (page 230)
1 large Russet potato, peeled and cut into ¼-inch dice
Salt
¼ cup chives cut into ½-inch lengths

1. Heat a large saucepan over medium heat. Add the oil and swirl to coat the bottom of the pan. When the oil shimmers, add the onions and garlic and sauté, stirring, until very brown, about 10 minutes. Add the brown sugar, white pepper, celery, and carrots. Season with the salt and sauté, stirring, until the carrots brown lightly, about 8 minutes. Add the stock, reduce the heat to low, and simmer until the vegetables are very soft, about 30 to 45 minutes. Transfer to a food processor and puree. Stir in the butter and correct the seasonings.

2. To make the potatoes, heat a large, deep skillet over medium heat. Add the curry oil and heat to 375° F. Add the potatoes and shallow-fry, turning as necessary, until golden brown and crispy, about 7 minutes. Drain the potatoes on paper towels and season with salt while still hot.

3. Divide the soup among 4 soup plates. Mound the potatoes in the plates so some of each portion is visible above the soup, garnish with the chives, and serve.

Many Onion Soup
with Steamed Coriander Scallops

Almost everyone loves French onion soup, myself included. But classics can be reenvisioned. My version contains not just one onion type but five—red and yellow onions, leeks, shallots, and scallions. (There's also a Crispy Onion garnish.) This plus fresh scallops given a curry-scented steaming result in a wonderful, deeply flavored soup (and one that's lighter than its predecessor). Try it as a simple supper served with a crisp side salad.

BEVERAGE TIP: RICH, DRY SAUVIGNON BLANC FROM POUILLY-FUMÉ OR SANCERRE (CROCHET "LE CHENE")

SERVES 4

2 tablespoons canola oil
1 large red onion, cut into $1/4$-inch slices
1 large yellow onion, cut into $1/4$-inch slices
2 leeks, white parts only, well washed and julienned
5 shallots, cut into $1/4$-inch slices
8 scallions, white and green parts, 6 cut into 1-inch lengths,
    2 cut into 2-inch lengths
$1/4$ cup Dijon mustard
1 cup dry red wine
$1/4$ cup Worcestershire sauce
Salt and freshly ground black pepper
1 tablespoon finely chopped fresh thyme, or $1/2$ tablespoon dried,
    plus 4 sprigs fresh, for garnish
6 cups Chicken Stock (page 14) or low-sodium canned broth
12 large sea scallops
$1/4$ cup coarsely ground coriander, toasted (see Tip, page 75)
$1/2$ cup Madras curry powder

Crispy Onions (page 212), for garnish

1. Heat a large saucepan over medium heat. Add the oil and swirl to coat. When the oil shimmers, add the onions, leeks, and shallots and sauté, stirring, until brown, about 10 minutes. Add the 1-inch scallion pieces, mustard, wine, and Worcestershire sauce, stir, lower the heat, and cook until reduced by three-fourths, about 10 minutes. Season with the salt and pepper to taste and add the chopped thyme and stock. Reduce the heat to simmer and cook until reduced by one-fourth, about 30 minutes. Correct the seasonings and keep warm.

2. Place the scallops on a cutting board. Using the tip of a paring knife, make a $\frac{1}{4}$-inch slit down through the center of each. Insert a 2-inch section of scallion into each scallop. Spread the coriander on a dish. Season the scallops with the salt and roll the outside edges in the coriander.

3. Set up a steamer. When the water is boiling, add the curry powder to it and stir to dissolve. Steam the scallops over the curry water until just cooked through, about 3 to 5 minutes.

4. Ladle the onion soup into 4 soup plates and, with a spoon, mound the onions in each. Lean 3 scallops against the onions, garnish with the thyme sprigs and crispy onions, and serve.

MING'S TIP: AVOID OVERSTEAMING THE SCALLOPS; YOU WANT THEM TO REMAIN MOIST AND THE SCALLIONS TO HOLD THEIR SHAPE.

Thai-Spiced Mussel Soup
with Leeks and Carrot Spaghetti

Until I went to France I never really liked mussels. The ones I'd had were breaded and broiled so their texture wasn't inviting. Steamed in wine with garlic, however, as they were in Normandy, they were a revelation.

That approach governed the creation of this mussel soup, which is fragrant with Thai aromatics and warmed with chiles. I've had a lot of fun with this, cutting carrots to resemble noodles (I use an inexpensive, readily available Japanese turning slicer but you can julienne the carrots if you like) and adding sweet leeks. The result is a tantalizing soup that's one of the best mussel dishes I know.

BEVERAGE TIP: BIG, RICH RIESLING (ALSATIAN ZIND HUMBRECHT OR HUGEL)

SERVES 4

3 tablespoons canola oil

1 large onion, sliced $\frac{1}{4}$ inch thick

2 lengthwise slices galangal about $\frac{1}{4}$ inch thick, or 4 $\frac{1}{4}$-inch-thick slices fresh
   ginger, cut as long as possible

2 serrano or Thai bird chiles, with stems and seeds, cut into $\frac{1}{4}$-inch slices

4 lemongrass stalks, white parts only, sliced $\frac{1}{8}$ inch thick

4 kaffir lime leaves, cut into $\frac{1}{8}$-inch ribbons

2 tablespoons Thai fish sauce *(nam pla)*

8 cups Chicken Stock (page 14) or low-sodium canned broth

Salt and freshly ground white pepper

1 pound mussels, preferably Prince Edward Island, scrubbed and debearded

2 large leeks, white parts only, well washed and julienned

1 large carrot, cut into "spaghetti" using a turning slicer or finely julienned

1. Heat a wok over high heat. Add 1 tablespoon of the oil and swirl to coat. When the oil shimmers, add the onion and cook, stirring, until brown, about 3 minutes. Add the galangal, chiles, lemongrass, and lime leaves, stir, and add the fish sauce. Add the stock, reduce the heat, and simmer until reduced by one-fourth, about 20 to 30 minutes. Strain into a bowl, season with the salt and pepper to taste, and keep hot.

2. Reheat the wok over high heat. Add the remaining 2 tablespoons of oil and swirl to coat. When the oil shimmers, add the mussels and cook, stirring occasionally until the mussels start to open. Add the leeks and carrot and allow to cook until tender-crisp, about 3 minutes. Season with salt and pepper to taste. Add the reserved stock mixture, correct the seasonings, and heat. Discard any unopened mussels, divide among 4 large soup bowls, and serve.

MING'S TIP: I STRAIN THE SOUP TO REMOVE THE LEMONGRASS, GALANGAL, AND OTHER TOO-TOUGH-TO-EAT FLAVORINGS BEFORE IT IS COMBINED WITH THE MUSSELS. THAI COOKS WOULD SKIP THE STRAINING STEP, KNOWING THAT DINERS WOULD AVOID EATING THE FLAVORINGS. FOR AN AUTHENTIC PRESENTATION, PUT YOUR GUESTS IN THE KNOW AND SERVE THE SOUP AS THE THAIS DO.

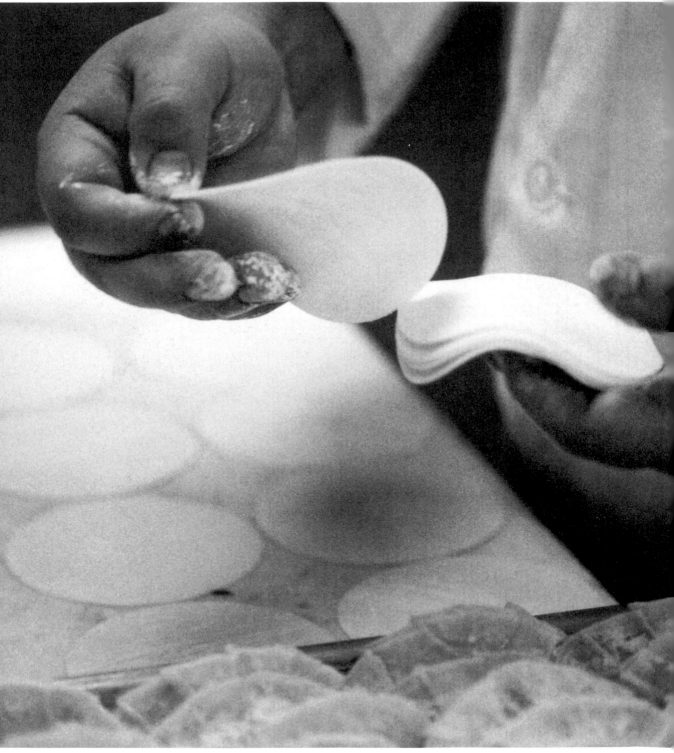

Chapter 2

Dim
Sum

THERE ARE FEW CULINARY OUTINGS I ENJOY MORE THAN A DIM SUM BRUNCH. I GET TO SAMPLE A WIDE VARIETY OF DUMPLINGS, BUNS, SPRING ROLLS, AND OTHER SUPREMELY SAVORY "LITTLE EATS." THE DIM SUM MENU IS A "TASTING" THAT DOESN'T QUIT, THE BEST WAY I KNOW TO ENJOY WONDERFUL FOOD IN A LEISURELY EATING RITUAL. THE SMALL PORTIONS EXCITE BUT NEVER TIRE MY APPETITE—AND THERE'S ALWAYS MORE!

To bring these pleasures home, I've created my own dim sum menu. Some of the dishes on it, like my mother's Pork and Ginger Pot Stickers, are traditional—they couldn't be improved. But others have been reworked to make them particularly exciting to modern palates. Smoky Turkey Shu Mai in a Sweet Pea Broth and Mushroom and Leek Spring Rolls with Mint Dipping Sauce are examples of old favorites brought to a new taste level. Prosciutto and Asian

Pear "Maki," Crab Lemongrass Tartlettes, and Spinach Tofu Napoleons with Spicy Miso Dressing borrow from tapas, antipasti, and Japanese eating traditions to satisfy my love of mixed culinary marriages. In rethinking dim sum I haven't neglected American small eats either; traditional shrimp cocktail is reborn as Tempura Shrimp Cocktail, a starter that's really fun to eat.

The dim sum challenge is, of course, all those little dishes—the tea house array—that can require as much work to produce as a regular entree. First of all, some attitude adjustment is in order. To enjoy dim sum, you needn't cook for days. Pick and choose one or two of the recipes that follow, make enough for a group, and enjoy a completely special eating experience. The Salmon Roll Tempura with caramelized leeks, soy syrup, and wasabi oil and the Asparagus-Crusted Ahi Tuna would make a delicious small grazing menu.

Remember, too, that dim sum make wonderful appetizers or hors d'oeuvre. There's no better way to get an evening going than by serving any of the rolls, the Crab and Fennel Wontons, and the Rock Shrimp Lollipops with Spicy Almond Sauce—all of which can be easily managed in a crowd. The rule of thumb is mix and match to provide a range of textures, tastes, and temperatures. Present the dim sum and others in bamboo steamers that you've lined with red-leaf lettuce or shredded romaine and pass the sauces separately. People will happily dig in.

Crab Lemongrass Tartlettes

I love classic quiche Lorraine, but sometimes find it too rich. Though this version contains its share of cream, the impression it makes is of sweet, lemongrass-flavored crab. The tartlettes are made with purchased frozen puff pastry, so their assembly is easy. These make an outstanding hors d'oeuvre, one that disappears quickly.

BEVERAGE TIP: CHAMPAGNE OR SPARKLING WINE (VEUVE CLICQUOT, PACIFIC ECHO)

SERVES 6

$\frac{1}{2}$ pound lump crabmeat, picked over
4 lemongrass stalks, white parts only, finely chopped
4 eggs
$\frac{1}{2}$ cup heavy cream
2 scallions, white and green parts, sliced $\frac{1}{8}$ inch thick
Salt and freshly ground white pepper
$\frac{1}{2}$ pound frozen puff pastry dough, thawed

1. In a medium bowl, combine the crab, lemongrass, eggs, cream, and scallions and season with the salt and pepper. Mix and set aside.

2. Preheat the oven to 350°F. Unfold the sheet of puff pastry and cut six 3 × 3-inch squares. Prick the squares with a fork at $\frac{1}{2}$-inch intervals. Spray a muffin tin with 2-inch cups with nonstick cooking spray and press a pastry square into each. Line each tartlette with foil, fill with rice or beans to keep the pastry from buckling, and bake until the sides of the pastry are golden, about 10 minutes. Remove the foil and continue to bake until the bottoms are golden, about 5 minutes more.

3. Divide the crab mixture among the tartlettes and bake just until the tip of a knife or cake tester inserted in the filling comes out clean, 12 to 15 minutes. Serve warm or at room temperature.

MING'S TIP: FOR A GREAT LUNCH DISH, FILL A HOMEMADE OR FROZEN PIE SHELL WITH A DOUBLE RECIPE OF THE CRAB MIXTURE AND BAKE.

Lobster and Mango Summer Rolls

The Vietnamese make summer rolls with a shrimp-based filling. My version is more deluxe and the lightest way to eat lobster I know. I love the way the mango adds just enough sweetness while the lime's acidic tang balances the sense of richness.

For all its refinement, this dish is easily made, especially if you purchase lobster tails—just mix everything, roll, and go. You can hold the rolls in the fridge for one hour, individually wrapped in plastic, if you need to delay things a bit.

BEVERAGE TIP: LIGHTLY OAKED CHARDONNAY (NEW ZEALAND SEPPELT, QUPE)

MAKES 8 ROLLS

2 limes, peeled and separated into segments
1 tablespoon Thai fish sauce *(nam pla)*
1 teaspoon light brown sugar, packed
$\frac{1}{2}$ pound pea sprouts
16 fresh Thai or sweet basil leaves
Salt and freshly ground black pepper
8 6- to 8-inch round rice paper wrappers
Meat from 2 cooked lobster tails, quartered lengthwise to make 8 strips
1 large mango, peeled and cut into slices the length of the fruit

1. In a large bowl, combine the lime segments, fish sauce, and brown sugar and mix, breaking up the segments. Add the pea sprouts and basil and toss. Season with salt and pepper to taste.

2. Soak the rice paper wrappers in warm water until they are pliable, 2 to 3 minutes. Drain on a clean dish towel, turning each sheet once.

3. Place a sheet of the rice paper on a work surface. Place $\frac{1}{4}$ cup of the filling on the lower third of the sheet. Top with 1 piece of the lobster and 2 strips of mango. Roll as shown on page 53, rolling as tightly as possible. Place seam side down. Repeat to make 7 more rolls; some filling will remain. Allow the rolls to rest about 2 minutes before serving.

4. To serve, divide the remaining filling among 4 plates. Slice each roll on the bias into 2 pieces, place 2 rolls on each mound of salad, and serve.

Steamed Chicken and Shiitake Buns

Deeply satisfying, steamed meat-filled buns are a popular dim sum and snack throughout China. The universal characteristic of all Chinese buns is a yeast dough; I use a classic formula for the bun dough in this recipe, but have refined the traditional pork filling (here chicken based) with shiitakes and some truffle oil. Making the filling "wealthier" has made the buns particularly delicious.

Note that the open-topped buns rise in the fridge only long enough for them to puff around their filling.

BEVERAGE TIP: FRUITY, CHILLED GAMAY (BEAUJOLAIS NOUVEAU GEORGES DUBOEUF, NOVEMBER TO JANUARY) OR JASMINE TEA

MAKES 8 BUNS

FILLING
2 tablespoons canola oil

1 tablespoon finely chopped garlic

1 tablespoon finely chopped fresh
   ginger

1 pound shiitakes, stemmed and caps sliced
   $\frac{1}{4}$ inch thick

Salt and freshly ground black pepper

1 pound ground chicken

$\frac{1}{3}$ cup chopped chives

1 tablespoon white truffle oil

BUN DOUGH
2 tablespoons sugar

$\frac{3}{4}$ cup warm water

$1\frac{1}{2}$ teaspoons (1 package) active dry yeast

$1\frac{1}{2}$ teaspoons melted lard or vegetable shortening (see Tip)

$2\frac{1}{2}$ cups sifted all-purpose flour

Ginger Dipping Sauce (page 235)

1. To make the filling, heat a medium skillet over high heat. Add the oil and swirl to coat the bottom of the pan. When the oil shimmers, add the garlic and ginger and sauté, stirring, until soft, about 2 minutes. Add the shiitakes and sauté until soft, about 6 minutes. Season with the salt and pepper to taste and allow to cool. Transfer the mixture to a medium bowl, add the chicken, chives, and truffle oil, and stir to blend. Correct the seasonings and chill.

2. To make the dough, combine the sugar and warm water in a small bowl and stir to dissolve. Add the yeast and allow to foam, about 10 minutes. (If the mixture doesn't foam, the yeast is old; begin again with fresh yeast.) Add the lard.

3. In a food processor, combine the flour and the yeast mixture. Turn on the machine and add up to 5 cups of cold water slowly until a ball forms. If the dough is too sticky, add more flour.

4. Transfer the dough to a floured work surface. Knead the dough until smooth and elastic, about 10 to 12 minutes. With your palms, roll the dough into a cylinder about 2 inches in diameter and 16 inches long. Cut the cylinder into eight 2-inch pieces. Take one piece and flatten it with your hands. Using a rolling pin or your hands, lightly roll into a disk about 3 inches in diameter and $\frac{1}{2}$ inch thick.

5. Place a heaping tablespoon of the chicken mixture in the center of the dough. Encircle the filling with dough, but allow the tops of the buns to remain open. Repeat with the remaining pieces of dough and filling. Cover the buns with a damp kitchen cloth and allow to rise, refrigerated, until the dough has puffed up around the filling, about $1\frac{1}{2}$ hours.

6. Set up a steamer. When the water boils, add the buns all at once and steam until the filling is cooked and the buns appear shiny, 10 to 12 minutes. Serve with the dipping sauce.

MING'S TIP: DO USE LARD FOR THE BUN DOUGH; ONLY A SMALL AMOUNT IS NEEDED AND IT ADDS DELICIOUS FLAVOR. HOWEVER, VEGETABLE SHORTENING WILL WORK, TOO.

Pan-Fried Chive and Shrimp Buns

Freshly pan-fried buns, made following the pot sticker technique, are venerable Chinese treats. I remember visiting my grandparents in Taiwan and seeing outdoor griddles filled with them. There were many variations; one of my favorites was called *goubuli baozi*, which means "not even dogs would look at them." They were, in fact, completely delicious, as are these, with their savory shrimp and chive filling.

BEVERAGE TIP: SOFT, MELLOW CHENIN BLANC FROM VOUVRAY OR MONT LOUIS

MAKES 16

1½ teaspoons finely chopped fresh ginger

1 pound rock shrimp, rinsed and drained, or regular shrimp, peeled and deveined, either roughly chopped

2 cups chopped Chinese chives or regular chives

2 eggs

1½ teaspoons toasted sesame oil

Salt and freshly ground black pepper

Bun dough (page 42)

2 tablespoons canola oil

2 cups Chicken Stock (page 14) or low-sodium canned broth or water

Spicy Soy Dipping Sauce (page 233)

DIM SUM

1. In a medium bowl, combine the ginger, shrimp, chives, eggs, and sesame oil and season with salt and pepper to taste. Mix thoroughly.

2. Following the instructions in Step 4, page 43, knead and roll the dough into a cylinder about 2 inches in diameter, but cut the dough into 1-inch pieces. Roll one piece of the dough into a circular wrapper 3 inches in diameter and ¼ inch thick. To fill, place 1 tablespoon of the filling in the center of the wrapper. Encircle the filling with the dough, pleat the edge of the wrapper to bring the top folds together, then pinch and twist them to seal. Repeat with the remaining pieces of dough and fillings. Cover the buns with a damp kitchen towel and allow them to rest, refrigerated, until puffed, about 1½ hours.

3. Heat a large skillet over medium heat. Add the oil and swirl to coat the bottom of the pan. When the oil shimmers, add 8 of the buns flat sides down and brown them, about 5 minutes. Add 1 cup of the stock and cover the pan immediately to avoid splattering. Allow the buns to steam until the liquid has completely evaporated and the bottoms have recrisped, about 10 minutes. Check after 5 minutes; if the stock has evaporated but the buns are not yet cooked, add more stock in ¼-cup increments. If the buns are done but stock remains in the pan, drain it and allow the bottoms to crisp. Serve with the dipping sauce.

Pork and Ginger Pot Stickers
with Spicy Soy Dipping Sauce

The recipe for these fried dumplings was passed down to me by my mom, Iris Tsai, and I wouldn't think of changing it. Some things are perfect as they are.

Like bread, the wrappers used in this are one of those things that are best homemade, but unlike bread, they're fast to prepare. Filling and pleating the dumplings is easy, too; after the first couple of dumplings, your fingers will know the way.

Browned and crisped on their bottoms, steamed, and recrisped, these have a great textural mix. Needless to say, they make perfect hors d'oeuvre.

BEVERAGE TIP: LAGER (TSINGTAO, SHANGHAI, SINGHA) OR JASMINE TEA

MAKES 20 TO 25 POT STICKERS

FILLING
4 cups finely chopped napa cabbage
1 tablespoon salt
$\frac{1}{2}$ pound ground pork (not too lean)
2 tablespoons finely chopped
   fresh ginger
$1\frac{1}{2}$ tablespoons finely chopped garlic
2 tablespoons soy sauce
3 tablespoons toasted sesame oil
1 egg, lightly beaten

DOUGH
2 cups water
4 cups all-purpose flour
$\frac{1}{2}$ teaspoon salt

2 tablespoons canola oil
Spicy Soy Dipping Sauce (page 233)

1. To make the filling, combine the cabbage and $1\frac{1}{2}$ teaspoons of the salt in a large bowl and toss together; set aside for 30 minutes. Transfer the cabbage to a clean dish towel or cheesecloth, gather the ends of the cloth together, and twist to squeeze as much water as possible from the cabbage (this will make the filling more cohesive.) In a second large bowl, combine the cabbage with the pork, ginger, garlic, soy sauce, sesame oil, the remaining $1\frac{1}{2}$ teaspoons of salt, and egg and mix.

(recipe continues)

2. To make the dough, bring the water to a boil. In a large stainless-steel bowl, combine the flour and salt. Slowly add the boiling water in $1/4$-cup increments, mixing with chopsticks until a ball is formed and the dough is no longer too hot to handle. All the water may not be needed. Knead the dough on a floured work surface until it becomes smooth and elastic, 15 to 20 minutes. Form the dough into a ball, return it to the bowl, and cover it with a damp cloth. Allow the dough to rest for 1 hour.

3. To form the wrappers, add more flour to the work surface. Divide the dough in half. Shape one portion into a log and roll it back and forth under your palms to make a thin sausage shape measuring about 1 inch in diameter. Cut into $1/2$-inch pieces. One by one, stand each piece on end, flatten the piece with your palm, and roll out to form a circular wrapper about 3 inches in diameter and $1/16$ of an inch thick. Repeat with the remaining dough.

4. To fill the pot stickers, place about $1/2$ tablespoon of the filling in the center of each wrapper. Avoid getting filling on the edges of the wrapper, which would prevent proper sealing. Fold each wrapper in half to form a half-moon shape. Seal the top center of each dumpling by pressing between the fingers and, starting at the center, make 3 pleats, working toward the bottom right. Repeat, working toward the bottom left corner. Press the dumplings down gently on the work surface to flatten the bottoms.

5. Heat a large nonstick skillet over high heat. Add the oil and swirl to coat. When the oil shimmers, add the pot stickers, flattened bottoms down, in rows of five, and cook in batches without disturbing until brown, about 6 minutes. Add about $1/2$ cup of water and immediately cover to avoid splattering. Lift the cover and make sure about $1/8$ inch of water remains in the pan; if not, add a bit more. Steam until the pot stickers are puffy yet firm and the water has evaporated, 8 to 10 minutes. If the water evaporates before the pot stickers are done, add more in $1/4$-cup increments. If the pot stickers seem done but water remains in the pan, drain it and return the pan to the stove top.

6. Continue to cook over high heat to allow the pot stickers to recrisp on the bottom, 2 to 3 minutes. Transfer the pot stickers to a platter and serve with the dipping sauce.

MING'S TIP: WHEN ROLLING OUT THE WRAPPERS, MAKE THE EDGES A LITTLE THINNER THAN THE CENTERS. THAT WAY, WHEN THE EDGES ARE FOLDED OVER THEMSELVES TO ENCLOSE THE FILLING, THEY'LL STILL BE THE SAME THICKNESS AS THE REST OF THE WRAPPER.

Spinach Tofu Napoleons
with Spicy Miso Dressing

These free-form napoleons, built with layers of satiny tofu and crispy raw spinach, make a great appetizer. They're truly healthful, but I like them best for their play of textures and the kick of the spicy miso dressing.

BEVERAGE TIP: SPARKLING CHENIN BLANC FROM SAUMUR OR VOUVRAY (CHATEAU MONCONTOUR)

SERVES 4

¼ cup rice wine vinegar
1 tablespoon soy sauce
2 tablespoons yellow miso *(shinsū miso)*
1 tablespoon sambal oelek
½ tablespoon sugar
2 tablespoons chopped Pickled Ginger (page 238), plus 4 whole pieces
1 teaspoon toasted sesame oil
½ cup canola oil
Salt and freshly ground black pepper
½ cup chopped scallions, green parts only
3 cups spinach leaves cut into ¼-inch ribbons
1-pound package firm tofu, cut into very thin lengthwise slices
1 tablespoon toasted sesame seeds (page 5)

1. In a blender, combine the vinegar, soy sauce, miso, sambal oelek, sugar, and chopped pickled ginger and blend until smooth. With the machine running, drizzle in the sesame and canola oils to form an emulsion. Season with salt and pepper to taste, and transfer to a large bowl, setting aside 4 tablespoons.

2. Add the scallions and spinach to the bowl with the dressing and gently combine. To shape the napoleons, place a slice of tofu on a plate and add a layer of spinach. Top with a second slice of tofu, continue with a second layer of spinach and a final layer of tofu. Repeat with the remaining tofu and spinach to make 3 more napoleons. Drizzle each serving with 1 tablespoon of the reserved dressing. Garnish with the whole pickled ginger and toasted sesame seeds and serve.

Smoky Turkey Shu Mai
in a Sweet Pea Broth

I'm a great lover of shu mai, those open-topped dumplings traditionally filled with a pork and shrimp mixture. For this East-West version, I use turkey and pureed chipotles in adobo—smoked jalapeños in a vinegar-based sauce—for the filling. (The chipotles and not the turkey provide the smoky flavor.) These savory dumplings pair beautifully with the fresh, bright green broth in which they're served. Laced with a little chile oil, the shu mai make a sensational starter or light lunch.

BEVERAGE TIP: CHILLED GAMAY (CRU BEAUJOLAIS FROM BROUILLY, MOULIN-A-VENT)

SERVES 4

BROTH
2 tablespoons canola oil
2 cups roughly chopped yellow onions
2 garlic cloves, crushed
2 cups Chicken Stock (page 14) or low-sodium canned broth
Salt and freshly ground white pepper
2 cups fresh English peas or frozen peas
1 cup spinach leaves, well washed and tough stems removed
4 tablespoons ($\frac{1}{2}$ stick) butter

FILLING
1 pound ground turkey
1 tablespoon pureed chipotles in adobo (see Tip)
1 egg
$\frac{1}{4}$ cup heavy cream
4 tablespoons ($\frac{1}{2}$ stick) butter, roughly chopped and frozen
4 scallions, green parts only, sliced $\frac{1}{8}$ inch thick
Salt and freshly ground black pepper

12 square wonton wrappers
4 teaspoons Chile Oil (page 230), for garnish

1. To make the broth, heat a medium saucepan over medium heat. Add the oil and swirl to coat the bottom of the pan. When the oil shimmers, add the onions and garlic, reduce the heat to medium-low, cover, and cook until the vegetables are soft and their moisture is released, about 8 minutes. Add the stock and season to taste with the salt and pepper. The broth should be salty.

2. Increase the heat to high and bring to a boil. Add the peas and spinach and cook until soft, 6 to 8 minutes, adding the spinach for the last 2 minutes. With a hand or standard blender, puree the mixture. Add the butter and puree until very smooth. Correct the seasonings. Keep warm over very low heat.

3. To make the filling, in a food processor, combine the turkey, pureed chipotle, egg, and cream, and puree. Add the butter all at once and pulse just to blend. Transfer the mixture to a chilled bowl and fold in the scallions. Season with the salt and pepper to taste.

4. To form the shu mai, hold 1 wonton wrapper in your hand as shown on page 178. Place about $\frac{1}{2}$ tablespoon of the filling in the center of the wrapper. Following the photos, bring the sides of the wrapper up around the filling, pleating the wrapper as you go. Tap the dumpling against the work surface to flatten it. Repeat with the remaining wrappers and filling.

5. Set up a steamer. Line the steamer baskets with lettuce leaves or spray with vegetable spray to prevent sticking. Add the shu mai, and steam until they soften and fat gathers near their openings, about 8 minutes.

6. Divide the shu mai among 4 soup plates. Add the broth, drizzle with the chile oil, and serve.

MING'S TIPS: MAKE SURE TO COOK THE PEAS IN STOCK THAT IS SUFFICIENTLY SALTY; THIS IS WHAT MAINTAINS THE BRIGHT COLOR OF THE PEAS.

PUREE A SMALL CAN OF THE CHIPOTLES IN ADOBO BEFOREHAND AND STORE IT IN A TIGHTLY SEALED CONTAINER FOR UP TO 3 MONTHS. LEFTOVERS MAKE A FIERY ACCOMPANIMENT TO BURGERS, RIBS, OR CHICKEN.

Mushroom and Leek Spring Rolls
with Mint Dipping Sauce

These rolls are a Blue Ginger favorite, developed after a stay in France, where I took my postgraduate degree in leeks. Such a great onion!

The rolls are easy to fill and form. Just make sure to drain the filling thoroughly to ensure a dry, cohesive mixture and to seal the rolls well with the egg wash so they won't break open during frying.

These are, of course, perfect for parties.

BEVERAGE TIP: LAGER (TSINGTAO, SHANGHAI, SINGHA)

MAKES 10 SPRING ROLLS

2 tablespoons canola oil, plus additional for deep-frying
1 tablespoon finely chopped garlic
1 tablespoon finely chopped fresh ginger
2 serrano chiles, stemmed and finely chopped
$\frac{1}{2}$ cup hoisin sauce
2 cups thinly sliced shiitake mushroom caps
2 large leeks, white parts only, well washed and julienned
Salt and freshly ground black pepper
$\frac{1}{2}$ cup chopped fresh cilantro
1 cup chopped scallions, white and green parts
1 cup bean threads, soaked in warm water to cover until soft, 10 to 15 minutes, drained well, and cut into 2-inch pieces
1 1-pound package lumpia/menlo wrappers or egg roll or spring roll wrappers
1 egg beaten with $\frac{1}{4}$ cup water, for egg wash

Mint Dipping Sauce (page 234)

1. Heat a wok or skillet over high heat. Add the oil and swirl to coat the pan. When the oil is hot, add the garlic, ginger, and chiles and cook until soft, about 2 minutes. Do not allow the aromatics to burn. Reduce the heat to medium, add the hoisin sauce, and cook until it loses its raw taste, about 3 minutes. Add the shiitakes and leeks and cook until soft, about 6 minutes. Season with the salt and pepper to taste, transfer the mixture to a strainer, and with a large spoon, press the mixture well to drain it thoroughly. Cool.

2. Transfer the filling mixture to a medium bowl and add the cilantro, scallions, and bean threads. Stir to blend.

3. Dampen a kitchen towel. Place 5 wrappers on a work surface with 1 point of each near you and cover the remainder with the cloth to prevent drying. Place about $\frac{1}{4}$ cup of the filling on the wrappers just above the near corners. Bring the corner nearest you up over the filling and roll halfway; brush the edges with egg wash, then fold in the side corners and continue rolling to enclose the filling completely. Roll as tightly as possible. Cover with the cloth and allow the rolls to rest, seam side down; this permits the egg to set. Fill and roll the remaining wrappers, cover, and allow the rolls to rest at least 2 minutes.

4. Fill a fryer or heavy medium pot one-third full with the oil and heat to 350°F over high heat. Add the spring rolls 4 to 6 at a time and fry them until golden, turning as needed, about 5 minutes. Remove them with a slotted spoon and drain on paper towels. Slice the rolls on the diagonal or in half, if you wish, and serve hot with the sauce for dipping.

Salmon Roll Tempura

To make this tempting riceless sushi I use traditional Japanese maki- and tempura-making techniques and a Westernized filling that includes caramelized leeks. People reluctant to take the raw-fish plunge find these particularly to their liking.

BEVERAGE TIP: FRESH, FRUITY, SLIGHTLY SWEET GROLLEAU BLEND ROSÉ (FROM ANJOU)

SERVES 4

1 tablespoon canola oil, plus additional for deep-frying
4 large leeks, white parts only, well washed and julienned
Salt and freshly ground white pepper
1 cup mirin (Japanese sweet sake)
4 toasted nori sheets
4 salmon fillets, about 4 ounces each, lightly pounded to ¼ inch thick
2 cups rice flour
4 cups club soda
Wasabi Oil (page 228)
Soy Syrup (page 236)

1. Heat a large skillet or wok over medium heat. Add the 1 tablespoon of oil and swirl to coat the pan. When the oil shimmers, add the leeks and sauté, stirring occasionally, until soft and browned, 6 to 8 minutes. Season with salt and pepper to taste, add the mirin, and cook to evaporate the liquid, about 6 minutes. Cool.

2. Arrange a sheet of the nori, shiny side down, on a rolling mat. Have a small bowl of water handy. Place a salmon fillet on the bottom half of the nori sheet and season with salt and pepper. Arrange a quarter of the leeks on the upper one-third of the salmon. Roll as shown on page 79, wet the edge, and press the mat to seal. Repeat with the remaining nori, salmon, and leeks. Allow the maki to rest, seam side down, for 2 minutes.

3. Fill a fryer or heavy medium pot one-third full with the oil and heat over high heat to 375°F. Place the flour in a medium bowl and slowly whisk in the club soda until the mixture resembles a light pancake batter. Dip the rolls in the batter and fry all at once, turning as necessary, until golden, 4 to 6 minutes. Remove the rolls with a mesh spoon and drain them on paper towels. Season to taste with the salt and pepper.

4. With a sharp knife, cut the maki as described on page 55. Divide the rolls among 4 plates, garnish with the wasabi oil and soy syrup, and serve.

Prosciutto and Asian Pear "Maki"

I'm pushing the sushi envelope with this recipe—there's no fish, rice, or even nori used here. But the maki-rolling technique, accomplished with a bamboo rolling mat, is needed to make this Eastern play on the classic prosciutto and melon pairing. Here, the "melon" is Asian pear, and the combination of the sweet fruit and the salty ham is wonderful.

BEVERAGE TIP: BRIGHT, CITRUSY PINOT GRIGIO FROM COLLIO (BORGO CONVERITI)

SERVES 4

1/2 cup balsamic vinegar
1/4 cup Chinese black vinegar
2 Asian pears or 1 pear and 1 apple, peeled and julienned
Juice of 1 lime
1 heaping teaspoon cracked black peppercorns
8 large thin slices prosciutto, preferably prosciutto di Parma
1/4 cup chives cut into 1/2-inch lengths

1. In a small nonreactive saucepan, combine the vinegars and bring to a boil over high heat. Turn down the heat and simmer until the mixture is reduced by three-fourths or until syrupy, about 20 minutes. The mixture will thicken as it cools.

2. In a medium bowl, combine the julienned pears and lime juice and season with 2 pinches of the pepper. Mix.

3. Cover the bottom half of a sushi rolling mat with 2 slices of the prosciutto overlapping side by side. Evenly arrange about one-fourth of the pears over the top third of the prosciutto. To roll, lift the mat and, compressing it against the filling, bring the bottom edge of the prosciutto toward the top as shown on page 79. Continue to roll very tightly. The prosciutto will adhere to itself. Transfer the completed roll to a cutting board and repeat with the remaining prosciutto and pears.

4. With a spoon, drizzle some of the reduced vinegar syrup across a serving plate in a zigzag pattern. With a sharp knife, slice each maki in half. Cut one half straight across into 3 pieces and cut the other half diagonally into 2 pieces. Garnish with the remaining cracked peppercorn and chives, and serve.

Seafood Spring Roll Sticks
with Citrus Dipping Sauce

If you've been to Italy you've no doubt seen *grissini*—thin crisp bread sticks—served in tall glasses. That presentation inspired me to create these sticklike spring rolls which are also served in a glass. I've filled them with a mixture of scallops, rock shrimp, and Chilean sea bass, but if you prefer, you can make the filling for these with just one kind of seafood; just triple the quantity.

BEVERAGE TIP: LIGHT, CITRUSY SAUVIGNON BLANC (NEW ZEALAND CLOUDY BAY, MORGAN)

MAKES 16 TO 20 ROLLS

FILLING
1 pound rock shrimp or regular shrimp, peeled
$\frac{1}{2}$ pound Chilean sea bass fillet, cut into 1-inch dice
$\frac{1}{2}$ pound bay scallops
1 egg
1 tablespoon finely chopped fresh ginger
1 teaspoon toasted sesame oil
$\frac{1}{2}$ cup scallions, white and green parts, sliced $\frac{1}{8}$ inch thick
$\frac{1}{4}$ cup chopped fresh cilantro
Salt and freshly ground black pepper

16 to 20 lumpia/menlo wrappers or spring roll wrappers
1 egg beaten with $\frac{1}{4}$ cup water, for egg wash
Canola oil, for deep frying

Citrus Dipping Sauce (page 235)

MING'S TIP: THE ROLLS FREEZE WELL, SO IT PAYS TO MAKE EXTRA TO HAVE THEM ON HAND. THEY DON'T HAVE TO BE DEFROSTED BEFORE COOKING, BUT WHEN FRYING THEM, PUT THEM IN THE HOT OIL FOR 2 MINUTES, REMOVE THEM TO ALLOW RESIDUAL HEAT TO WARM THEM THROUGH, ABOUT 2 MINUTES, THEN RETURN THE ROLLS TO THE OIL TO FINISH COOKING.

1. To make the filling, combine the shrimp, bass, scallops, egg, ginger, and sesame oil in a food processor. Pulse just to chop ingredients finely; do not puree. Transfer to a large bowl and fold in the scallions and cilantro. Season with salt and pepper to taste.

2. Have a small bowl of water handy. Place a lumpia wrapper on a work surface with a corner near you. Place about 2 tablespoons of the filling a little above the corner and bring the near corner of the wrapper over the filling to enclose it. Brush the edges with egg wash, roll tightly toward the middle of the wrapper, then fold in the sides and continue to roll to make a sticklike spring roll ¼ to ½ inch in diameter. Make the roll as thin as possible. Rest the roll seam side down for 2 minutes and repeat with the remaining wrappers and filling.

3. Fill a fryer or heavy medium pot one-third full with the oil and heat over high heat to 350°F. Add half the rolls and fry until golden brown, about 5 minutes. Remove with a large-mesh spoon and drain on paper towels. Repeat with the remaining rolls. Stand the rolls in a large glass and serve with the dipping sauce on the side.

D
I
M

S
U
M

Crab and Fennel Wontons
with Mango-Lime Puree

Tropical fruit and seafood are a great combination, a point this dish really makes. But the flavor playoffs don't end there. The wontons are served with a raw fennel salad whose crispness is a great foil for the cooked fennel in the filling.

BEVERAGE TIP: TROPICAL SAUVIGNON BLANC (PETER MICHAELS, AUSTRALIAN LENSWOOD)

SERVES 4

PUREE
1 ripe mango, peeled and cut into chunks
Juice of 1 lime
1 teaspoon sambal oelek
$\frac{1}{2}$ cup canola oil
Salt and freshly ground white pepper

2 medium fennel bulbs, 1 finely diced, 1 shaved paper-thin, fronds
    reserved for garnish
1 tablespoon honey
Juice of 2 limes
$\frac{1}{4}$ cup chopped chives
4 dashes Tabasco sauce
1$\frac{1}{2}$ teaspoons extra-virgin olive oil
$\frac{1}{2}$ pound lump crabmeat, picked over
Salt and freshly ground white pepper
1 package thin, square wonton skins
1 egg beaten with $\frac{1}{4}$ cup water,
    for egg wash
Canola oil, for deep-frying

1. To make the puree, combine the mango, lime juice, and sambal oelek in a blender and blend well. With the machine running, add the oil slowly to create an emulsion. Transfer to a small bowl and season with salt and pepper to taste.

2. In a large bowl, combine the diced fennel, honey, half of the lime juice, the chives, Tabasco sauce, and olive oil. Mix; set aside for 10 minutes, then stir in the crab. Season with salt and pepper to taste.

3. Place 1 wonton skin on a work surface with 1 corner nearest you. Place $\frac{1}{2}$ tablespoon of the filling in the center of the skin, moisten the far sides with the egg wash, and fold the bottom half over the top to create a triangular dumpling. Bring the left and right sides under the dumpling, moisten the points with the egg wash, and pinch together to seal. Repeat with the remaining skins and filling.

4. In a medium bowl, combine the shaved fennel and the remaining lime juice. Season with salt and pepper and set aside.

5. Fill a fryer or medium heavy pot one-third full with the oil. Heat to 375°F over high heat. Add the wontons 6 at a time and fry until golden brown, about 3 minutes. Remove with a large-mesh spoon and drain on paper towels.

6. Divide the shaved fennel among 4 plates. Top with 3 wontons, garnish with the mango puree and fennel fronds, and serve.

MING'S TIP: THE FENNEL FOR THE SALAD GARNISH SHOULD BE SHAVED ALMOST PAPER-THIN. USE A MANDOLINE OR SHARP, THIN-BLADED KNIFE. IF YOU CAN'T MANAGE THE REQUIRED DEGREE OF THINNESS, START THE FENNEL'S "MARINATION" IN THE LIME JUICE ABOUT 20 MINUTES BEFORE SERVING TO SOFTEN.

DIM SUM

Oyster Corn Fritters
with Two-Vinegar Emulsion

I had my first hush puppy, the predecessor of this dish, at a Red Lobster—not exactly an auspicious introduction to that Southern specialty but good enough to excite my interest. I've had fun experimenting with them since then. Served with a tart vinegar emulsion, these fritters please everyone. They're particularly great for people who like the idea of raw oysters better than the reality: the oysters are cooked, but still retain their plump freshness.

These make a great Asian oyster po' boy served on sourdough bread with Dijon-Sambal Aïoli (page 237), lettuce, and tomatoes.

BEVERAGE TIP: SPARKLING WINE (JORDAN'S J)

MAKES 20 FRITTERS

EMULSION
2 cups balsamic vinegar
$\frac{1}{2}$ cup Chinese black vinegar
1 cup canola oil
Salt and freshly ground black pepper

8 eggs, separated
4 cups polenta or yellow cornmeal
4 cups 2 percent milk
1 cup canola oil, plus additional for frying
2 bunches scallions, green parts only, cut into $\frac{1}{8}$-inch slices
4 serrano chiles, finely chopped
4 cups corn kernels, preferably fresh, or frozen and defrosted
1 tablespoon brown sugar
$1\frac{1}{2}$ teaspoons salt, plus more as needed
$1\frac{1}{2}$ teaspoons black pepper
1 cup all-purpose flour
20 large oysters, freshly shucked
1 baby romaine lettuce, cut into $\frac{1}{4}$-inch ribbons

1. To make the emulsion, combine the vinegars in a medium nonreactive saucepan and reduce over low heat by three-fourths or until syrupy, about 20 to 30 minutes. Transfer to a blender, start the machine, and add the oil slowly to form an emulsion. Season with salt and pepper to taste and set aside.

2. Whip the egg whites until firm peaks form. In a large nonreactive bowl, combine the egg yolks, polenta, milk, 1 cup oil, the scallions, chiles, corn, brown sugar, $1\frac{1}{2}$ teaspoons salt, and the pepper and stir gently to blend. The mixture should have the consistency of thick pancake batter. If it's too thin, add a little more polenta; if too thick, add more milk. Keep in mind that the mixture will thicken on standing. Fold in the whites.

3. Fill a fryer or heavy medium pot one-third full with the oil and heat to 400°F. Place the flour on a plate and have the batter handy. Dredge the oysters lightly in the flour, dip in the batter, and fry 6 to 8 at a time until golden brown, 2 to 3 minutes until golden brown. Remove with a large-mesh spoon, drain on paper towels, and sprinkle with salt.

4. Divide the romaine among 4 plates and drizzle the emulsion around the portions. Top the emulsion with the oysters and serve.

MING'S TIP: YOU CAN USE FROZEN CORN KERNELS, BUT I HIGHLY RECOMMEND THAT YOU TAKE THE TROUBLE TO PREPARE FRESH. TO REMOVE THE KERNELS FROM FRESH CORN, SLICE THE LARGER END OFF EACH EAR AND STAND EACH ON A CUTTING BOARD. CUT STRAIGHT DOWN THE COBS WITH A SHARP KNIFE, REMOVING SEVERAL KERNEL ROWS AT A TIME. FROZEN KERNELS, IF USED, SHOULD BE AS MOISTURE FREE AS POSSIBLE TO AVOID THEIR "EXPLODING" WHEN FRIED. TO ACHIEVE THIS, DEFROST THEM OVERNIGHT IN A STRAINER OVER A SMALL BOWL IN THE FRIDGE.

DIM SUM

Tempura Shrimp Cocktail
with Two Purees

No offense, but I find the traditional American shrimp cocktail—boiled shrimp, ketchupy sauce—less than exciting. I've remade this starter in East-West style and paired it with avocado puree and a chipotle-fired tomato sauce—my versions of guacamole and salsa. I tucked everything into a martini glass (it's called a cocktail, isn't it?) with freshly fried tortilla chips. Voilà!

The tempura coating is delicate. Don't be alarmed if the shrimp appear to have been unbattered in places after frying; this translucence is normal. They'll still be GB&D, as we say at the restaurant—golden brown and delicious.

BEVERAGE TIP: MODERATE SPICY PINOT GRIS (ALSATIAN WEINBACH OR TRIMBACH)

SERVES 4

TOMATO PUREE
2 tablespoons canola oil
1 medium onion, roughly chopped
1 tablespoon chopped garlic
2 medium tomatoes, roughly chopped, or 1 cup drained canned plum tomatoes
$\frac{1}{2}$ to 1 tablespoon chopped chipotles in adobo sauce, according to heat preference
Salt and freshly ground black pepper

AVOCADO PUREE
2 ripe avocados, roughly chopped
1 jalapeño pepper, stemmed and seeded
Juice of 1 lime
Salt and freshly ground black pepper
$\frac{1}{4}$ cup chopped fresh cilantro
1 tablespoon finely chopped shallots

2 flour tortillas or best-quality tortilla chips
1 teaspoon ancho chile powder
Salt
2 cups rice flour
2 to 3 cups club soda
Canola oil, for deep-frying
12 large shrimp, peeled except for tail and deveined (see Tip, page 102)
2 cups romaine lettuce cut into $\frac{1}{8}$-inch ribbons
1 cup mesclun (optional), for garnish
8 chives, for garnish

1. To make the tomato puree, heat a small skillet over medium heat. Add the oil and swirl to coat the pan. When the oil shimmers, add the onion and garlic and sauté, stirring, until brown, about 6 minutes. Add the tomatoes and the chipotles to taste and cook, stirring, until the tomatoes are soft and their liquid has evaporated, about 10 minutes. Transfer to a food processor and puree. Season with salt and pepper to taste. Set aside.

2. To make the avocado puree, combine the avocados with the jalapeño and lime juice in a food processor and puree. Season with salt and pepper to taste and fold in the cilantro and shallots. Set aside.

3. Cut the tortillas, if using, into long-sided triangles the length of the tortillas and about 1 inch wide. In a small bowl, combine the chile powder and salt, mix well, and set aside. Place the flour in a medium bowl and stir in sufficient club soda to produce a pancake batter–like mixture.

4. Fill a fryer or heavy medium pot one-third full with the oil and heat to 375°F. Add the tortilla triangles and fry until golden brown, about 3 minutes. Drain well on paper towels, season with chile powder and salt, and set aside.

5. Reheat the oil to 375°F, dip the shrimp in the batter, drain any excess, and fry in 2 batches until golden brown, 3 to 5 minutes. Remove with a large-mesh spoon and drain on paper towels. Season with salt to taste.

6. Place a small mound of the romaine in each of 4 martini glasses. Add dollops of the purees side by side and insert 3 chips upright into each portion. Hang 3 shrimp off the rims of each of the glasses, pushing them very gently into the glasses to adhere, and garnish with the mesclun and chives.

MING'S TIP: THIS IS EASY TO DO ONCE YOU GET THE PUREES PREPARED, AND YOU CAN DO THAT AHEAD. THE TOMATO PUREE, AND THEREFORE THE DISH, IS BEST MADE IN SUMMER WHEN TOMATOES ARE AT THEIR PEAK. AT OTHER TIMES, IF FRESH TOMATOES ARE BELOW PAR, USE BEST-QUALITY CANNED WHOLE PLUM TOMATOES.

New Hamachi Sashimi
with Curry Oil

I call this Sashimi 101 because the hamachi is served part-raw, part-cooked, making it perfect entry-level raw fish eating. The half-cooking is accomplished by the curry oil, which is heated and spooned onto the raw fish just before it's served, partially searing it. This method, based on the Chinese cooking technique called flashing, imparts richness and great flavor. A final touch of soy syrup enlivens the dish. The fish must be absolutely fresh. If the hamachi in your market is not up to par, buy tuna, salmon, or whatever sashimi-grade fish meets the freshness standard.

BEVERAGE TIP: CHILLED SAKE (PREFERABLY A JI-SAKE)

SERVES 4

4 2-ounce hamachi fillets (yellowtail)
Fleur de sel or regular sea salt
Coarsely ground black pepper
2 tablespoons chopped chives
2 teaspoons Soy Syrup (page 236) or kechap manis
$\frac{1}{4}$ cup Curry Oil (page 230)
$\frac{1}{2}$ tablespoon finely julienned fresh ginger

1. Wrap each piece of hamachi loosely in plastic film. Place on a work surface and using a meat pounder or mallet, pound the fish gently to about $\frac{1}{8}$-inch thickness.

2. Unwrap the hamachi and transfer each flattened fillet to a serving plate. Season the fish lightly with salt and pepper and sprinkle with the chives. Drizzle each serving with about $\frac{1}{2}$ teaspoon of the soy syrup in a zigzag pattern.

3. In a small skillet over high heat, heat the curry oil until very hot, about 5 minutes. Stir in the ginger, remove from the stove, and immediately spoon a bit of the oil over one portion of fish. The fish should sizzle when the oil hits it; if not, return the skillet to the stove, reheat the oil. Spoon 1 tablespoon of the hot oil over each portion and serve at once.

MING'S TIP: THE HAMACHI IS WRAPPED IN PLASTIC AND POUNDED LIGHTLY. ONCE THAT IS ACCOMPLISHED, YOU CAN STORE THE FISH FOR FINISHING LATER IN ITS WRAPPER, REFRIGERATED, FOR UP TO 4 HOURS.

Asparagus-Crusted Ahi Tuna
with Asparagus Vinaigrette

David Burke of Manhattan's Park Avenue Cafe was, I believe, the first to make aspara-gus-crusted tuna. I've borrowed his method, adding sesame seeds to the coating, and serve the fish with an asparagus vinaigrette. And because more is often more, I spear each tuna portion with an asparagus stalk before frying it.

This isn't hard to prepare, but the fish must be absolutely fresh. Insist on #1 grade ahi tuna and check to make sure that the fish you're offered is deeply and consistently red in color; that it's moist but never sticky to the touch; and that it smells fresh, like the sea itself, never fishy. Above all, buy from a fish merchant you trust.

BEVERAGE TIP: HERBACEOUS, VEGETAL SAUVIGNON BLANC (SOUTH AFRICAN MULDERBOSCH)

SERVES 4

24 medium asparagus spears, 8 cut $^{1}/_{16}$ inch thick
$^{1}/_{4}$ cup canola oil, plus additional for deep-frying
2 teaspoons toasted sesame oil
1 tablespoon Dijon mustard
Juice of 1 lemon
Salt and freshly ground black pepper
1 pound #1 grade ahi tuna, cut into 4
    2 × 1-inch portions
1 cup rice flour
$^{1}/_{2}$ tablespoon sesame seeds, plus $^{1}/_{2}$ tablespoon
    toasted (see page 5), for garnish
4 egg whites, beaten until foamy

1. Bring a large quantity of salted water to a boil. Fill a medium bowl with water and add ice. Boil the whole asparagus spears until tender-crisp, about 3 minutes. Drain and transfer to the ice water. When the spears are cold, drain well, setting aside 4 spears.

2. Cut the top 2 inches from the remaining 12 asparagus spears, set aside, and roughly chop the remaining spears. In a small bowl, combine the $\frac{1}{4}$ cup canola oil and the sesame oil and mix. In a blender, combine the chopped asparagus, the mustard, and the lemon juice. Blend, slowly adding the mixed oils. Season the vinaigrette with the salt and pepper to taste and set aside.

3. To prepare the tuna, insert a metal skewer into one short side of each tuna portion and push it through the opposite end. Work the skewer to create a small channel, and push 1 of the reserved asparagus spears through each tuna portion. Allow 1 inch of stalk to protrude on either side.

4. Fill a fryer or heavy medium pot one-third full with the canola oil and heat over high heat to 400°F. Meanwhile, season the tuna generously with salt and pepper. Spread the rice flour on a plate and dredge the tuna in it. Add the sliced asparagus and raw sesame seeds to the egg whites and mix well. When the oil is hot, coat each tuna piece in the egg white mixture and deep-fry, turning with tongs as necessary, just until the coating is golden brown, 2 to 3 minutes. Do not allow the tuna to overcook; it should remain rare in the center. Remove the tuna with a mesh spoon and drain on paper towels.

5. Toss the reserved asparagus tops with half of the vinaigrette. Divide the tops among 4 plates. Halve the tuna portions along the length of the asparagus and place on top of the arranged asparagus. Drizzle the plate with the remaining vinaigrette. Garnish with the toasted sesame seeds and serve.

MING'S TIP: DON'T OVERCOOK THE TUNA; IT SHOULD REMAIN RARE AND COOL IN THE CENTER. THE TEMPERATURE CONTRAST BETWEEN THE EXTERIOR AND INTERIOR OF THE TUNA IS PART OF THE PLEASURE OF THIS DISH.

DIM SUM

Rock Shrimp Lollipops
with Spicy Almond Sauce

Whenever I sample a dish that intrigues me, I immediately think about how I might rein-terpret it. These simply made lollipops—spicy shrimp puree molded around lemongrass stalks and then fried—began just that way. Their ancestor was a traditional Vietnamese specialty of sugarcane coated with shrimp paste. I've added coconut, lemongrass, and other good things to the paste and included a complementary pesto-style sauce.

BEVERAGE TIP: SPARKLING CHENIN BLANC FROM SAUMUR OR VOUVRAY (CHATEAU MONCONTOUR)

SERVES 6 TO 8

SAUCE
1 cup slivered almonds
1 tablespoon sambal oelek
¼ cup fresh cilantro leaves, plus 3 sprigs for garnish
¼ cup fresh Thai or sweet basil leaves, plus 3 sprigs for garnish
1 tablespoon Thai fish sauce *(nam pla)*
Juice of 1 lime
¼ cup peanut oil
Salt and freshly ground black pepper

1½ pounds rock shrimp or regular shrimp, peeled
3 shallots, peeled and quartered
3 Thai bird chiles
1 cup unsweetened shredded coconut
1 tablespoon brown sugar, packed
2 tablespoons finely chopped lemongrass, white parts only, plus 12 3-inch
    lemongrass stalks, green parts only
5 kaffir lime leaves, julienned
Juice of 1 lime
Salt and freshly ground black pepper
1 cup rice flour
1 cup canola oil

1. Preheat the oven to 300°F. Spread the almonds on a baking sheet and toast, tossing once, until brown, 15 to 20 minutes. Watch carefully because the almonds burn easily. Allow to cool. Set aside 1 tablespoon for garnish.

2. To make the sauce, combine the toasted almonds, sambal oelek, cilantro and basil leaves, fish sauce, lime juice, and peanut oil in a food processor. Puree to make a smooth sauce. Add a little water, if necessary, to achieve a pancake batter–like consistency. Season with salt and pepper to taste and set aside.

3. In a food processor, combine the shrimp, shallots, chiles, coconut, brown sugar, chopped lemongrass, lime leaves, and lime juice. Process until well combined; the mixture should have the consistency of ground meat. If too thin, add more coconut; if too thick, thin with lime juice and/or oil. Season lightly with salt and pepper. With wet hands mold the shrimp mixture onto the lemongrass stalks, leaving 1½ inches exposed for a "handle."

4. Spread the rice flour on a large plate. Heat the oil in a large skillet over high heat. Dredge the lollipops in the flour and shallow-fry them, turning once, until golden brown, about 6 minutes. Drain on paper towels and allow to cool slightly. Salt lightly.

5. With a spoon, drizzle the sauce across a large platter in a zigzag pattern. (You may not need it all; reserve extra for another use.) Top with the lollipops, garnish with the basil and cilantro sprigs, and the reserved almonds, and serve.

MING'S TIP: YOU MAY SUBSTITUTE 4-INCH WOODEN SKEWERS FOR THE LEMONGRASS STALKS. IF YOU DO, SOAK THE SKEWERS IN WATER FOR 30 MINUTES TO PREVENT THEM FROM BURNING.

DIM SUM

Chapter 3

Rice and Noodles

SOME CHEFS FINISH THEIR TRAINING WITH AN APPRENTICE-SHIP IN A FRENCH KITCHEN. I WENT TO OSAKA AS A KITCHEN APPRENTICE TO MASTER SHORT-GRAIN SUSHI RICE.

Until then, long-grain rice—and the Chinese dishes that featured it—were my bread and butter. I can't remember a home meal from my childhood days that wasn't accompanied by a pot of steaming rice, and we often enjoyed real fried rice, as in the traditional Mandarin version on page 83. My grandfather was also adept at turning out the most toothsome lo mein, produced, incongruously, with an Italian pasta machine.

But learning to make sushi rice, the foundation of Japan's great contribution to world eating, became my goal. At Osaka's restaurant Matsuri, I learned the sushi rice technique I present here in a simplified but in no way compromised version. I also discovered the incredibly varied sushi rice repertoire—the maki rolls and other delights that are a feast for the eye as well as the palate.

My quest to translate these for American home cooks meant acknowledging some obstacles. These include getting properly fresh catch and pleasing diners who fear raw fish. To overcome such difficulties, I've devised counterparts to uncooked seafood rolls like Smoked Salmon and Jicama Maki Sushi. These are guaranteed to satisfy sushi novices and old hands alike. I also offer Grilled Sushi Rice with Soy Ginger Glaze, a savory rice bite that's a perfect use for any sushi rice you may have left over.

The Japanese prize noodles too, of course. I'm a great udon noodle lover and like to serve these tasty wheat noodles in a lemongrass broth (see page 88), which is great for slurping. When it comes to noodles, though, my heart probably belongs to China. Whether the Chinese invented noodles or not (and according to my Food Network colleague Mario Batali, they did), the rice, wheat, and bean thread noodles they've devised are central to the informal, meal-in-one cooking I love best. Shrimp Curried Noodles, Sweet and Spicy Beef Noodles, and Shrimp and Haricots Verts Shanghai Noodles are savory examples of these dinner-in-a-pot dishes that are also easy on the cook. And in salute to the great stir-fried noodle dishes I've enjoyed through the years, I give you the spicy, shiitake-packed Chicken Chow Mein My Way, a real chow mein, as opposed to the many chop suey versions that go around. Like the other noodle and rice dishes in this chapter, the chow mein is the body-and-soul nourishing eating that only rice and noodles can provide. As a cook, I always return to these culinary fundamentals.

A Word About Rice Cookers

There are over 2.5 billion Asians, and most of those who cook rice use rice cookers—with reason! Of course, you can make rice beautifully without a cooker, but cookers make flawless rice effortlessly.

Using a cooker is simplicity itself. You put washed rice into the cooker, add water "up to Mt. Fuji" (see page 74), cover, and turn on the machine. The machine cooks the rice automatically, turning the heat off at exactly the right moment for perfectly done rice. The best models hold the rice in readiness until it's needed.

The cookers come in various sizes, from 1 cup to professional models that accommodate great quantities of rice; home cooks will want models that can handle 4 to 6 cups of raw rice. The cookers can also double as steamers, making them convenient for preparing vegetables or steaming buns. Rice cookers are available in most appliance stores and large Asian markets.

Sushi Rice

In France, the first thing you do in a professional kitchen is peel potatoes; in Japan, you make sushi rice. My introduction to this process came from Chef Kobayashi, a renowned sushi master with whom I studied in Osaka.

The traditional method involves cooking the medium-sticky short-grain sushi rice to a deliciously chewy texture. The rice is then turned in a porous wooden bowl, which absorbs moisture and helps it to become glossy. To further ensure a fine finish, the rice is fanned after being tossed with its vinegar flavoring—a bit of a feat for a solo cook!

Here I've simplified the method without sacrificing the flavor or texture of the finished rice.

MAKES 6 CUPS

4 cups short-grain Japanese sushi rice
1 cup rice wine vinegar
$\frac{1}{4}$ cup mirin (Japanese sweet sake)
$\frac{1}{2}$ cup sugar

1. Place the rice in a bowl or rice cooker insert and add water to cover it generously. Swish the rice in the water in a single direction to rinse off residual starch. Drain the water, refill the bowl or insert, and swish again. Repeat until the water is clear. Do not rub the rice together with your hands because it could break the grains.

2. Drain the rice and if not using a rice cooker, place it in a medium saucepan fitted with a tight lid. If using a rice cooker, dry the outside of the insert and place it in the cooker. Flatten the rice with a palm and without removing your hand, add water until it just touches the middle and highest knuckle of your hand. This is the "Mt. Fuji" method. If using a rice cooker, turn it on and allow the rice to cook. In a saucepan, cover and bring the water to a boil over high heat, 10 to 15 minutes. Reduce the heat to medium and simmer for 30 minutes. Turn off the heat and let the rice stand, covered, to plump, for 20 minutes.

3. Meanwhile, in a small nonreactive saucepan, combine the vinegar, mirin, and sugar and heat over medium heat until hot, about 5 minutes; do not allow the mixture to boil. Keep hot.

4. Invert the rice into a large stainless-steel or wooden bowl. Don't include any browned rice that may have formed at the bottom of the pan. Using a wood or rubber spatula, gently fold half of the vinegar mixture into the rice. Use a light, lifting motion to avoid mashing the rice. Taste; the rice should have a pleasingly sweet-acidic edge. If necessary, fold in more of the vinegar mixture.

5. Dampen a clean dish towel. With your hands, gently push the rice together to form a loose mound. (Spread out rice would become dry.) Cover with the towel and allow the rice to rest for 20 minutes to develop its flavor. The rice is now ready to use.

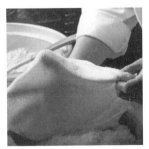

Grilled Sushi Rice
with Soy Ginger Glaze

This dish, which I learned to make in Osaka, is an ingenious way to use cooked sushi rice. The rice is formed by hand into triangular cakes, filled with pickled ginger, sealed, and quickly grilled. While cooking, the cakes are brushed with a soy ginger glaze. The cakes leave the grill with a smoky-savory taste and are served wrapped in lettuce leaves. They make a great light appetizer.

BEVERAGE TIP: MEDIUM-DRY, FRUITY, CHILLED SAKE (GEKKEIKAN "HORIN" OR "HAIKU")

MAKES 6 CAKES

2 cups Sushi Rice (page 74)
¼ cup julienned Pickled Ginger (page 238)
¼ cup Soy Ginger Glaze (page 236)
1 tablespoon sesame seeds
6 leaves red leaf lettuce, for serving

1. Heat an outdoor grill or preheat the broiler. To form the cakes, wet your hands. Take about one-sixth of the rice and compress it between your hands. Use your fingers to mold the rice into a 2-inch-high by 2-inch-thick triangular shape. Flip the rice mass and continue to mold, compressing the rice only enough to shape it. Repeat to make 6 cakes in all, wetting your hands well before forming each. (See photograph on page 70.)

2. With a finger, make shallow holes halfway through one side of each of the triangles and fill with the pickled ginger. Cover the holes over with rice and let rest for 5 minutes.

3. Grill or broil the cakes until browned, 3 minutes. Brush with the glaze, turn, and cook 3 minutes more. Alternatively, line a baking tray with foil and oil it lightly. Place the triangles on the foil and broil until browned, brushing the triangles with the glaze before turning them, about 4 minutes per side. Sprinkle with the sesame seeds, wrap each triangle in a lettuce leaf, and serve.

MING'S TIP: FORMING THE RICE INTO TRIANGLES TAKES SOME PRACTICE, BUT PRACTICE MAKES PERFECT. KEEP YOUR HANDS WET AS YOU WORK AND DON'T COMPRESS THE RICE SO TIGHTLY THAT YOU MASH THE GRAINS.

Shiitake and Spinach Ura Maki

Ura maki are inside-out rolls. Rather than enclosing a filling inside a rice-covered nori sheet, ura maki feature the nori and filling rolled within the rice. The result is not only delicious but also wonderful to look at.

BEVERAGE TIP: MEDIUM-DRY, FRUITY, CHILLED SAKE (GEKKEIKAN "HORIN" OR "HAIKU")

MAKES 4 ROLLS

2 tablespoons canola oil
1 teaspoon finely chopped fresh ginger
2 cups fresh shiitake caps cut into $\frac{1}{4}$-inch slices
1 tablespoon soy sauce
1 tablespoon rice wine vinegar
$\frac{1}{2}$ teaspoon toasted sesame oil
1 teaspoon sugar
1 large bunch spinach, stemmed, blanched, and chopped
Salt and freshly ground white pepper
1 teaspoon vinegar
4 toasted nori sheets
4 cups Sushi Rice (page 74)

1. Heat a medium skillet over high heat. Add the oil and swirl to coat the pan. When the oil shimmers, add the ginger and sauté, stirring, until soft, about 3 minutes. Add the shiitakes and sauté until soft, about 6 minutes. Drain off any liquid, and set aside.

2. In a medium bowl, combine the soy sauce, vinegar, sesame oil, and sugar and stir to blend. Add the spinach, stir to coat, and season with the salt and pepper to taste.

3. Fill a small bowl with water and add the vinegar. Place a nori sheet shiny side down on a sushi mat with one long edge toward you. Wet your hands and pat a $\frac{1}{4}$-inch layer of the sushi rice over the nori. Wrap a second rolling mat in plastic wrap, place the mat over the rice and, holding a palm against it, flip the rice. Remove the first rolling mat; the nori side will now be facing you. Cover the top one-third of the nori with the spinach and top with a line of shiitakes and roll as shown on page 79. Repeat with the remaining nori and filling. Allow the maki to rest, seam side down, for 2 minutes then cut each roll into 5 pieces as described on page 78.

Smoked Salmon and Jicama Maki Sushi

As much as I enjoy sushi, the chef in me has always wished that maki rolls had more textural contrast. I've made up for that in this maki version by adding crispy jicama to its salmon-based vegetable filling. Jicama is a vegetable I first used in maki while cooking in New Mexico. It also adds a nice sweetness.

The maki rolling technique takes a little practice, but isn't difficult to learn. Do invest in a bamboo rolling mat (called a *maki-su*).

BEVERAGE TIP: CHILLED SAKE OR CHAMPAGNE (VEUVE CLICQUOT)

SERVES 4

1 teaspoon vinegar
4 toasted nori sheets
4 cups Sushi Rice (page 74)
4 thin slices smoked salmon cut into $\frac{1}{4}$-inch strips
1 cup jicama, peeled and cut into strips $\frac{1}{4}$ inch thick
   and as long as the vegetable
$\frac{1}{4}$ cup Pickled Ginger (page 238)
$\frac{1}{4}$ cup Wasabi Oil (page 228)
$\frac{1}{4}$ cup Soy Syrup (page 236)

1. Fill a small bowl with water; add the vinegar. Place 1 sheet of nori shiny side down on the sushi mat with one long edge toward you. Wet your hands and pat a $\frac{1}{4}$-inch layer of the rice over the bottom half of the nori.

2. Cover the rice with one-fourth of the salmon strips and top with one-fourth of the jicama and pickled ginger. Drizzle a thin line of wasabi oil over the filling. To roll, lift the mat, compressing it against the filling as you roll the bottom edge in on itself. Continue rolling toward the top edge until only $\frac{1}{4}$ inch of the nori remains unrolled. Moisten a finger and wet the edge of the nori. Press the mat to seal the roll. Repeat with the remaining nori and filling. Allow the maki to rest, seam side down, for 2 minutes.

3. With a sharp knife, slice each maki in half. Cut one half straight across into 3 pieces and cut the other half diagonally into 2 pieces. With a spoon, drizzle additional wasabi oil and the soy syrup onto plates in a zigzag pattern, arrange the maki pieces over, and serve.

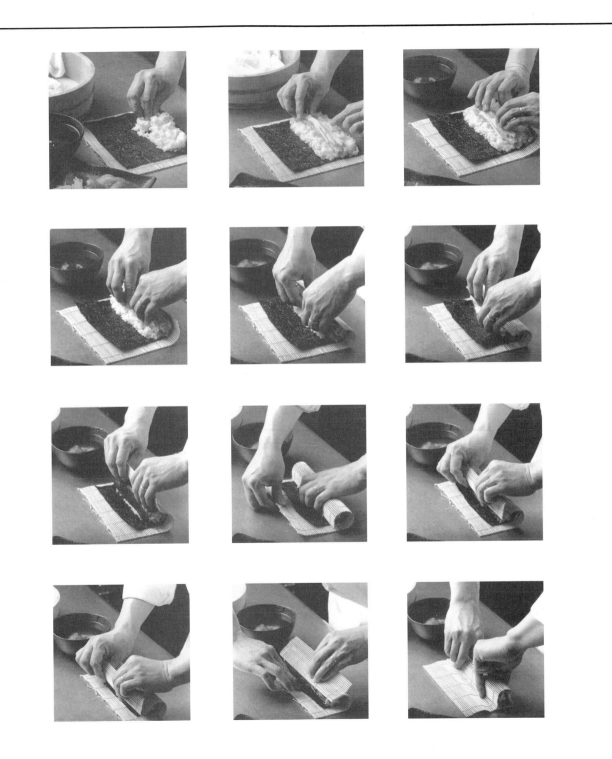

Spicy Crab Handrolls

Here is another contender from my make-sushi-and-sashimi-accessible repertoire. Though similar to the sushi bar favorite, spicy tuna maki, the seafood involved is cooked, not raw. Crab is close to my heart, not only because of my Chinese culinary roots but also because of its light sweetness. A touch of honey and sambal oelek gives a nice twist to the seafood, which is also enhanced by crunchy cucumber.

BEVERAGE TIP: CHILLED SAKE OR SEMILLON (AUSTRALIAN BROKENWOOD)

SERVES 4

8 ounces lump crabmeat, picked over
1 1/2 teaspoons sambal oelek
1/4 cup chopped fresh cilantro leaves
1 tablespoon chopped chives
1 tablespoon honey
1 tablespoon canola oil
Salt and freshly ground pepper
1 teaspoon vinegar
4 toasted nori sheets, halved lengthwise
2 cups Sushi Rice (page 74)
1/2 cup peeled, seeded, and julienned cucumber

1. In a medium bowl, combine the crab, sambal oelek, cilantro, chives, honey, and canola oil, and toss lightly. Season with the salt and pepper to taste.

2. Fill a small bowl with water and add the vinegar. Place a half-sheet of the nori vertically on a work surface, shiny side down. Spread about 1/2 cup of the rice on the lower half of the nori, patting it down lightly. Top with one-fourth of the seasoned crab, placing it diagonally across the rice from the upper left corner to the bottom right. Place one-fourth of the cucumber on the crab, fold the lower left-hand corner of the nori toward the right side to enclose the filling, and continue to roll toward the nori's left side to form a cone. Wet a finger in the water and moisten the top 1/2 inch of the nori's edge to seal the cone. Repeat with the remaining nori, rice, and filling. Serve immediately.

Crab and Herb Salad Maki

A sweet-tart crab salad, brightened with the taste of basil, is the basis for this delectable maki—one of my all-time favorites. Though the salad excels as a filling for maki, it's also great on its own, piled on lettuce. Or use it to make the world's best crab roll—toast a bun, butter it well, fill it with the salad, and I'll be right over.

BEVERAGE TIP: CHILLED SAKE OR SAUVIGNON BLANC (MICHEL LYNCH)

MAKES 4 ROLLS

1 tablespoon honey

1 tablespoon Dijon mustard

1½ tablespoons fresh lemon juice

1 tablespoon canola oil

1 pound lump crabmeat, picked over

¼ cup chopped fresh cilantro

¼ cup chopped flat-leaf parsley

¼ cup fresh basil cut into ⅛-inch ribbons

1 shallot, finely chopped

Salt and freshly ground black pepper

1 teaspoon vinegar

4 toasted nori sheets

4 cups Sushi Rice (page 74)

1. In a medium bowl, combine the honey, mustard, lemon juice, and oil and whisk to mix. Add the crab, cilantro, parsley, basil, and shallot and season with the salt and pepper to taste. Mix lightly and correct the seasonings.

2. Fill a small bowl with water and add the vinegar. Place a nori sheet shiny side down on a sushi rolling mat with one long edge toward you. Wet your hands and pat a ¼-inch layer of the sushi rice over the bottom half of the nori.

3. Cover the top one-third of the rice with one-fourth of the crab mixture. Roll as illustrated on page 81 and press the mat to seal the roll. Allow the maki to rest, seam side down, for 2 minutes. Repeat with the remaining nori and filling. With a sharp knife, slice each maki into 5 pieces as described on page 78 and serve immediately.

Traditional Mandarin Fried Rice

I'm passionate about fried rice: it's the first real dish I ever made. This traditional version contains Chinese sausage, ginger, garlic, and softly cooked egg. Peas don't belong in this authentic recipe, though their use has become almost automatic even among Chinese. Use day-old or leftover rice for this, as freshly made rice gets mushy when it's stir-fried. If you must use fresh-made rice, "dry" it by spreading it on a baking sheet and putting it in the freezer until cool, 30 minutes.

BEVERAGE TIP: CRISP SAUVIGNON BLANC (NEW ZEALAND CLOUDY BAY)

SERVES 4

4 tablespoons canola oil
3 eggs, beaten lightly
2 tablespoons finely chopped garlic
2 tablespoons finely chopped fresh ginger
1 la chang (Chinese sausage), cut into $\frac{1}{8}$-inch dice, or
   4 strips cooked bacon, crumbled
1 bunch scallions, white and green parts chopped and reserved separately
5 cups cold cooked rice
2 tablespoons soy sauce
$\frac{1}{2}$ teaspoon white pepper
Salt, if needed

1. Heat a wok or large nonstick skillet over high heat. Add 2 tablespoons of the oil and swirl to coat the pan. When the oil shimmers, add the eggs, which will puff up. Allow to set, about 5 seconds, and using a wok spatula or similar tool, push the sides of the egg mass toward the center to allow uncooked egg to reach the pan and solidify. Flip the mass, allow it to set, about 5 seconds, and slide it onto a dish; do *not* overcook. With the edge of the spatula, break the eggs into small pieces. Set aside.

2. Add the remaining 2 tablespoons of the oil to the wok and swirl to coat the pan. When the oil shimmers, add the garlic and ginger and stir-fry until soft, about 2 minutes. Add the la chang, the white parts of the scallions, and the rice and toss thoroughly until heated through. Add the soy sauce, pepper, and reserved eggs and toss. Correct the seasonings, adding the salt if necessary, transfer to a platter, and garnish with the scallion greens. Serve immediately.

Sticky Rice Pouches
with Garlic-Flashed Scallops

I devised this dish of lotus leaf–wrapped rice, scallops, and sausage in tribute to my beloved Grandma, Nai-Nai.

Nai-Nai used to prepare *zongzi*—traditional rice packets that were tricky to tie up properly and needed to be steamed forever. I could never quite get Grandma's knack, but the dish was delicious and I set about reinventing it. The result, which is easier and quicker, features both fresh and dried scallops, a delicacy much prized by the Chinese. It also uses the Chinese technique of hot-oil flashing (see page 64) to sear the fresh scallops and add great taste.

These pouches make an impressive first course and get lots of "oohs" and "ahs" when they're "flashed" tableside.

BEVERAGE TIP: BIG, DRY, BUTTERY CHARDONNAY (PATZ & HALL)

SERVES 4

POUCHES
3 cups short-grain Japanese sushi rice
1/4 cup dried scallops
2 la chang (Chinese sausage), cut into 1/8-inch dice
1/2 cup scallions, white and green parts, sliced 1/4 inch thick
1/3 cup oyster sauce
1/4 cup chopped fresh cilantro
Salt and freshly ground black pepper
4 lotus leaves, soaked in water to cover until pliable, about 30 minutes (see Tip)

12 large sea scallops
Salt and freshly ground black pepper
2 tablespoons canola oil
1/2 cup peanut oil
16 garlic cloves, thinly sliced
1/4 cup fresh cilantro leaves, for garnish

1. In a medium bowl, combine the rice with enough water to cover it generously. Swish the rice in the water in a single direction to wash it of residual starch. Drain the water, refill the bowl, and swish again. Repeat until the water is clear when the rice is swished.

2. Drain the rice and place it in a rice cooker or medium saucepan fitted with a tight lid. Flatten the rice with a palm and without removing your hand, add water until it rises to the highest knuckle of your hand. Add the dried scallops.

3. Turn on the rice cooker if using. Otherwise, cover the saucepan and bring to a boil over high heat. Reduce the heat to medium-low and simmer, covered, for 30 minutes. Turn off the heat and let the rice stand, covered, to plump, for about 20 minutes. Transfer the rice and scallops to a large bowl and cool.

4. Remove the scallops and shred them by hand. Return the scallops to the rice and add the la chang, scallions, oyster sauce, and cilantro. Season with salt and pepper to taste and mix lightly.

5. To form the pouches, place 4 lotus leaves on a work surface. Place 1 cup of the filling in the center of each. Fold the bottoms up to enclose the filling and the tops down to cover the bottoms. Fold the left and right sides under the pouches.

6. Set up a steamer and steam the packages until hot, about 15 minutes. Meanwhile, season the scallops with salt and pepper to taste. Heat a medium skillet over hot heat; add the canola oil and swirl to coat. When the oil shimmers, add the scallops and sauté over high heat without moving until brown and crispy, 2 to 3 minutes. Turn and cook on the second side 3 minutes more. Remove and keep warm.

7. Meanwhile, divide the pouches among 4 plates. Using the point of a sharp knife, slit an H with a long center bar in each and fold back the wrapper. Place 3 of the sautéed scallops on top of each portion.

8. Wipe out the skillet and return to the stove over medium heat. Add the peanut oil and swirl to coat. Add the garlic and sauté, stirring, until light brown, 3 to 5 minutes. Immediately flash the scallops with the hot oil and garlic. Garnish with the cilantro leaves and serve.

MING'S TIP: IF YOU CAN'T GET LOTUS LEAVES, BANANA LEAVES OR CORN HUSKS LIKE THOSE USED FOR TAMALES MAY BE SUBSTITUTED WITH EXCELLENT RESULTS.

RICE AND NOODLES

Shrimp and Haricots Verts Chow Fun

This satisfying noodle stir-fry uses the Chinese cooking technique aptly called velveting. The process involves coating ingredients before they're cooked with a mixture of cornstarch, oil, and sometimes egg whites. I've upped the velvet ante by adding coriander seeds to the coating mixture, which add crispness, and using sesame oil to round out the flavor of the shrimp.

BEVERAGE TIP: LIGHT OAKED CHARDONNAY (LANDMARK, HANZELL)

SERVES 4 TO 6

1 pound haricots verts or slender green beans

1 pound large shrimp, peeled and deveined

1 tablespoon cornstarch

1 teaspoon coarsely ground coriander seeds (see Tip)

1 teaspoon toasted sesame oil

4 tablespoons canola oil

1 tablespoon finely chopped garlic

1 tablespoon finely chopped fresh ginger

1 large red onion, thinly sliced

Salt and freshly ground
    black pepper

1 cup Chinese dried black mush-
    rooms, soaked in a bowl of warm
    water to cover until soft, about 20
    minutes, and stemmed

1/4 cup oyster sauce

1/2 cup Chicken Stock (page 14) or
    low-sodium canned broth

1 pound fresh chow fun or rice stick
    noodles, soaked in warm water
    and drained

1/4 cup finely diced red bell pepper

1. Fill a medium bowl with cold water and add ice. Bring a large pot of salted water to a boil. Add the haricots verts and cook until tender-crisp, about 2 minutes. Drain the beans and add to the ice water. When cold, drain again and set aside.

2. In a medium bowl, combine the shrimp, cornstarch, coriander seeds, and sesame oil. Stir to coat the shrimp evenly and set aside.

3. Heat a large wok over high heat. Add 2 tablespoons of the oil and swirl to coat the pan. When the oil shimmers, add the shrimp and stir-fry for 2 minutes only; they will not be cooked through. Remove to a side dish and wipe out the wok with a paper towel.

4. Add the remaining 2 tablespoons of oil to the wok. Add the garlic, ginger, and onion and stir-fry until lightly colored, about 3 minutes. Season with salt and pepper to taste.

5. Add the mushrooms, oyster sauce, and chicken stock. Allow the mixture to come to a boil and cook over high heat for 3 minutes. Add the noodles and beans and the shrimp, and stir gently just to blend the ingredients; you don't want to break up the noodles. Continue to toss over high heat until the shrimp cook through, 3 to 5 minutes. Serve immediately. Garnish with red bell peppers.

MING'S TIPS: THE SHRIMP GET COOKED TWICE HERE—A PRELIMINARY STIR-FRY, AND A FINAL COOK-THROUGH WITH THE OTHER INGREDIENTS. BE SURE NOT TO COOK THE SHRIMP ENTIRELY THE FIRST TIME AROUND.

TO GRIND THE CORIANDER SEEDS COARSELY, USE A SPICE GRINDER OR CLEAN COFFEE GRINDER, PROCEEDING CAREFULLY SO THE SEEDS AREN'T OVERGROUND. IF USING A COFFEE GRINDER, CLEAN IT WELL.

RICE AND NOODLES

Udon Noodles
with Lemongrass Clam Broth

I grew up on soupy noodle dishes and always loved them. Here's a warming example that includes Manila clams, udon noodles, lemongrass, and, for fire, Thai chiles.

BEVERAGE TIP: RICH, TANGY SAUVIGNON BLANC FROM POUILLY-FUMÉ (DAGUENEAU-PUR SANG)

SERVES 4

1 tablespoon canola oil
2 pounds Manila or littleneck clams, shells scrubbed
6 lemongrass stalks, white parts only, thinly sliced
4 ¼-inch-thick slices fresh ginger
2 Thai bird chiles
1 large onion, thinly sliced
Salt and freshly ground black pepper
⅓ cup mirin (Japanese sweet sake)
4 cups Chicken Stock (page 14) or low-sodium canned broth
2 packages (8 ounces each) fresh udon noodles
3 cups spinach leaves
1 tablespoon butter
1 tablespoon fresh lemon juice

1. Heat a large, heavy-bottomed pot over high heat. Add the oil and swirl to coat the pan. When the oil shimmers, add the clams and cook, stirring, until the clams begin to open, about 2 minutes. Add the lemongrass, ginger, chiles, and onion and continue to cook, stirring, 5 minutes more. Remove the clams as they open, 4 to 6 minutes; discard any that do not open. Season the broth with the salt and pepper, add the mirin, and cook until the liquid is reduced by about by one-fourth, about 5 minutes.

2. Add the stock, reduce the heat, and simmer the broth until reduced by one-fourth, about 30 minutes. Strain the broth, return to the pot, and bring to a boil. Add the noodles, spinach, clams in their shells, and butter and stir. Cook just until the ingredients are hot, about 5 minutes. Add the lemon juice and stir. Serve immediately.

Shrimp Curried Noodles

At Blue Ginger, Amy Trujillo, one of my sous chefs, makes copious quantities of the curry paste featured in this recipe. Though we use the paste in other recipes, it really makes a statement in this dish, as a flavoring for wheaty Shanghai noodles, rock shrimp, and bok choy. Combined, they make a quick and savory yet soothing dish-in-one.

BEVERAGE TIP: SPICY GEWÜRZTRAMINER (ALSATIAN SCHLUMBERGER)

SERVES 2 TO 4

1 cup snow peas or sugar snap peas
1/2 pound Shanghai noodles
2 tablespoons canola oil
1/2 cup Curry Paste (page 240)
2 tablespoons coconut milk
2 tablespoons fresh lime juice
2 tablespoons Thai fish sauce *(nam pla)*
1/2 pound rock shrimp, rinsed and drained
1 cup chopped Chinese chives or regular chives
1 cup mung bean sprouts
1 red bell pepper, cored, seeded, and julienned
2 heads bok choy, well cleaned and julienned

1. Fill a large bowl with water and add ice. Bring a large pot of salted water to a boil. Add the snow peas to the boiling water and cook until tender-crisp, about 3 minutes. Strain the peas from the pot, reserving the water, and add them to the bowl of ice water. When cold, remove, drain, and set aside. Add more water and ice to the bowl.

2. Return the water in the pot to a boil, add the noodles, and cook until al dente, about 10 minutes. Drain the noodles and transfer them to the ice water. Allow to cool, drain, and transfer to a bowl. Toss with the canola oil and set aside.

3. Heat a large wok over high heat. Add the curry paste, coconut milk, lime juice, and fish sauce and stir to blend. Add the shrimp and simmer until just cooked, about 2 minutes. Add the reserved noodles, chives, bean sprouts, bell pepper, bok choy, and snow peas; toss to coat the noodles; and heat fully, about 3 minutes. Correct the seasonings and serve.

Sweet and Spicy Beef Noodles

This Tsai-family standard called *zha jiang mian* was the spaghetti and meatballs of my youth. I remember well the satisfaction it provided, with its crisp vegetables and black bean–spiked sauce. And, thinking about it, I can't fail to recall Yeh-Yeh, my paternal grandfather, who would accompany his helping with mouthfuls of raw garlic cloves. We all copied him—to keep everyone on the same social footing!

This is great informal eating, wonderful in cold weather when you crave something filling.

BEVERAGE TIP: SLIGHTLY CHILLED CABERNET FRANC (CHINON, BOURGUEIL)

SERVES 4

3 tablespoons canola oil
3 Thai bird chiles, finely chopped
¼ cup finely chopped garlic
1 tablespoon finely chopped fresh ginger
1 tablespoon fermented black beans, rinsed and drained
1 red onion, finely diced
⅔ cup hoisin sauce
1 pound ground beef (not too lean)
½ cup Shaoxing rice wine
2 cups Chicken Stock (page 14) or low-sodium canned stock, or water
1 pound fresh or dried Shanghai noodles or other egg noodles (see Tip)
1 cucumber, peeled, seeded, and julienned
2 carrots, peeled and julienned
2 cups mung bean sprouts

1. Heat a large saucepan over high heat. Add the oil and swirl to coat the bottom of the pan. When the oil shimmers, add the chiles, garlic, ginger, beans, and onion and sauté, stirring, until the vegetables are soft, about 5 minutes. Add the hoisin sauce and cook, stirring, to remove any raw taste, about 2 minutes. Add the beef and cook, stirring, until it browns, about 6 minutes, and then add the wine and stock.

2. Reduce the heat to low and simmer until the mixture has a saucelike consistency, stirring occasionally, about 45 minutes. Correct the seasonings.

3. Bring a large pot of salted water to a boil. Add the noodles and cook until al dente, about 5 minutes for fresh, 10 to 15 minutes for dried. Drain well and divide among 4 bowls. Ladle on the sauce, top with the cucumber, carrots, and sprouts, and serve.

MING'S TIPS: I RECOMMEND SHANGHAI NOODLES FOR THIS, BUT YOU COULD USE WONTON NOODLES, LO MEIN, OR EVEN NON-ASIAN PASTA, LIKE SPAGHETTI OR FETTUCCINE.

TO MAINTAIN THEIR CRISPNESS, THE VEGETABLES ARE ADDED AFTER THE NOODLES ARE SAUCED. KEEP THIS TECHNIQUE IN MIND WHEN PREPARING SIMILAR DISHES THAT MIGHT OTHERWISE LACK TEXTURAL VARIETY.

RICE AND NOODLES

Chicken Chow Mein
My Way

Chicken chow mein, that much abused warhorse of Chinese-American cooking, has a thoroughly respectable ancestry. The Chinese have always stir-fried noodles with savory accompaniments. I remember my dad concocting great dishes using leftover boiled noodles and fresh vegetables. My version, featuring bok choy and shiitake mushrooms, takes the dish a step further. It's the way chicken chow mein *should* be made.

BEVERAGE TIP: FRUITY, BRIGHT PINOT NOIR (ANCIEN, DUTTON RANCH)

SERVES 4

2 tablespoons cornstarch
1/4 cup Shaoxing wine or dry sherry
1/2 cup oyster sauce
1 tablespoon finely chopped fresh ginger
1 bunch scallions, white and green parts, sliced 1/8 inch thick
1 teaspoon freshly ground black pepper plus additional
1 tablespoon sambal oelek
1 pound chicken meat, preferably from legs and thighs, cut into 1/2-inch pieces
1 pound fresh or dried lo mein (egg noodles)
5 tablespoons canola oil
6 garlic cloves, thinly sliced
2 cups quartered fresh shiitake mushroom caps
4 heads bok choy, cored and cut into 1/2-inch slices
1 cup Chicken Stock (page 14) or low-sodium canned broth
Salt

1. In a large bowl, combine the cornstarch and wine and mix. Stir in the oyster sauce, ginger, scallions, the 1 teaspoon pepper, and the sambal oelek. Add the chicken, stir to coat, and allow to marinate covered and refrigerated for at least 2 hours and preferably overnight.

2. Bring a large pot of salted water to a boil. Fill a bowl with water and add ice. Add the lo mein to the boiling water and cook until al dente, about 5 minutes for fresh, 10 to 15 minutes for dried. Drain and transfer the noodles to the ice water. When cold, drain and toss with 1 tablespoon of the oil. Set aside.

3. Heat a wok over high heat. Add 2 tablespoons of the oil and swirl to coat. When the oil shimmers, add the garlic and shiitakes and stir-fry until the mushrooms are soft, about 4 minutes. Remove the mushrooms and set aside. Add the remaining 2 tablespoons of the oil and, when hot, add the chicken and stir-fry until almost cooked through, 6 to 8 minutes. Add the bok choy and stir-fry until crisp-tender, about 3 minutes. Add the stock and season with the salt and pepper to taste. Add the reserved shiitakes and the noodles. Stir to coat, and heat through, about 5 minutes. Correct the seasonings and serve.

MING'S TIP: IF YOU CAN'T FIND BOK CHOY, USE ANY OTHER CHINESE CABBAGE LIKE NAPA CABBAGE.

RICE AND NOODLES

Poached Prawn and
Soba Noodle Salad

Consider this a pasta salad—with a difference. Rather than the typical mayonnaise-y dressing, I present soba (noodles with true character) combined with shrimp and cucumber, scallions, and a touch of pickled ginger. This is a fantastic light, summery dish.

BEVERAGE TIP: MEDIUM-DRY, CHILLED SAKE (PREFERABLY A JI-SAKE OR GEKKEIKAN'S "HAIKU")

SERVES 4

2 bay leaves

1 tablespoon black peppercorns

1 tablespoon salt

8 cups water

1 lemon, halved

12 large shrimp, peeled except for the tails, and deveined (see Tip, page 102)

SALAD

½ pound dried soba noodles

¼ cup rice wine vinegar

1 teaspoon toasted sesame oil

2 tablespoons light miso

½ tablespoon sugar

½ cup canola oil

Salt and freshly ground black pepper

2 tablespoons chopped Pickled Ginger (page 238),
    or 1 tablespoon finely chopped ginger

½ cup chopped scallions, green parts only

1 English cucumber, julienned

1 red bell pepper, cut into ⅛-inch dice

1. Fill a medium bowl with water and add ice. In a medium pot, combine the bay leaves, peppercorns, salt, and water. Squeeze the lemon halves directly into the pot, add the squeezed rinds, and bring to a boil over high heat. Reduce the heat, add the shrimp, and cook until just done, 3 to 5 minutes. Check the shrimp after 3 minutes; they must not overcook. Drain the shrimp and transfer immediately to the ice water. When cold, drain on paper towels and reserve in the refrigerator.

2. To make the salad, bring a large quantity of salted water to a boil. Refill the bowl with water and more ice. Add the noodles to the boiling water and cook until al dente, about 8 minutes. Drain and transfer to the bowl. When the noodles are cold, drain well and set aside.

3. In a medium bowl, combine the vinegar, sesame oil, miso, and sugar and mix. Whisk in the oil slowly to make an emulsion and season with salt and pepper to taste. Add the pickled ginger and scallions; stir. Add the cucumber, bell pepper, reserved shrimp, and noodles, and toss to coat well. Correct the seasonings.

4. Transfer to a large serving platter or pasta bowls, making certain some of the shrimp are arranged on top, and serve.

Chapter 4

Seafood

I GREW UP IN DAYTON, OHIO, WHICH ISN'T EXACTLY SEASIDE,

SO WE DIDN'T OFTEN HAVE ACCESS TO SWEET, FRESH

SEAFOOD.

Now, of course, I get to cook and eat as much fresh seafood as I like. A lot of the time, this means shrimp. Shrimp are so adaptable—you can grill, bake, broil, deep- and stir-fry them—and they're fast to fix. I like to give shrimp the simplest treatments while pairing them with strong, aromatic flavors. Asian Pesto Grilled Shrimp, a basil and peanut-sauced shrimp specialty, is an example, as is Wok-Flashed Salt and Pepper Shrimp with Lemon Basmati Rice, a quick stir-fry featuring brined unshelled shrimp and a tart rice accompaniment.

Like shrimp, scallops require only the simplest treatments. I like to sear them best of all. I'm partial, also, to easily cooked mussels. Spicy Black Bean Mussels with Rice Stick Noodles is my take on a classic Chinese pairing; the addition of lime and tomatoes provides a great Thai-Western savor.

I'm sometimes asked to suggest "nonfishy" fish dishes. I smile to myself because I know that fish is only fishy tasting when it's old or overcooked, but in such cases I'm happy to recommend skate, a fish I adore. Tasting something like scallops, but with a sweetness and special texture all its own, skate pleases fish lovers and the fish-averse alike. Chile Skate Wings in Banana Leaves, my play on a fiery Singapore classic, and Cornmeal-Crusted Skate with Citrus Brown Butter Vinaigrette, a bow to the French "brown butter" approach to skate, are two completely different ways of cooking this great fish. Reluctant fish lovers also fall under the spell of fish cooked whole, and few people have resisted the pleasures of Whole Crispy Red Snapper with Mango Pineapple Sauce and Spicy Chinese Long Beans or Herb-Crusted Trout with Shiitake Sticky Rice and Shiso Oil.

Of all the seafood dishes I offer, however, I'm perhaps most fond of my signature miso-marinated Chilean sea bass (page 186). It's the most popular Blue Ginger dish and I'd probably eat it every night, myself, if it weren't for the other fish and shellfish I'd miss!

Seafood

Asian Pesto Grilled Shrimp

This simple dish is loaded with flavor. Pesto is, of course, an Italian creation, and shrimp are the most commonly used seafood in Chinese cooking. (I won't tell you how many shrimp I've prepped in Chinese kitchens near and far.) The two—pesto and shrimp—are wonderful together, especially when the pesto receives the East-West treatment.

BEVERAGE TIP: REFRESHING, BONE-DRY CHARDONNAY FROM CHABLIS (DOMAINE MOREAU & FILS)

SERVES 4

PESTO
¾ cup roasted peanuts
4 serrano chiles
3 garlic cloves
1 tablespoon finely chopped fresh ginger
Juice of 4 limes
2 tablespoons Thai fish sauce *(nam pla)*
½ cup peanut oil
½ tablespoon salt
1 tablespoon sugar
2 cups fresh Thai basil leaves
1 cup fresh mint leaves

12 large shrimp, peeled, deveined, and brined (see Tip, page 102)
2 tablespoons canola oil
Salt and freshly ground black pepper
4 cups baby or regular romaine cut in ¼-inch ribbons

1. To make the pesto, combine the peanuts, chiles, garlic, ginger, lime juice, fish sauce, oil, salt, and sugar in a food processor and process to a smooth puree. Add the basil and mint and puree again. Do not overmix. (Excessive mixing can heat the mixture, "cooking" the basil, turning it dark.) Correct the seasonings and set aside.

2. Prepare an outdoor grill or preheat the broiler. Coat the shrimp lightly with the oil and season with salt and pepper to taste. Grill outdoors, or broil, turning once, until the shrimp are just cooked through, about 5 minutes.

3. Divide the lettuce among 4 plates, place 3 shrimp on top of each salad portion, drizzle liberally with the pesto, and serve.

Spicy Shrimp
with Mangoes and Snow Pea Salad

This pungent shrimp and mango stir-fry veers away from China, my home base, toward Southeast Asia. The Chinese don't cook with mangoes usually, but other Asians do, often as a sweet complement to dishes with heat. That's their role here.

BEVERAGE TIP: TROPICAL SAUVIGNON BLANC (AUSTRALIAN LENSWOOD)

SERVES 4

SALAD

$1/2$ pound snow peas, strings removed

1 tablespoon Dijon mustard

2 tablespoon rice wine vinegar

$1/4$ cup canola oil

1 tablespoon canola oil

2 medium red onions, thinly sliced

1 2-inch piece fresh ginger, julienned

Salt and freshly ground black pepper

$1\frac{1}{2}$ tablespoons sambal oelek

$1\frac{1}{2}$ pounds large shrimp, peeled, deveined, and brined (see Tip, page 102)

Juice of 2 limes

2 ripe mangoes, peeled, 8 $1/8$-inch slices reserved for garnish, remaining mango cut into $1/4$-inch dice

1. Fill a large bowl with cold water and add ice. Bring a medium pot of salted water to a boil, add the snow peas, and cook until tender-crisp, about 5 minutes. Using a slotted spoon, transfer the peas to the ice water to cool. Drain and set aside.

2. In a medium bowl, whisk together the mustard, vinegar, and oil. Set aside.

3. Heat a wok over high heat. Add the oil and swirl to coat the pan. When the oil shimmers, add the onions and ginger and stir-fry until the onions have browned, about 8 minutes. Season with the salt and pepper to taste.

4. Add the sambal oelek and shrimp and stir-fry until the shrimp are cooked through, about 6 minutes. Add the lime juice, stir, and add the diced mango; heat until warmed through. Correct the seasonings.

5. Toss the snow peas with the vinaigrette and correct the seasonings. Divide the stir-fry among 4 plates and top with the snow pea salad. Garnish with mango slices and serve.

Wok-Flashed Salt and Pepper Shrimp
with Lemon Basmati Rice

As a kid I loved shrimp so much I would eat them shell and all, realizing perhaps that most of their flavor is in the shell. (Or maybe I was just more hungry than patient!)

This dish, based on a traditional Chinese favorite, uses unshelled shrimp for just that reason. The shrimp are brined in a salt-water bath to ensure they remain plump and moist, then dredged in a mixture of salt and three kinds of pepper, and quickly stir-fried. Served with tart, lemony rice, the dish is great informal eating—just the thing to make after work when you feel like something easygoing but delicious.

BEVERAGE TIP: CRISP, TROPICAL SAUVIGNON BLANC NEW ZEALAND (CLOUDY BAY PETER MICHAELS)

SERVES 4

1½ pounds large shrimp
1 tablespoon freshly ground black pepper
1 tablespoon freshly ground white pepper
1½ teaspoons ground Szechwan peppercorns
2 tablespoons coarse sea salt, preferably fleur de sel
¼ cup cornstarch
¼ cup canola oil
1 tablespoon finely chopped fresh ginger
5 garlic cloves, finely chopped
8 scallions, green and white parts, finely chopped
Lemon Basmati Rice (page 223)

MING'S TIP: WHENEVER SHRIMP ARE TO BE DEVEINED AS THEY ARE IN THIS RECIPE (WHETHER OR NOT THEY ARE PEELED), I RECOMMEND INCORPORATING THE CHINESE BRINING TECHNIQUE. THIS METHOD, WHICH INVOLVES SOAKING THE SHRIMP IN A SALT-WATER BATH WHILE THEY'RE PREPPED, ENSURES COOKED SHRIMP THAT ARE PLUMP AND MOIST. SEE STEP 1, OPPOSITE, FOR DETAILS.

1. Fill 2 medium bowls with water and add enough regular salt to each to give the water a definite saltiness. Add the shrimp to one bowl. To devein the shrimp without removing their shells, slit the back of each from the head to the tail with the point of a small sharp knife, open the shrimp, and remove the vein. Transfer the deveined shrimp to the second bowl of salted water. Drain the shrimp, rinse them very well, and drain again.

2. In a large bowl, combine the ground peppers, sea salt, and cornstarch and mix. Dredge the shrimp in the salt and pepper mixture.

3. Heat a wok over high heat, add the oil, and swirl to coat the pan. When the oil shimmers, add the ginger, garlic, and scallions and sauté, stirring, until fragrant, about 30 seconds. Add the shrimp and stir-fry 4 to 6 minutes.

4. Mound the rice on an oval platter, top with the shrimp, and serve.

Wasabi Seafood Salad

Tuna salad, that great mainstay of quick lunches, was actually the jumping-off point for this. I was looking for a way to produce an equally straightforward but considerably more luxurious version of the old tried-and-true tuna dish. The traditional mayo dressing gave way to a piquant wasabi-flavored vinaigrette—much lighter and more interesting than its ancestor.

If you lack time or the financial wherewithal, you can make a delicious version of this using pan-seared fresh tuna or salmon.

BEVERAGE TIP: SPARKLING WINE (SCHRAMSBERG, DOMAINE CHANDON)

SERVES 4

2 fresh lobster tails
12 large shrimp, deveined
2 tablespoons freshly grated wasabi, or 1 tablespoon prepared horseradish mixed
    with 2 teaspoons wasabi paste
1 tablespoon soy sauce
Juice of 1 lemon
1 teaspoon sugar
⅓ cup canola oil
¼ pound lump crabmeat, picked over
4 cups mizuna or tatsoi lettuce, or 2 cups mesclun plus 2 cups watercress
4 plum or 2 large round tomatoes, sliced
Salt and freshly ground black pepper
2 ounces daikon sprouts

1. Bring a large pot of salted water to a boil. Fill a medium bowl with water and add ice. Add the lobster tails to the boiling water and boil until just cooked through, 5 to 7 minutes. With tongs, transfer the lobster to the ice water; retain the cooking water. When cool, drain the lobster tails, crack the shells, and remove the meat. Quarter the meat and set aside.

2. Return the water in the pot to a boil and add water and ice to the bowl if necessary. Add the shrimp, and cook until just done, 3 to 5 minutes. Check the shrimp after 3 minutes; they must not overcook. Drain the shrimp and transfer immediately to the ice water. When cold, drain on paper towels and peel.

3. In a small bowl, combine the wasabi, soy sauce, lemon juice, and sugar and whisk to blend. Whisk in the oil to make a light emulsion.

4. In a large bowl, combine the crabmeat, lobster meat, shrimp, mizuna, and tomatoes. Add the dressing, season with the salt and pepper, and toss to blend.

5. Divide the salad among 4 plates. Garnish with the daikon sprouts and serve.

MING'S TIP: I RECOMMEND FRESHLY GRATED WASABI FOR THIS. THE DIFFERENCE BETWEEN IT AND THE POWDERED AND PREPARED VERSION IS SIMILAR TO THAT BETWEEN FRESH GINGER AND THE POWDERED VARIETY. HAVING SAID THAT, HOWEVER, YOU SHOULD KNOW THAT THE LATTER IS CONSIDERABLY EASIER TO FIND, AND ITS USE WILL NOT COMPROMISE THIS DISH IN ANY WAY.

Crispy Scallops
with Carrot–
Star Anise Syrup

This is one of the dishes we opened Blue Ginger with, and it's been a hit from the start. The carrot syrup is not only beautiful but also delicious. It gives an impression of richness, yet doesn't contain the butter or cream you'd expect. The spicy eggplant caviar recalls a French aubergine puree; actually, it's more like baba ghannouj, but hot. Include sweet seared scallops and you've got a dish that's light but satisfying and full of flavor.

BEVERAGE TIP: BRIGHT CHARDONNAY (CHALONE)

SERVES 4

SYRUP
4 cups fresh carrot juice
2 star anise
1 cup canola oil
Salt and freshly ground white pepper

2 large eggplants
1 teaspoon ground cumin
3 tablespoons canola oil
½ cup shallots cut into ¼-inch slices
1 tablespoon finely chopped garlic
1 tablespoon sambal oelek
1 tablespoon honey
2 tablespoons butter
Salt and freshly ground black pepper
2 tablespoons chopped scallions, white and green parts
2 tablespoons chopped fresh cilantro
20 large sea scallops
¼ cup Curry Oil (page 230)
¼ cup chives cut into ½-inch lengths
Russet Crisps (see Variation, page 219)

1. To make the syrup, combine the carrot juice with the star anise in a large nonreactive saucepan. Bring to a simmer over low heat and cook slowly until 90 percent of the juice has evaporated and only a foam remains, 30 to 45 minutes. Be careful not to reduce the juice too quickly or it will darken. Remove the anise and scrape the foam into a blender while still warm. Blend, adding the oil slowly to make an emulsion. Season with the salt and pepper to taste, cool, and set aside.

2. Preheat the oven to 375°F. Place the eggplants on a baking sheet and roast, turning once, until soft, about 45 minutes. When cool enough to handle, scoop the flesh from the skin into a medium bowl and set aside.

3. In a small skillet, heat the cumin over high heat, stirring constantly, until fragrant, about 5 minutes. Transfer to a small bowl and set aside.

4. Heat a medium skillet over high heat. Add 1 tablespoon of the oil and swirl to coat the pan. When the oil shimmers, add the shallots and garlic and sauté, stirring, until brown, about 6 minutes. Add the sambal oelek, honey, toasted cumin, and the eggplant, mix well, and continue to cook until the eggplant liquid is reduced slightly, 6 to 8 minutes. Transfer the mixture to a food processor and puree. Add the butter, process to blend, and season with the salt and pepper to taste. Transfer to a medium bowl and fold in the scallions and cilantro. Keep warm.

5. Season the scallops with salt and pepper. Heat a medium skillet over high heat. Add the remaining 2 tablespoons of oil and swirl to coat the pan. When the oil shimmers, add the scallops and sear, turning once, until brown and just cooked through, about 6 minutes. Remove the scallops and keep warm.

6. Divide the eggplant among 4 plates and surround with the scallops. Drizzle over the carrot syrup and curry oil, garnish with the chives and potato crisps, if using, and serve.

MING'S TIP: USE A JUICER TO GET THE FRESH CARROT JUICE YOU NEED FOR THIS, OR BUY THE JUICE IN A HEALTH FOOD STORE. DON'T USE CANNED JUICE—IT TASTES TINNY WHEN REDUCED.

Spicy Black Bean Mussels
with Rice Stick Noodles

I've always enjoyed dishes that combine mussels and black beans, a traditional Chinese pairing. I've joined the two here, with the addition of Thai basil leaves and a shot of fresh lime—a bow to Thailand. The inclusion of tomatoes—we're traveling West, now—adds freshness and color.

I recommend Prince Edward Island mussels for this dish—they're particularly tender and sweet—but any mussel will work well. To serve, arrange the mussels on top of each portion "to be closer to the gods"—a Chinese practice that also makes the dish look more bountiful.

BEVERAGE TIP: FRUITY RIESLING, NOT BONE DRY (AUSTRALIAN GROSSET, ALSATIAN TRIMBACH)

SERVES 4

2 tablespoons canola oil

2 pounds mussels, preferably Prince Edward Island, scrubbed, beards removed

1 tablespoon finely chopped garlic

1 tablespoon finely chopped fresh ginger

4 serrano or Thai bird chiles, stemmed and minced

1 tablespoon fermented black beans, rinsed and drained

$\frac{1}{2}$ cup dry white wine

2 medium tomatoes, or 4 canned, cut into $\frac{1}{4}$-inch dice

1 tablespoon Thai fish sauce *(nam pla)*

2 cups Chicken Stock (page 14) or low-sodium canned broth

8 ounces rice stick noodles, soaked in warm water to cover until softened, about 30 minutes

1 cup fresh Thai or sweet basil leaves

1 bunch chives, cut into $\frac{1}{2}$-inch lengths

2 tablespoons butter

Salt and freshly ground white pepper

2 limes, halved

1. Heat a wok over high heat. Add the oil and swirl to coat the pan. When the oil shimmers, add the mussels and stir-fry until some of the mussels open, about 5 minutes. Add the garlic, ginger, chiles, and black beans and stir-fry until fragrant, about 2 minutes. Add the wine, cover, and cook until all the mussels have opened, 3 to 5 minutes. Add the tomatoes, fish sauce, chicken stock, and drained noodles. Toss and add the basil, chives, and butter. Toss again. Season with the salt and pepper to taste.

2. Transfer the mixture to large pasta bowls, and arrange the mussels on top of each portion. Squeeze lime juice over and serve.

MING'S TIP: I SOMETIMES ADD A BIT OF BUTTER TO A COMPLETED DISH, AS I DO IN THIS RECIPE, TO PROVIDE LIGHT ENRICHMENT AND TO ROUND OUT FLAVORS. KEEP THIS CLASSIC FRENCH TECHNIQUE IN MIND FOR YOUR OWN COOKING.

SEAFOOD

Grilled Ponzu-Marinated Snapper
with Ginger Pea Sprout Salad

I first discovered ponzu, the Japanese citrus sauce, in Osaka. I thought it was a kind of vinegar (*su* means "vinegar" in Japanese), but was delighted to learn differently. In this dish I use ponzu as part of an aromatic marinade for snapper fillets, which are then grilled and served with a sprightly pea sprout salad.

This dish is something like a quick ceviche; the marinade partially "cooks" the snapper, so the fillets grill quickly. You can have this dish, salad and all, on the table in about half an hour.

BEVERAGE TIP: TART, CLEAN SAUVIGNON BLANC (POUILLY-FUMÉ)

SERVES 4

½ cup ponzu, or ¼ cup each lime and lemon juices
1 tablespoon finely chopped fresh ginger
¼ cup soy sauce
1 teaspoon toasted sesame oil
4 skinless snapper fillets, about 6 ounces each
Salt and freshly ground black pepper

VINAIGRETTE
2 tablespoons Dijon mustard
2 tablespoons rice wine vinegar
¾ cup canola oil
Salt and freshly ground black pepper

2 tablespoons Pickled Ginger (page 238), julienned
4 cups pea sprouts

MING'S TIP: DON'T EXCEED THE SPECIFIED MARINATING TIME FOR THE FISH, OR THE FLESH WILL BECOME TOO MUSHY OR BREAK APART WHEN THE FILLETS ARE GRILLED.

1. In a baking dish just large enough to hold the fillets, combine the ponzu, ginger, soy sauce, and sesame oil. Stir to blend, add the fish, and turn to coat. Allow to marinate for 10 minutes only.

2. Prepare an outdoor grill. Season the fish with salt and pepper to taste, spray the grill with nonstick cooking spray, and grill over very high heat until grill marks form, about 3 minutes. Rotate the fillets and grill for 3 minutes more. Turn the fish and grill on the second side just until done, about 4 minutes. Alternatively, heat a grill pan over high heat and brush with 2 tablespoon of canola oil. Grill the fillets as above, rotating and turning the fillets once, 10 minutes total.

3. Meanwhile, to make the vinaigrette, whisk together the mustard, vinegar, and oil in a medium bowl. Season with salt and pepper. Set aside half the vinaigrette, add the pickled ginger and the pea sprouts to the remainder, and toss. Correct the seasonings.

4. Divide the salad among 4 plates and top each portion with a fillet. Drizzle the plate with the remaining vinaigrette and serve.

Teriyaki Salmon
with Mirin Cucumber Salad

When people think of cooked Japanese food, teriyaki dishes usually come to mind. The key to great teriyaki is to keep glazing the food with the marinade as it grills or broils, as I do when I prepare the salmon in this dish. A cool and crunchy cucumber salad is a terrific counterpoint to the salmon's richness.

   You can plate the salads up to 20 minutes before serving, if you like. This dish makes perfect summer eating.

BEVERAGE TIP: MEDIUM-DRY, CHILLED SAKE (PREFERABLY A JI-SAKE OR GEKKEIKAN'S "HAIKU")

SERVES 4

SALAD
1 1/2 teaspoons wasabi powder
1 tablespoon mirin (Japanese sweet sake)
1 tablespoon rice wine vinegar
1 teaspoon sugar
1/2 cup canola oil
Salt and freshly ground black pepper

1 cup soy sauce
Juice and zest of 2 oranges
3 tablespoons brown sugar
4 garlic cloves, peeled and left whole
1 tablespoon finely chopped fresh ginger
1 tablespoon white sesame seeds
4 skinless salmon fillets (about 6 ounces each), preferably center cut
2 large English cucumbers, julienned

1. To make the salad, combine the wasabi powder and mirin in a medium bowl and mix to make a paste. Whisk in the vinegar and sugar. Whisk in the oil and season with the salt and pepper. Taste and correct the seasonings, if necessary.

2. To make the salmon, combine the soy sauce, orange juice and zest, brown sugar, garlic, and ginger in a medium saucepan. Bring to a boil over high heat and simmer slowly until reduced by half or syrupy, about 15 minutes. Remove from the heat, stir in the sesame seeds, and cool. Transfer to a baking dish, add the salmon, turn to coat, and marinate for 1 hour.

3. Prepare an outdoor grill or preheat the broiler. If cooking outdoors, spray the grill with nonstick cooking spray. Grill the salmon over high heat, or broil, turning once, until the flesh is slightly charred, about 4 minutes per side. Brush the fish with the remaining teriyaki sauce as it cooks. The fish will be medium-rare to medium.

4. About 10 minutes before serving, toss the cucumbers with enough of the vinaigrette to coat them completely. Correct the seasonings and set aside. Divide the salad among 4 plates. Place a salmon fillet on top of each portion and serve.

MING'S TIP: WHEN BUYING SALMON FILLETS, ALWAYS ASK FOR CENTER CUT. THESE ARE MORE TENDER THAN SECTIONS TAKEN FROM NEAR THE TAIL, WHICH GET MORE EXERCISE AND ARE THEREFORE TOUGHER.

S
E
A
F
O
O
D

Whole Crispy Red Snapper
with Mango Pineapple Sauce and Spicy Chinese Long Beans

It's very Chinese to serve fish whole, especially for New Year's, when it's said to ensure abundance in the coming year. Red snapper is particularly good this way, especially when it's partnered with a mango-based accompaniment—my interpretation of sweet-and-sour sauce—and dry-fried long beans.

The whole fish, presented at the table, is impressive. I well remember my mother's and grandmother's delight at having whole fish to eat; they'd fight over the cheeks and tail, which the Chinese consider delicacies. Even if you don't prize those parts of the snapper, the rest of the fish and its savory accompaniments make great eating.

BEVERAGE TIP: SPICY GEWÜRZTRAMINER (ALSATIAN SCHLUMBERGER)

SERVES 3 TO 4

SAUCE
2 tablespoons canola oil
1 tablespoon finely chopped
    lemongrass, white parts only
3 shallots, thinly sliced
2 tablespoons Thai fish sauce *(nam pla)*
1 small pineapple, peeled, cored, and cut into ¼-inch dice
2 mangoes, peeled and cut into ¼-inch dice
Juice of 1 lime
Salt and freshly ground black pepper

MING'S TIP: WHEN CHOOSING WHOLE FISH AT THE MARKET, LOOK FOR SWEET-SMELLING SPECIMENS WITH BRIGHT SKIN, RED GILLS, INTACT SCALES, AND NO SURFACE BROWNING. CLEAR EYES ARE NOT A RELIABLE SIGN OF FRESHNESS—IN SOME SPECIES, THEY CAN CLOUD RIGHT AFTER DEATH.

2 cups rice flour
1 tablespoon ground cumin
1 tablespoon ancho chile powder
1 tablespoon ground coriander
1 tablespoon ground fennel
Canola oil, for deep-frying
1 large yellow onion, sliced thinly
1 red snapper, about 3 pounds, cleaned, with head and tail left on
Salt
Spicy Chinese Long Beans (page 206)

1. To make the sauce, heat a medium skillet over medium heat. Add the oil and swirl to coat the bottom of the pan. When the oil shimmers, add the lemongrass and shallots and sauté, stirring, until soft, 4 to 6 minutes. Add the fish sauce, stir, and add the pineapple, mangoes, and lime juice and heat through. Season with salt and pepper to taste and keep warm.

2. Heat the oil to 375°F. Mix the flour with the cumin, chile powder, coriander, and fennel in a large baking dish. Dredge the onions in the seasoned flour and fry until golden brown, about 5 minutes. Transfer to paper towels to drain. Reheat the oil to 375°F. Dredge both sides of the fish well in the flour, shake off any excess, and fry, turning once, until golden brown and cooked through, about 8 minutes. With a large-mesh spoon, transfer the fish to paper towels to drain, season lightly with the salt, and keep warm.

3. Mound the long beans on a serving platter large enough to hold the snapper. Top with the fish and surround with the sauce. Garnish with the onions and serve.

Chile Skate Wings in Banana Leaves

This meal-in-one dish was inspired by a trip I took to Singapore, where skate with chiles is a big favorite. It's my play, also, on cooking *en papillote,* that easy French technique for cooking fish and vegetables or other foods in sealed paper pouches.

Here, skate wings are seasoned with a spicy chile-fired paste, placed on top of grilled eggplant, rice, and tomatoes, and enclosed in banana leaves. The packages are opened at table and diners are greeted with bursts of fragrant steam; the filling is a medley of flavors and textures.

This is great for parties, as you can assemble the bundles beforehand and hold them until you're ready to cook.

BEVERAGE TIP: LAGER (SINGHA, FOSTER'S) OR EXOTIC MULLER-THURGAU (SOKOL BLOSSER)

SERVES 4

CHILE PASTE

6 shallots, roughly chopped

1 tablespoon freshly ground black pepper, plus additional as needed

2 serrano chiles

3 Thai bird chiles

1 tablespoon sambal oelek

6 garlic cloves, peeled

2 lemongrass stalks, white parts only, chopped

2 tablespoons finely chopped fresh ginger

1 tablespoon sugar

1 tablespoon kosher salt, plus additional as needed

Juice of 2 limes

1 tablespoon Worcestershire sauce

$\frac{1}{4}$ to $\frac{1}{2}$ cup canola oil

1 medium eggplant, cut into 8 $\frac{1}{4}$-inch slices

2 tablespoons canola oil, plus additional as needed

Salt and freshly ground black pepper

2 large red onions, thinly sliced

4 large banana leaves (about 16 × 16 inches)

3 cups cooked jasmine or other long-grain rice

2 medium tomatoes, cut into $\frac{1}{4}$-inch slices

$\frac{1}{2}$ cup Thai or sweet basil leaves

4 skate wing fillets, skinned, about 6 ounces each

$\frac{1}{4}$ cup scallions, white and green parts, sliced $\frac{1}{8}$ inch thick

8 wooden skewers, soaked in water for 30 minutes

MISO BROTH WITH TATSOI-ENOKI SALAD (PAGE 18).

OPPOSITE: MING'S PHO (PAGE 16). ABOVE: CORN LEMONGRASS SOUP WITH LOBSTER SALAD (PAGE 28). LEFT: ASIAN GAZPACHO WITH CILANTRO-JICAMA CREAM (PAGE 20).

LEFT, FROM TOP TO BOTTOM: STEAMED
CHICKEN AND SHIITAKE BUNS (PAGE 42) AND
PAN-FRIED CHIVE AND SHRIMP BUNS (PAGE 44).
ABOVE: SPINACH TOFU NAPOLEONS WITH SPICY
MISO DRESSING (PAGE 49). RIGHT: ASPARAGUS-
CRUSTED AHI TUNA WITH ASPARAGUS
VINAIGRETTE (PAGE 66).

ABOVE: TEMPURA SHRIMP COCKTAIL WITH TWO
PUREES (PAGE 62). RIGHT: ROCK SHRIMP LOLLIPOPS
WITH SPICY ALMOND SAUCE (PAGE 68).

ABOVE: SCALLOPS ON THE HALF SHELL WITH WASABI
LIME VINAIGRETTE (PAGE 176). RIGHT: AHI TUNA
PARFAIT WITH TWO CAVIARS (PAGE 170).

OPPOSITE: LOBSTER AND MANGO SUMMER ROLLS
(PAGE 41). ABOVE: SMOKY TURKEY SHU MAI IN A
SWEET PEA BROTH (PAGE 50). LEFT: SALMON ROLL
TEMPURA (PAGE 54).

ABOVE: NEW HAMACHI SASHIMI WITH CURRY OIL
(PAGE 64). RIGHT, CLOCKWISE FROM TOP LEFT:
SHIITAKE AND SPINACH URA MAKI (PAGE 77), CRAB
AND HERB SALAD MAKI (PAGE 82), SMOKED SALMON
AND JICAMA MAKI SUSHI (PAGE 78), SPICY CRAB
HANDROLLS (PAGE 80), GRILLED SUSHI RICE WITH SOY
GINGER GLAZE (PAGE 76).

ABOVE: UDON NOODLES WITH LEMONGRASS CLAM
BROTH (PAGE 88). RIGHT: SHRIMP CURRIED
NOODLES (PAGE 89). OPPOSITE: STICKY RICE
POUCHES WITH GARLIC-FLASHED SCALLOPS (PAGE
84). OVERLEAF: FOIE GRAS AND MOREL SHU MAI
WITH CARAMELIZED SAUTERNES-SHALLOT BROTH
AND TRUFFLED EDAMAME PUREE (PAGE 177).

1. To make the chile paste, combine the shallots, pepper, chiles, sambal oelek, garlic, lemongrass, ginger, sugar, salt, lime juice, and Worcestershire sauce in a food processor. Process, adding the oil through the feed tube gradually until the mixture is pastelike. You may not need all the oil. Correct the seasonings with the salt and pepper and set aside.

2. Prepare an outdoor grill. Coat the eggplant lightly with the oil, season it with salt and pepper, and grill over high heat, turning once, until browned, about 5 minutes per side. Alternatively, heat a medium skillet over medium heat, add 2 tablespoons of the oil, and swirl to coat the pan. Season the eggplant with salt and pepper to taste. When the oil shimmers, add the eggplant and sauté, turning once, until the eggplant is brown on both sides, about 10 minutes. Set aside.

3. Heat a medium skillet over medium heat or, if the eggplant was sautéed, return the skillet to medium heat. Add the 2 tablespoons of oil and swirl to coat the pan. Add the onions, season with salt and pepper to taste, and sauté, stirring, until brown, 8 to 10 minutes.

4. If not completing the dish outdoors, preheat the oven to 350°F. Place a banana leaf on a work surface. In the center place 1 eggplant slice and cover with one-fourth of the rice. Top the rice with one-fourth of the tomato slices and the basil and season with salt and pepper to taste. Cover with a second slice of the eggplant, one-fourth of the onions, and 1 skate wing. Spread the skate generously with the paste and strew with one-fourth of the scallions. Fold the top one-third of the leaf over the filling and the bottom one-third over the top. Seal the sides of the leaf by working skewers in and out through them. Repeat to make 3 more packages and grill outdoors until brown, turning once, 6 to 8 minutes per side, or place on a baking sheet and bake until the packages are very hot to the touch, 15 to 20 minutes.

5. To serve, transfer the packages to plates. With the point of a sharp knife, cut an *H* with a long center bar through the top of each bundle and fold back the leaf edges.

MING'S TIP: AS WRAPPERS, TOUGH BANANA LEAVES ARE BETTER INSULATORS THAN THEIR PAPER EQUIVALENTS, SO THIS DISH IS JUST ABOUT FOOLPROOF. (THE LEAVES ALSO CONTRIBUTE FLAVOR.) YOU COULD, HOWEVER, SUBSTITUTE FOIL OR BUTTERED BAKING PARCHMENT FOR THE LEAVES.

S
E
A
F
O
O
D

Cornmeal-Crusted Skate and Pea Sprout Salad
with Citrus Brown Butter Vinaigrette

The French dish of seared skate with *beurre noisette*—a brown butter sauce—was my starting point for this deliciously light dish. Here, you get the joy of skate, a sweet white-fleshed fish with wonderful flavor—and a brown butter–based vinaigrette that's tangy with orange, lime, and lemon juices. The accompanying salad is made with pea sprouts; these are usually available in Chinatown markets. (If you can't get them, substitute blanched snap peas.)

BEVERAGE TIP: TOASTED HONEY, VANILLAN CHARDONNAY (RAMEY, DOMAINE LATOUR-GIRAUD)

SERVES 4

VINAIGRETTE

10 tablespoons butter

1 cup fresh orange juice

1/4 cup fresh lime juice

1/4 cup lemon juice

2 tablespoons Dijon mustard

2 shallots, roughly chopped

Salt and freshly ground black pepper

1 cup cornmeal

4 skate wing fillets, skinned, about 6
   ounces each

Salt and freshly ground black pepper

3 tablespoons canola oil

1/2 pound pea sprouts, or 1 cup
   blanched snap peas

1/4 cup orange segments

1/4 cup lime segments

1/4 cup lemon segments

1 tablespoon pink peppercorns, crushed

1. To make the vinaigrette, heat the butter in a small skillet over low heat until it browns, 30 to 45 minutes. Watch carefully as the butter can burn quickly. It will smell like buttered popcorn.

2. In a blender, combine the orange, lime, and lemon juices, mustard, and shallots and blend until pureed. With the machine running, add the browned butter slowly to make an emulsion. Be careful, as the mixture may foam up when the hot butter is added. Do not add the dark butter solids from the bottom of the pan. Season with salt and pepper and set aside.

3. Place the cornmeal in a large shallow dish. Season the skate with salt and pepper to taste and dredge in the cornmeal. In a large nonstick skillet, heat the oil over medium heat. Add the skate and sauté, turning once, until golden brown, about 8 minutes. Drain on paper towels.

4. Toss the pea sprouts with the vinaigrette to coat lightly and season with the salt and pepper to taste. Place the salad on a round serving platter, top with the fish, and surround with the citrus segments. Drizzle the segments with the remaining vinaigrette, and garnish with the pink peppercorns.

Herb-Crusted Trout
with Shiitake Sticky Rice and Shiso Oil

This recipe was inspired by the Japanese dish of panko-breaded fried pork cutlet called *tonkatsu. Tonkatsu* can be a little heavy; with trout, this dish is light and delicate.

BEVERAGE TIP: CRISP PINOT BLANC (STEELE)

SERVES 4

RICE
2 tablespoons canola oil
1 teaspoon finely chopped garlic
1 tablespoon finely chopped
   fresh ginger
Salt and freshly ground black pepper
2 cups thinly sliced shiitake mushrooms
4 cups unflavored cooked sushi rice, hot
   (page 74)

1 cup panko or bread crumbs
1 teaspoon ground coriander
$1/3$ cup shiso leaves cut into $1/16$-inch
   ribbons
2 cups all-purpose flour
2 eggs, beaten
Canola oil, for frying
4 skinless trout fillets, about 4
   ounces each
Salt and freshly ground black pepper
4 tablespoons Shiso Oil (page 229)

1. To prepare the rice, heat a medium saucepan over medium heat. Add the oil and swirl to coat the pan. When the oil shimmers, add the garlic and ginger and sauté, stirring, until the garlic begins to color, about 2 minutes. Season with salt and pepper, add the shiitakes, and sauté, stirring occasionally, until soft, about 8 minutes. Keep warm.

2. Place the hot rice in a medium bowl, add the shiitake mixture, and combine. Correct the seasonings. Form the rice into 4 triangles (see page 70) or pack it lightly into 4 bowls or ramekins.

3. On a deep plate, combine the panko, coriander, and shiso and stir to mix. Spread the flour on a second plate and arrange the beaten eggs next to it in a small bowl.

4. Fill a fryer or a heavy medium pot one-third full with the oil and heat over high heat to 350°F. Meanwhile, dredge the fillets in flour, dip in the eggs, and coat with the panko mixture. Add the fillets to the oil and fry until golden, turning the fish once with tongs, 6 to 8 minutes. Remove with a large-mesh spoon, drain on paper towels, and season with salt and pepper to taste. Keep warm.

5. Drizzle 4 plates with the shiso oil and divide or unmold the rice among them. Add the fillets and serve.

Seared Arctic Char
with Wild Mushroom Ragout and Truffle Oil

Wild mushrooms and fish have an affinity for one another, especially when the fish is arctic char, which has delicately delicious flesh. The mushroom ragout, flavored with red wine and dark soy sauce, beautifully complements the char's sweetness.

The char, cooked on one side only, is served partially raw. This is a wonderful way to eat fish. It's always wise to tell your fish seller that you intend to eat fish raw, and to receive his or her approval of your selection. If you're uncomfortable with the idea of eating raw fish, turn the fillets and cook them about 4 additional minutes.

BEVERAGE TIP: RASPBERRY, MINTY PINOT NOIR (TURLEY)

SERVES 4

1 tablespoon coarse sea salt, preferably fleur de sel
2 tablespoons coarsely ground black pepper
4 very fresh arctic char fillets, skin on, about 6 ounces each
2 tablespoons canola oil
2 cups well-washed spinach cut into $1/4$-inch ribbons
Wild Mushroom Ragout (page 211)
White truffle oil
$1/4$ cup fresh chives cut into $1/2$-inch lengths

1. Combine the salt and pepper on a plate large enough to accommodate the fillets. Place the fillets skin side down on the mixture and press down gently to coat the skin completely.

2. Heat a large skillet over high heat. Add the oil and swirl to coat the pan. When the oil shimmers, add the char skin side down and sear until well crisped, 6 to 8 minutes. The flesh should be only partially cooked through.

3. Divide the spinach among 4 plates. Top with the mushroom ragout and cover with the char. Drizzle with the truffle oil, garnish with the chives, and serve.

MING'S TIP: WHEN FISH IS COOKED ON THE SKIN SIDE ONLY, IT BROWNS ON THE EXTERIOR AND THE FLESH COOKS TO GRADATIONS OF DONENESS. BITING INTO THE FISH, YOU ENJOY THE CRISPY SKIN, THE "MEDIUM-RARE" FLESH UNDERNEATH IT, AND AT THE TOP, THE UNCOOKED SASHIMI-LIKE MEAT.

Chapter 5

Birds

CHICKEN GETS SHORT SHRIFT ON MANY RESTAURANT MENUS.
IT'S A SHAME SOME CHEFS FIND IT UNINSPIRING. CHICKEN
AND OTHER BIRDS ARE AMONG THE BEST COOKING CANVASES.
PERHAPS IT HAS TO DO WITH MY DEVOTION TO THE CHINESE
AND FRENCH TABLES, WHERE CHICKEN IS CELEBRATED, BUT I
LOVE THE BIRD AND ALWAYS LOOK FOR NEW WAYS TO PRE-
PARE IT.

Take, for example, Braised Chicken Curry with Yams, a hearty sweet-hot stew,
or Hoisin-Marinated Chicken with Napa Slaw, my Asian barbecued chicken.
These savory recipes reveal my penchant for deeply flavorful chicken dishes
that are also simple to fix. Classic Roast Chicken with Sticky Rice Stuffing is
another straightforward but delicious dish. Chicken needs to be imaginatively
treated, but you shouldn't do much *to* it.

You must, however, begin with a flavorful bird. Early on, I learned that slow-
raised and unprocessed chicken was the prerequisite for the best chicken
dishes. The poultry markets of Chinatown still offer freshly butchered birds of
superior quality, but getting them is impractical for most cooks. What you

want, therefore, is chemical-free chicken that has been allowed enough growing time to produce flavorful meat—and that, if frozen (most poultry available to us is at some point), hasn't been held that way for long. Your best bet is organically raised birds (which are usually free-range) and kosher chickens. Look for birds labeled "fresh," which are usually frozen for the shortest period of time.

People think of chicken as "everyday," duck and turkey as dress-up. There *is* something special-occasion about these birds, the former because of its rich meat, the latter, probably, because of its size.

But duck and turkey—conveniently sold in parts—are readily available in our markets and no more difficult to prepare than chicken. Red-Roast Duck with Baby Bok Choy (a fragrant braise, actually), and Turkey Breast with Three-Pea Fried Rice are two such exciting but accessible dishes. "A Turkey in Every Pot" might be my new cooking slogan, and the grilled breast should convince you of its culinary logic.

Squab and quail make perfect entry-level game eating. I think of squab as "little duck"—it has something of the latter's rich flavor, but a special character of its own. Pomegranate-Marinated Squab with Thai Quince Chutney, which is paired with a Roasted Garlic and Sweet Potato Hash, and Grilled Quail with Sambal and Braised Green Papaya are game dishes everyone loves. Like the other birds in this chapter, quail and squab invite imaginative treatment and make delicious eating.

Braised Chicken Curry
with Yams

This is an easy, hearty, and inexpensive dish—good, one-pot cooking. It has a nice balance of hot and sweet—thank the yams for providing the latter—and is quickly prepared. Serve it with basmati rice and you're in business.

BEVERAGE TIP: CLEAN, EXOTIC MULLER-THURGAU (SOKOL BLOSSER)

SERVES 4

2 pounds chicken thighs
Salt and freshly ground black pepper
2 tablespoons canola oil
2 large onions, roughly chopped
1 tablespoon finely chopped garlic
1 tablespoon finely chopped fresh ginger
$\frac{1}{3}$ cup Madras curry powder
1 banana, peeled and quartered
2 bay leaves
4 cups Chicken Stock (page 14) or low-sodium canned broth
3 large yams, peeled and roughly chopped

1. Season the chicken with salt and pepper. Heat a large Dutch oven or heavy-bottomed pot over high heat, add the oil, and swirl to coat the bottom of the pot. When the oil shimmers, add the chicken pieces and brown them well on all sides, about 10 minutes. Don't skimp on this step; not only does it add color, it renders the fat.

2. Remove the chicken and pour off excess fat, leaving only enough to coat the pot. Add the onions, garlic, and ginger and sauté until soft, about 8 minutes. Add the curry powder and cook, stirring, just until the curry is fragrant, about 2 minutes; do not burn. Return the chicken to the pot and add the banana, bay leaves, and stock. Correct the seasonings and bring to a boil. Reduce the heat and simmer gently until the chicken meat almost falls from the bone, $1\frac{1}{2}$ to 2 hours. During the last 30 minutes of cooking, add the yams and cook through. Serve.

Hoisin-Marinated Chicken
with Napa Slaw

This is my Asian barbecued chicken. It's an outstanding summer dish, not only because it's cooked outdoors and is excellent for a gathering but because it's served with a light, fresh slaw, a perfect contrast to the spicy-sweet chicken.

You can, and should, marinate the chicken ahead—overnight isn't too long. And you can double this dish; people can't seem to get enough of it.

BEVERAGE TIP: CHILLED GAMAY FROM FLEURIE OR CHIROUBLES (CRU BEAUJOLAIS)

SERVES 4

2 cups hoisin sauce
4 tablespoons sambal oelek
2 bunches scallions, white and green parts, chopped
1 cup dry red wine
1/2 cup finely chopped garlic
1/2 cup finely chopped fresh ginger
2 teaspoons freshly ground black pepper
4 chicken breasts with drumettes (first wing joints) attached and 4 chicken leg-thigh pieces
Salt
Napa Slaw (page 207)

1. In a nonreactive baking dish just large enough to hold the chicken, combine the hoisin sauce, sambal oelek, scallions, wine, garlic, ginger, and pepper and mix. Add the chicken, turn to coat, cover, and marinate, refrigerated, at least 4 hours and preferably overnight.

2. Heat an outdoor grill or preheat the broiler. Spray the grill with nonstick cooking spray. Season the chicken with the salt to taste and grill or broil it, turning once, until brown and the juices run clear when pricked with a fork at the joint, 12 to 15 minutes.

3. Divide the slaw and chicken among 4 plates and serve.

MING'S TIP: BECAUSE HOISIN CONTAINS SUGAR, THE MARINADE BURNS EASILY. WHEN GRILLING THE CHICKEN, WATCH CAREFULLY TO AVOID FLARE-UPS. HAVE A SPRAYER WITH WATER HANDY JUST IN CASE.

Braised Chicken
with Shiitakes and Snap Peas

This is a wonderful stir-fry—almost. I say almost because it's not really a stir-fry. It begins like one—aromatics and chicken thighs are added to a wok and both are colored—but it ends as a braise, since longer cooking is needed to cook the bone-in thighs properly.

The thighs—my favorite chicken part because of their great flavor and excellent meat-to-bone ratio—are dished up with sugar snap peas and shiitakes. This is one-pot cooking at its best.

BEVERAGE TIP: MEDIUM-BODIED GRENACHE ROSÉ FROM TAVEL OR LESSER KNOWN LIRAC

SERVES 4

1 tablespoon toasted sesame oil
$\frac{1}{2}$ cup oyster sauce
2 tablespoons cornstarch
8 chicken thighs
$\frac{1}{2}$ pound sugar snap peas
Salt and freshly ground black pepper
   plus cracked black peppercorns, for garnish
2 tablespoons canola oil
1 tablespoon finely chopped garlic
1 tablespoon finely chopped fresh ginger
4 scallions, white and green parts,
   sliced $\frac{1}{8}$ inch thick and reserved separately
2 cups shiitake mushroom caps cut in $\frac{1}{4}$-inch slices
$\frac{1}{2}$ cup Chicken Stock (page 14) or low-sodium canned broth

1. In a medium baking dish, combine the sesame oil, oyster sauce, and cornstarch and mix. Add the chicken, turn to coat, and allow to marinate, covered, about 30 minutes.

2. Fill a bowl with cold water and add ice. Bring a large pot of salted water to a boil, add the snap peas to the boiling water, and cook until tender-crisp, 2 to 3 minutes. Drain and transfer the peas to the bowl. When cold, drain and set aside.

3. Remove the chicken from the marinade and season with the salt and ground pepper. Heat a large wok over high heat. Add the oil and swirl to coat the pan. When the oil shimmers, add the garlic, ginger, and white parts of the scallions and stir-fry until fragrant and lightly brown, about 3 minutes. Add the chicken and shiitakes and sauté, turning as necessary, until both are brown, about 8 minutes. Add the stock and cook until the liquid is reduced by half, about 20 minutes. Add the reserved peas, stir until heated through, about 2 minutes, and correct the seasonings. Divide among 4 plates, garnish with the cracked peppercorns and scallion greens, and serve.

MING'S TIPS: YOU CAN USE LEGS OR LEG-THIGH COMBINATIONS IN PLACE OF THE CHICKEN THIGHS CALLED FOR HERE.

SUGAR SNAP PEAS QUICKLY GO BEYOND CRISP-TENDER TO MUSHY, SO TAKE EXTRA CARE NOT TO OVERCOOK THEM DURING THEIR PRELIMINARY BLANCHING. THEY WILL RECEIVE MORE HEAT JUST BEFORE THEY'RE SERVED.

Classic Roast Chicken
with Sticky Rice Stuffing

Necessity really *is* the mother of invention. I was roasting a turkey one Thanksgiving and was about to make a stuffing when I discovered I had no bread. I had to improvise, with this aromatic, sticky-rice stuffing the result. Paired with chicken, it is now a great favorite in our house—my version of an American classic.

BEVERAGE TIP: BALANCED CHARDONNAY FROM MACON (MACON CLESSÉ DOMAINE BON-GRAN)

SERVES 4

1 6-pound chicken (preferably free-range), washed and patted dry
3 tablespoons canola oil
Salt and freshly ground black pepper
1 tablespoon finely chopped garlic
1 tablespoon finely chopped fresh ginger
5 scallions, white and green parts, sliced ⅛ inch thick
1 jalapeño or 2 serrano chiles, finely chopped
2½ cups cooked Sushi Rice (page 74), at room temperature
2 tablespoons Scallion Oil (page 229), for garnish

1. Preheat the oven to 550°F.

2. Rub the chicken inside and out with 1 tablespoon of the oil and season inside and out with the salt and pepper. Choose a roasting pan with a rack that will hold the chicken comfortably but not snugly. Place the chicken, breast side up, on the rack in the pan and roast, turning the pan once back to front, until brown, about 25 minutes.

3. Meanwhile, heat a small skillet over medium heat. Add the remaining 2 tablespoons of oil and swirl to coat the pan. When the oil shimmers, add the garlic, ginger, scallions, and jalapeño and sauté, stirring, until the vegetables have browned, about 5 minutes. Add to the rice and mix lightly. Correct the seasonings.

4. When the chicken has browned, remove from the oven and stuff with the rice. Reduce the oven temperature to 325°, drape the chicken with foil to keep it from getting too brown, and return it to the oven until done, or a wing can be moved back and forth with ease, 45 to 55 minutes more.

5. Carve the chicken into serving pieces. Mound the rice onto a platter and top with the chicken pieces. Drizzle the chicken and rice with the scallion oil and serve.

MING'S TIP: I ALWAYS ROAST BIRDS AT A HIGH TEMPERATURE INI-
TIALLY TO BROWN THEM, THEN LOWER THE HEAT TO COOK THEM
THROUGH. I FIND THIS ENSURES JUICY POULTRY WITH CRISPY SKIN.
ALSO I STUFF CHICKEN OR TURKEY HALFWAY THROUGH ITS COOKING
TO ENSURE THAT THE BIRD'S INSIDE GETS COOKED THOROUGHLY.
WEAR CLEAN RUBBER GLOVES TO PROTECT YOUR HANDS WHEN
STUFFING THE HOT BIRD.

Pomegranate-Marinated Squab
with Thai Quince Chutney

Squab is the regal bird of Asian cuisine. I think of it as duck with more finesse—a slightly gamy yet delicate bird that's perfect for special occasions. In this dish, squab is marinated in a bath that includes pomegranate molasses, the dark, tangy syrup that is native to the Middle East and now widely available. The bird is then seared and served with a garlicky hash and fiery-tart chutney.

Served on a mound of Roasted Garlic and Sweet Potato Hash, this makes a wonderful meal, but you could also serve half-portions for an appetizer or first course.

BEVERAGE TIP: BLEND OF SYRAH, GRENACHE, CLAIRETTE, AND MORE (CHATEAUNEUF-DU-PAPE)

SERVES 4

¼ cup pomegranate molasses
¾ cup soy sauce
¾ cup dry red wine
2 tablespoons finely chopped garlic
2 tablespoons finely chopped fresh ginger
¼ cup brown sugar, packed
8 boned squab half-breasts with leg-thighs and
   wing "drumsticks" (see Tip)
Salt and freshly ground black pepper
2 tablespoons canola oil
2 tablespoons butter
Roasted Garlic and Sweet Potato Hash (page 215)
4 heaping tablespoons Thai Quince Chutney (page 241)
2 tablespoons Scallion Oil, for garnish (page 229)

1. In a baking dish large enough to hold the squab, combine the molasses, soy sauce, wine, garlic, ginger, and brown sugar. Add the squab, turn to coat, and marinate, covered, about 1 hour.

2. Season the squab with the salt and pepper. Set aside the marinade. Heat a large skillet over medium heat. Add the oil and swirl to coat the bottom of the pan. Add the squab skin side down and cook until brown, about 4 minutes. Turn the squab and cook for 2 minutes more for medium-rare meat. Remove the squab and keep warm. Add the marinade to the pan, scrape the brown bits from the bottom of the pan with a wooden spoon, and reduce the liquid by half over low heat, about 6 minutes.

3. Right before serving, whisk the butter into the sauce and correct the seasonings. Mound the sweet potatoes at one end of a large oval serving platter. Place the squab crisscrossed along the platter and place the chutney near the squab. Drizzle over the sauce and the scallion oil and serve.

MING'S TIPS: THE RECIPE REQUIRES 8 BONED SQUAB HALF-BREASTS WITH LEG-THIGHS AND WING "DRUMSTICKS" ATTACHED. HAVE YOUR BUTCHER DO THIS, OR DO IT YOURSELF BY SPLITTING THE SQUABS AND RUNNING A SMALL SHARP KNIFE BETWEEN THE BREAST MEAT AND THE RIB BONES. AS YOU WORK, SEVER THE THIGH AND WING JOINTS WHERE THEY ARE ATTACHED TO THE CARCASS, FREEING THE HALF-BREASTS. REMOVE COLLAR AND WISHBONE FRAGMENTS AND THE WING FIRST JOINTS.

I STRONGLY BELIEVE THAT SQUAB SHOULD BE EATEN MEDIUM-RARE. COOKED THROUGH, IT TENDS TO ACQUIRE A LIVERISH FLAVOR. THE COOKING TIME HERE PRODUCES MEDIUM-RARE BIRDS. IF YOU LIKE YOUR SQUAB MORE FULLY COOKED, HOWEVER, SAUTÉ THEM FOR 4 ADDITIONAL MINUTES.

Grilled Quail
with Sambal and Braised Green Papaya

Quail is wonderful eating—and so is Thai green papaya salad. This dish, with its spicy-sweet quail and green papaya braise, is the result of my wanting to combine the two.

In working on this, the salad evolved into a braise; to make it, I treat the papaya like acorn squash, cooking it with brown sugar and a little stock until it becomes tender and delicious.

This is a dish to enjoy with friends. Remember, though, not to be Miss Manners with the quail. It needs to be eaten with the fingers—just dig in.

BEVERAGE TIP: FRUITY RIESLING, NOT BONE DRY (AUSTRALIAN GROSSET OR ALSATIAN HUGEL)

SERVES 4

¼ cup sambal oelek
2 tablespoons finely chopped garlic
2 tablespoons finely chopped fresh ginger
½ cup dry red wine
¼ cup chopped scallions, white and
   green parts
2 tablespoons molasses
½ cup canola oil
8 quail

PAPAYA
2 tablespoons butter
2 tablespoons brown sugar
2 medium green papayas, skinned,
   seeded, and cut into ½-inch dice
Salt and freshly ground black pepper
Juice of 1 lime
½ cup Chicken Stock (page 14) or
   low-sodium canned broth

Salt and freshly ground black pepper
4 teaspoons Chile Oil (page 230), for
   garnish

1. In a baking dish just large enough to hold the quail, combine the sambal oelek, garlic, ginger, wine, scallions, molasses, and oil. Add the quail, turn to coat, cover, and marinate, refrigerated, at least 6 hours and preferably overnight.

2. To prepare the papaya, in a medium saucepan combine the butter and brown sugar and cook over medium heat until the butter colors slightly, about 8 minutes. Add the papayas and cook, stirring occasionally, about 5 minutes. Season with the salt and pepper to taste, add the lime juice and stock; and simmer until the papaya is tender-firm and becomes somewhat translucent, 25 to 30 minutes. Correct the seasonings and set aside.

3. Prepare an outdoor grill or preheat the broiler. Season the quail with the salt and pepper to taste and grill over high heat or broil, turning as necessary, until the quail are done or the legs move freely, about 6 minutes. Do not overcook.

4. Divide the papaya among 4 dishes and top with the quail. Drizzle with the chile oil and serve.

MING'S TIP: YOU CAN USE FRESH OR FROZEN QUAIL. THE LONGER THE QUAIL MARINATE, THE BETTER THE FLAVOR. AND KEEP AN EYE ON THEM AS THEY GRILL; THEY CAN OVERCOOK QUICKLY.

Red-Roast Duck
with Baby Bok Choy

This spectacularly fragrant duck dish celebrates Chinese red roasting and French confit making.

A red roast, which is in fact a super braise, derives its special character from the use of dark soy sauce (the source of the duck's "red" color), Shaoxing wine, and rock sugar. The duck, red roasted until its meat is velvety, ends up confitlike, but without the stewing in fat that preparation entails. I've added baby bok choy and some chile heat to the duck, which underline the dish's Asian origins and ensure that people who eat it will be very, very happy.

BEVERAGE TIP: SPICY, DRIED-CHERRY SHIRAZ/SYRAH AUSTRALIAN (BROKENWOOD HER-MITAGE)

SERVES 4

1 bottle dry red wine
2 cups Shaoxing wine, or 1 cup dry
   sherry
1 cup dark soy sauce
3 cups soy sauce
4 cups water
1 large duck, about 6 pounds
2 boxes (about 3 pounds) rock sugar,
   or 2 cups dark brown sugar
1 5-inch piece fresh ginger, cut into
   $\frac{1}{4}$-inch slices
1 whole head garlic, unpeeled and
   halved horizontally
2 bunches scallions, white parts sliced into 3-inch lengths,
   green parts sliced $\frac{1}{8}$ inch thick
2 star anise
4 Thai bird chiles
2 cinnamon sticks
8 baby bok choy, halved and cored

1. In a large, deep pot, combine the wines, soy sauces, and water. Bring to a boil over high heat and add the duck. If the liquid doesn't cover the duck, add more water. Bring to a boil again, then reduce the heat and simmer, skimming the liquid until no more scum forms, about 30 minutes.

2. Add the rock sugar, ginger, garlic, long scallion pieces, star anise, chiles, and cinnamon sticks. Stir to dissolve the sugar and taste the liquid for sweetness. It should be pleasantly sweet; if not sweet enough, add more sugar. Place a second pot or stainless steel bowl half-filled with water into the first to keep the duck submerged (see Tips) and simmer until the duck is very tender and almost falling from the bones, $2\frac{1}{2}$ to 3 hours. Do not overcook or the meat will come apart. During the last 10 minutes of cooking, add the bok choy.

3. Using a large-mesh spoon, carefully remove the duck and bok choy to a platter and cover with foil to keep warm. Strain and skim the stock, return it to the pot, and reduce it over high heat until lightly syrupy, about 20 minutes.

4. Transfer the duck to a serving platter and surround it with the bok choy. Glaze the duck with the sauce, garnish it with the scallion greens, and serve.

MING'S TIPS: THE DUCK MUST BE KEPT SUBMERGED IN ITS BRAISING LIQUID WHILE IT COOKS. TO ACCOMPLISH THIS, FIND A POT OR STAINLESS STEEL BOWL THAT WILL FIT INTO THE BRAISING POT. FILL IT HALFWAY WITH WATER, AND PLACE IT ON THE DUCK TO WEIGH IT DOWN AS IT COOKS.

DON'T BE PUT OFF BY THE AMOUNT OF SUGAR I CALL FOR HERE; IT'S NEEDED TO GIVE THE DISH ITS MELLOW FLAVOR.

Turkey Breast
with Three-Pea Fried Rice

Turkey is a sadly underused meat; most of us have it at Thanksgiving and in sandwiches and that's it. I like turkey a lot and enjoy devising ways to use it, like this dish. I marinate this good, inexpensive cut in a fragrant bath, grill it, and serve it with fried rice that includes English peas and a crispy snow and snap pea salad. This dish is full of textural and flavor contrasts and, with its green accents, looks terrific. Start this a day in advance for the best flavor.

BEVERAGE TIP: VELVETY, SMOOTH MOURVEDRE BLEND ROSÉ FROM BANDOL (DOMAINE TEMPIER)

SERVES 4

1 tablespoon coriander seeds

2 tablespoons grainy mustard

1 cup dry red wine

$\frac{1}{2}$ cup extra-virgin olive oil

1 tablespoon chopped fresh thyme

1 tablespoon chopped fresh rosemary

1 tablespoon finely chopped garlic

$\frac{1}{2}$ tablespoon salt

1 tablespoon coarsely ground black
    pepper

1 4-pound turkey breast, skin
    removed

VINAIGRETTE

Juice of 1 lemon

Juice of 1 lime

Juice of 1 orange

$\frac{1}{4}$ cup extra-virgin olive oil

Salt and freshly ground black pepper

1 cup snow peas, strings removed

1 cup sugar snap peas, strings removed

1 cup English peas or frozen peas

4 tablespoons canola oil

3 eggs, beaten lightly

1 tablespoon finely chopped garlic

1 tablespoon finely chopped fresh ginger

4 cups cooked long-grain rice

1 bunch chives, cut into 2-inch lengths

1. Using a spice grinder or clean coffee grinder, grind the coriander seeds coarsely. In a large bowl, combine the mustard, wine, oil, thyme, rosemary, garlic, coriander, salt, and pepper. Mix, add the turkey breast, and turn to coat. Marinate the turkey, covered, for at least 6 hours and preferably overnight.

2. To make the vinaigrette, combine the lemon, lime, and orange juices in a small bowl. Whisk in the olive oil and season with the salt and black pepper to taste. Set aside.

3. Bring a large quantity of salted water to a boil. Fill a bowl with cold water and add ice. Add the snow peas and snap peas to the boiling water and cook until tender-crisp, 3 to 4 minutes. With a large-mesh spoon, transfer the peas to the ice water to cool. Remove the peas, drain well, and set aside. Add more ice to the bowl of water and return the water on the stove to a boil. Add the fresh or frozen peas and cook until just done, about 6 minutes for the fresh, 1 minute for the frozen. Drain, transfer the peas to a separate bowl, and when cold, drain and set aside.

4. Prepare an outdoor grill or preheat the broiler. Season the turkey breast with the salt and pepper and grill it covered or broil it, turning frequently, until just cooked through, or to an internal temperature of 160°F, about 30 minutes. Allow to rest for 15 minutes before slicing.

5. Heat a wok or large nonstick skillet over high heat. Add 2 tablespoons of the oil and swirl to coat the pan. When the oil shimmers, add the eggs, which will puff up. Stir constantly to scramble softly, about 10 seconds, and set aside.

6. Add the remaining 2 tablespoons of oil to the wok and swirl to coat the pan. When the oil shimmers, add the garlic and ginger and stir-fry until soft, about 2 minutes. Add the rice, eggs, chives, and reserved English or frozen peas and stir-fry to heat through, about 8 minutes. The stir-frying will break up the eggs. Correct the seasonings.

7. Toss the reserved snow and snap peas with the vinaigrette. Cut the turkey breast diagonally into ¼-inch slices. Divide the rice among 4 plates. Surround with the turkey, top with the salad, and serve.

MING'S TIP: TO AVOID BURNING THE TURKEY BREAST BEFORE IT'S COOKED THROUGH, GRILL IT OVER A MEDIUM FLAME. COVERING THE BREAST AS IT COOKS HELPS TO COOK IT EVENLY. IT CAN ALSO BE PAN-SEARED AND OVEN-ROASTED.

Chapter 6

Meat

I'M THE TALLEST TSAI IN MY FAMILY. WHEN PEOPLE ASK ME HOW I GOT THAT WAY, I SMILE AND SAY "MILK AND MEAT." MY DAD USED TO BUY COPIOUS QUANTITIES OF BEEF, WHICH IS SCARCE IN CHINA, AND WE'D ALL SIT DOWN TO SLABS OF IT FOR DELICIOUS SUNDAY DINNERS.

I still relish meat, but the big meat and potato plates I favored as a child have given way to dishes like Gingered Beef with Leeks and Asparagus in which meat is one element of a multi-ingredient entree. And though I still love a good steak I also adore deep-flavored beef braises made with inexpensive but delicious cuts. Savory Braised Oxtail with Preserved Lemon Polenta and Aromatic Braised Short Ribs with Napa Cabbage–Orzo Stew are as satisfying to eat as they're uncomplicated to cook.

It's often said that pork is the beef of China. My allegiances to the Asian table aside, I'm crazy for pork—when it's not overcooked. Properly prepared pork is succulent and pink inside with a sweet, delicate flavor. To achieve this end I like to brine nontenderloin pork cuts, a process whereby the meat receives a soak in a moisturizing salt-water solution before it's cooked. This "secret" step, used in Asian-Marinated Pork Loin with Gingered Sweet Potatoes and Five-Spice Apples produces marvelously juicy meat. Once you acquaint yourself with the brining process, you'll wonder how you cooked pork without it.

Lamb is my favorite "restaurant meat." I order it out often, not only for its flavor but also because it goes so well with red wines. I particularly appreciate New Zealand lamb, which is deliciously tender. Braised Curried Lamb Shanks with Three-Onion Couscous takes my lamb passion in a different, more down-to-earth direction.

I've been happy to note the renewed interest in venison. I first enjoyed this rich, hearty meat in Colorado, where it was grilled over a wood-burning fire, and I've been hooked ever since. Farm- and ranch-raised venison is increasingly available and excels in dishes like Spiced Venison with Parsnip Puree and Parsley Oil, the perfect "starter" dish for this wonderful meat. Too bad venison wasn't around when I was growing up; if it had been, there's no telling how tall I'd be.

Asian-Marinated Pork Loin
with Gingered Sweet Potatoes and Five-Spice Apples

Every element in this dish complements the others. The pork, brined to ensure moistness, is ideally set off by the spicy, slightly sweet potatoes, whose warm flavors are echoed by the lightly caramelized apples. This is pork, sweet potatoes, and applesauce—that favorite American triumvirate—from an East-West point of view.

I can't say enough about the virtues of brining, the process whereby meat, poultry, or seafood is soaked in salted water before cooking to increase internal moisture. For this recipe I add sugar, soy sauce, and other seasonings to the brining liquid so the meat is flavored as well as made moist.

BEVERAGE TIP: FRUITY, BRIGHT BLENDED RED FROM COTEAUX DU LANGUEDOC (PIC ST. LOUP)

SERVES 4

4 cups water
⅓ cup kosher salt
⅓ cup sugar
1 tablespoon dark soy sauce
1½ teaspoons toasted Szechwan peppercorns
1 tablespoon toasted black peppercorns, plus
    freshly ground black pepper
4 ¼-inch-thick slices fresh ginger
2 star anise
2 bay leaves
1 4-pound pork loin
2 tablespoons canola oil
Gingered Sweet Potatoes (page 217)
Five-Spice Apples (page 209)
¼ cup chives cut into 1-inch lengths, for garnish
2 tablespoons Chile Oil (page 230), for garnish

1. One day in advance, combine the water, salt, sugar, soy sauce, peppercorns, ginger, anise, and bay leaves in a deep baking dish large enough to hold the pork and stir to mix. Add the pork; if it is not covered, add more water. Cover and refrigerate overnight.

2. Preheat the oven to 375°F. Rinse the pork thoroughly with cold water, pat dry, and season with the ground pepper to taste. Heat a large skillet over high heat, add the oil, and swirl to coat the bottom of the pan. When the oil shimmers, add the pork and brown on all sides. Transfer the pork to a roasting pan and roast just until the the pork is hot through to the center (about 150°F internal temperature), 25 to 30 minutes. The interior of the pork will remain pink.

3. Allow the pork to rest for 10 minutes and cut into $\frac{1}{4}$-inch slices. Divide the gingered sweet potatoes among 4 plates, surround with the pork, and add the five-spice apples. Garnish with the chives, drizzle with the chile oil, and serve.

MING'S TIP: A BRINED LOIN WILL ROAST IN LESS TIME THAN AN UNBRINED LOIN; BECAUSE OF THE PROCESS, THE PORK REMAINS A DEFINITE PINK AFTER COOKING SO TAKE CARE NOT TO OVERCOOK.

M
E
A
T

Hoisin Pork Tenderloin Sandwiches
with Napa Slaw

I grew up enjoying hoisin-roasted pork—my mom would pack it into a Thermos and send it with me to school. At first I was embarrassed by my "different" lunch, but soon found myself fielding many requests for a taste. This led to bartering and, usually, more food than I'd begun with. Thanks, Mom!

Now I serve the hoisin-marinated pork as a sandwich with crispy napa slaw. It would be the runaway hit of any picnic.

BEVERAGE TIP: LAGER (TSINGTAO, SHANGHAI, SINGHA)

SERVES 4

1 cup hoisin sauce
2 tablespoons sambal oelek
2 tablespoons finely chopped garlic
2 tablespoons finely chopped fresh ginger
$\frac{1}{2}$ cup red wine
$\frac{1}{4}$ cup chopped scallions, white parts only
2 pork tenderloins (about 8 ounces each)
Salt and freshly ground black pepper
2 tablespoons canola oil
4 large sesame seed buns
Napa Slaw (page 207)

1. In a nonreactive baking dish large enough to hold the pork, combine the hoisin sauce, sambal oelek, garlic, ginger, wine, and scallions. Mix, add the pork, and turn to coat. Cover and marinate in the refrigerator for at least 3 hours and preferably overnight.

2. Preheat the oven to 350°F. Season the pork with the salt and pepper. Heat a large ovenproof skillet over high heat, add the oil, and swirl to coat the pan. When the oil shimmers, add the pork and brown, turning once, about 5 minutes. Transfer the pork to the oven and roast until just done, 150°F inside, about 12 to 15 minutes. The interior of the pork should remain pink. Allow the pork to rest for 5 minutes and cut into $\frac{1}{4}$-inch slices.

3. Halve the buns and toast lightly, if you wish. Top the bottoms with half of the slaw. Add 6 to 8 slices of pork per sandwich, top with the remaining slaw and bun halves. Cut the sandwiches in half and serve.

Gingered Beef
with Leeks and Asparagus

You've undoubtedly had beef with broccoli, an old faithful of Chinese-American cuisine. The dish can be very good, but I much prefer this take on it, with asparagus in place of the broccoli. Leeks, which are seldom used in Chinese cooking, add their subtle taste and texture to this simple but flavorful dish. Serve this with rice, of course.

BEVERAGE TIP: SPICY SYRAH FROM GIGONDAS (GUIGAL CHATEAU D'AMPUIS)

6 $\frac{1}{8}$-inch-thick slices fresh ginger

1 tablespoon toasted sesame oil

1 teaspoon freshly ground black pepper

$\frac{1}{4}$ cup canola oil

$\frac{1}{4}$ cup soy sauce

$\frac{1}{2}$ cup Shaoxing wine or dry sherry

1 pound flank steak, cut against the grain
  into $\frac{1}{8}$-inch slices

1 pound asparagus, ends trimmed and
  cut into 2-inch pieces

LEEKS

1 tablespoon canola oil

4 medium leeks, white parts only,
  well washed and julienned

1 tablespoon finely chopped garlic

2 tablespoons finely chopped fresh
  ginger

Salt and freshly ground black pepper

1. In a dish large enough to hold the beef, combine the ginger, sesame oil, pepper, canola oil, soy sauce, and wine. Stir to blend, add the beef, turn to coat, and marinate, covered, at least 1 hour and preferably overnight.

2. Bring a large quantity of salted water to a boil. Fill a large bowl with water and add ice. Add the asparagus to the boiling water and cook until tender-crisp, 4 to 6 minutes. Transfer to the bowl of ice water to cool. Drain well and set aside.

3. To make the leeks, heat a wok or large skillet over high heat. Add the oil and swirl to coat the pan. When the oil shimmers, add the leeks, garlic, and ginger and cook, stirring, until soft, about 3 minutes.

4. Drain the beef and stir-fry until just cooked through, about 4 minutes. Add the asparagus and stir-fry until thoroughly heated. Season with the salt and pepper to taste and serve immediately.

Mongolian Beef Sandwiches
with Black Bean Aïoli

These savory sandwiches take me back to the Mandarin Kitchen, my parents' restaurant in Ohio, and to one of its most popular dishes, Mongolian Beef. That dish was in such demand that my father juryrigged a portable barbecue to function like the restaurant's 80,000 BTU griddle to prepare the dish for catering dates. Everyone called it The Walking Mongolian Beef Show.

The beef in this sandwich receives a similarly delicious treatment. The resulting sandwich would make a cook's reputation when served at any informal gathering.

BEVERAGE TIP: LAGER (TSINGTAO, SHANGHAI, SINGHA)

SERVES 4

½ cup canola oil
1 tablespoon toasted sesame oil
½ cup soy sauce
½ cup Shaoxing wine or dry sherry
2 tablespoons finely chopped
  garlic
½ cup scallions, white and green
  parts, sliced 1 inch thick
½ tablespoon coarsely ground
  black pepper
2 pounds flank steak, sliced ¼
  inch thick against the grain

BLACK BEAN AÏOLI

2 cups plus 2 tablespoons canola oil
3 tablespoons finely chopped garlic
1 tablespoon finely chopped rinsed and
  drained fermented black beans
1 tablespoon finely chopped fresh ginger
2 tablespoons rice wine vinegar
2 egg yolks
Salt and freshly ground black pepper

2 tablespoons canola oil
2 large red onions, cut into ¼-inch slices
2 serrano chiles, stemmed and finely
  chopped with seeds
½ head green cabbage, cut into ¼-inch
  slices
1 red bell pepper, cored, seeded, and
  julienned
1 green bell pepper, cored, seeded, and
  julienned
2 carrots, thinly sliced
4 pita bread with pockets

1. In a medium nonreactive bowl, combine the canola and sesame oils, soy sauce, wine, garlic, scallions, and pepper. Add the beef, stir to coat, and marinate, refrigerated, at least 4 hours and preferably overnight.

2. Meanwhile, make the aïoli. Heat a medium skillet over medium heat. Add the 2 table-spoons of oil and swirl to coat the pan. When the oil shimmers, add the garlic, beans, and ginger and sauté, stirring, until soft, about 3 to 5 minutes. Add the vinegar and cook to reduce it by three-fourths, about 3 minutes. Allow to cool completely.

3. In a food processor, combine the vinegar mixture with the yolks and process. With the machine running, add the 2 cups of oil through the feed tube, slowly at first. When the mixture emulsifies, add the oil more quickly until the mixture is mayonnaise-like. Season with the salt and pepper to taste. If not using immediately, store in the refrigerator.

4. Preheat the oven to 250° F. Heat a wok over high heat. Add the oil and swirl to coat the pan. When the oil shimmers, add the onions and chiles and stir-fry until tender-crisp, about 3 minutes. Add the beef and stir-fry just until the beef is seared on the outside and rare within, about 5 minutes; do not overcook. Add the cabbage, red and green peppers, and carrots and stir-fry until tender-crisp, about 8 minutes.

5. Meanwhile, warm the pita breads in the oven. Cut a $\frac{1}{2}$-inch slice off one side of each pita and spread the insides with the aïoli. Stuff very generously with the beef and serve.

MING'S TIPS: UNLIKE CLASSIC AÏOLIS, THIS ONE USES GARLIC THAT'S COOKED BEFORE IT'S PUREED. DON'T SKIP THIS IMPORTANT STEP, WHICH ENSURES THAT THE FINISHED AÏOLI WILL BE MELLOW, AND THAT DINERS, HAVING EATEN IT, WON'T OFFEND!

IF MAKING THE SANDWICHES FOR A PICNIC OR OTHER OUTING, YOU CAN PREPARE THE FILLING AHEAD AND KEEP IT REFRIGERATED. PACK THE FILLING, AÏOLI, AND PITA SEPARATELY AND MAKE THE SAND-WICHES JUST BEFORE SERVING THEM.

Aromatic Braised Short Ribs
with Napa Cabbage–Orzo Stew

I love braised short ribs. They're a perfect dish for a gathering, which is why I've made this a large-quantity recipe.

Much depends on the liquid in which the ribs are cooked, and in this dish the square-cut ribs get the full savory treatment. Like most braises, the dish is quickly put together and cooks unattended, so you get to relax, too.

Don't be intimidated by the relatively long ingredient list. You probably have most of these in your pantry.

BEVERAGE TIP: VELVETY SMOOTH, ANISE-Y MERLOT (CASA LAPOSTOLLE)

SERVES 10 TO 12

½ cup ancho chile powder
¼ cup salt, plus additional as needed
2 tablespoons freshly ground black pepper, plus additional as needed
15 double-rib short ribs, cut into 3-inch-long pieces (have the butcher do this)
4 tablespoons canola oil
5 medium onions, cut into ½-inch dice
3 medium fennel bulbs, cored and cut into ½-inch dice, fronds reserved for garnish
4 celery stalks, cut into ½-inch dice
4 large carrots, peeled and cut into ½-inch dice
½ cup finely chopped garlic
½ cup finely chopped fresh ginger
½ cup fermented black beans, rinsed and drained
1 bottle dry red wine
1 1-pound can whole plum tomatoes with their juice
1 cup dark soy sauce
½ bunch fresh thyme, or 1 tablespoon dried
4 bay leaves
4 star anise

MING'S TIP: CABBAGE RELEASES A GOOD DEAL OF WATER AS IT COOKS. BE CAREFUL, THEREFORE, NOT TO ADD TOO MUCH STOCK TO THE STEW AS IT COOKS.

ORZO STEW

6 tablespoons butter

2 medium onions, cut into ¼-inch slices

1 pound orzo

2 heads napa cabbage, cut into ¼-inch ribbons

Salt and freshly ground black pepper

4 to 5 cups Chicken Stock (page 14), low-sodium canned broth, or
   water with 2 ladles of the rib cooking liquid added

1. In a small bowl, combine the chile powder, the ¼ cup salt, and the 2 tablespoons pepper and mix well. Season the ribs well with the mixture.

2. Heat a very large pot or Dutch oven over high heat. Add 2 tablespoons of the oil and swirl to coat the bottom of the pan. When the oil shimmers, add the ribs and brown on all sides, 10 to 12 minutes. Remove the ribs, wipe out the pan, and add the remaining 2 tablespoons of oil. When the oil shimmers, add the onions, fennel, celery, carrots, garlic, ginger, and black beans and sauté, stirring, until the vegetables are soft, about 10 minutes. Add the wine, stir, and cook to reduce the liquid by one-fourth, about 15 minutes. Add the tomatoes with their juice, soy sauce, thyme, bay leaves, and star anise. Return the ribs to the pot, add water to cover, and season with salt and pepper to taste. Bring the mixture to a boil, reduce the heat, and simmer slowly, covered, until the meat falls from the bones, 3 to 4 hours.

3. Carefully remove the ribs and keep them warm. Remove the anise, bay leaves, and fresh thyme sprigs, if using, from the sauce. Skim the sauce to remove the fat and heat over medium heat to reduce slightly, about 10 minutes. Using a hand blender or food processor, blend the sauce until smooth. Correct the seasonings.

4. Meanwhile, make the orzo stew. Heat a large saucepan over high heat. Add 2 tablespoons of the butter and swirl to coat the bottom of the pan. Add the onions and sauté, stirring, until soft, about 8 minutes. Add the orzo and cook, stirring occasionally, until well heated, about 5 minutes. Add the cabbage and sauté, stirring, until soft, 3 to 5 minutes. Season with salt and pepper to taste. Add the stock in 1-cup increments, allowing it to be absorbed by the orzo before adding more, and cook until the orzo is soft, 25 to 30 minutes. Keep in mind that the cabbage will release water; you may not need all the stock. Stir in the remaining 4 tablespoons of butter.

5. Mound the stew in a large bowl. Top with the ribs and ladle over the sauce. Garnish with the fennel fronds and serve.

Savory Braised Oxtail
with Preserved Lemon Polenta

The Chinese love oxtail. Besides enjoying it in bouillon and broths, they revere its tonic effects. (It is said to improve one's sex life; I make no promises.) I join the Chinese as a fan of this flavorful meat, which requires slow braising for a savory falling-from-the-bones specialty that people love.

The polenta helps to temper the richness of the oxtails.

BEVERAGE TIP: PEPPERY BLACKBERRY ZINFANDEL (RAVENSWOOD ALEXANDER VALLEY, ROSENBLUM)

SERVES 4

2 cups all-purpose flour
¼ cup salt
2 tablespoons freshly ground black pepper
12 large oxtails (6 to 8 pounds)
4 tablespoons canola oil
2 large onions, chopped
2 medium fennel bulbs, cored and roughly
   chopped
1 celery stalk, chopped
1 large carrot, peeled and chopped
2 tablespoons finely chopped fresh ginger
10 garlic cloves, peeled
4 lemongrass stalks, white parts only, pounded
   and finely chopped
2 cups Shaoxing wine
1 1-pound can plum tomatoes, drained
1 cup dark soy sauce
4 sprigs fresh thyme, or 1½ teaspoons dried
2 bay leaves
1 lemon, halved
Preserved Lemon Polenta (page 222)

1. On a platter, combine the flour, salt, and pepper and mix. Add the oxtails and dredge on all sides. Set aside.

2. Heat a Dutch oven or heavy medium pot over high heat. Add 2 tablespoons of the oil and swirl to coat the bottom of the pot. When the oil shimmers, add the oxtails and brown on all sides, about 10 to 12 minutes, working in batches if necessary. Remove the oxtails, wipe out the pot, and add the remaining 2 tablespoons of oil. When the oil shimmers, add the onions, fennel, celery, carrot, ginger, garlic, and lemongrass. Sauté, stirring, until soft, about 10 minutes. Add the wine, stir, and cook to reduce it by half, 6 to 8 minutes. Add the tomatoes, soy sauce, thyme, bay leaves, and lemon. Return the meat to the pot, add water to cover, and correct the seasonings. The liquid should be well seasoned. Bring to a boil, reduce the heat to low, and simmer, covered, until the meat falls from the bones, about 3 hours.

3. Remove the oxtails to a plate and skim the sauce to remove fat. Remove the bay leaves, lemons, and thyme sprigs, if using, and cook over high heat to reduce the sauce by one-fourth, 8 to 10 minutes. Using a hand or standard blender, puree the sauce. Correct the seasonings. Divide the polenta among 4 plates, top with the oxtails, spoon some of the sauce over, and serve.

MING'S TIP: OXTAILS ARE RELATIVELY INEXPENSIVE, SO TAKE ADVANTAGE OF THEM. HOWEVER, THIS DISH CAN ALSO BE MADE WITH THE VEAL SHANK PORTIONS USED FOR OSSO BUCO OR PORK SHANKS.

Five-Peppercorn Grilled Rib-Eye Steaks

Steak au poivre, which is often served with *frites,* is one of the classic dishes of the French bistro repertoire. The creamy mustard sauce, probably the most Gallic accompaniment in this book, is my interpretation of the classic beurre blanc; the addition of mustard and cream to the sauce provides great taste and also stabilizes it.

I love to serve the beef with a rich potato gratin. In tribute to the venerable American marriage of steak and mushrooms, there are shiitakes in the gratin—definitely an East-West pairing.

This dish is perfect for an informal dinner party.

BEVERAGE TIP: PEPPERY, MINTY ZINFANDEL (RAVENSWOOD PICKBERRY)

SERVES 4

STEAKS
3 heaping tablespoons black
   peppercorns
2 heaping tablespoons white
   peppercorns
1 heaping tablespoon green
   peppercorns
2 heaping teaspoons Szechwan
   peppercorns
1 heaping tablespoon pink
   peppercorns
4 rib-eye steaks, 10 to 12 ounces each
Kosher salt

MUSTARD SAUCE
1/2 cup red wine
5 shallots, cut into 1/4-inch slices
2 tablespoons grainy mustard
1/2 cup heavy cream
8 tablespoons (1 stick) butter, chilled
   and cut into rough cubes
Salt and freshly ground black pepper

1 tablespoon canola oil
Potato, Spinach, and Shiitake Gratin
   (page 221)
Crispy Onions (page 212)
Mustard Oil (page 228)

1. To make the steaks, combine the black, white, green, and Szechwan peppercorns in a spice grinder or clean coffee grinder and grind coarsely. Add the pink peppercorns and turn the machine on and off a few times to grind them. Season the steaks with salt and liberally with the pepper mix. Set aside.

2. To make the sauce, set up a double boiler. In a medium saucepan, combine the wine and shallots and heat over medium heat until the wine has evaporated entirely, about 8 minutes. Add the mustard and cook for 1 minute. Add the cream and cook to reduce the mixture by one-fourth, about 3 to 5 minutes. Transfer to a blender and puree. With the machine running, add the butter 1 cube at a time to make an emulsion. Season with the salt and pepper to taste, transfer the sauce to the double boiler, and keep warm.

3. Prepare an outdoor grill or preheat the broiler. Alternatively, preheat a grill pan shortly before cooking the steaks and brush it with the oil. Grill the steaks outdoors, broil, or grill them on the grill pan, turning once, until done to taste, 4 to 5 minutes per side for medium-rare. Allow the steaks to rest.

4. Place a portion of gratin on each of 4 plates and pour the mustard sauce around the gratin. Slice the steaks and arrange the slices around each gratin. Garnish with the crispy onions, drizzle with a little of the mustard oil, and serve.

MING'S TIP: FOR A NEAT AND ATTRACTIVE PRESENTATION, I CUT THE COOKED POTATOES USING A 3-INCH RING MOLD OR 2-OUNCE WATER CHESTNUT OR TUNA CAN WITH THE TOP AND BOTTOM REMOVED. YOU CAN, HOWEVER, SERVE THEM FAMILY-STYLE, FROM THE BAKING DISH.

Beef and Shiitake Stew
with Garlic Mashers

Maybe it's my northern Chinese heritage, but I'm a great fan of stews and braises, which are typical of that region. This hearty stew features beef, specifically hanger steak, the delicious, chewy cut the French call *onglet*. Hanger steak is wonderful grilled, but it benefits from stewing, too. This is hearty cold-weather fare.

BEVERAGE TIP: CABERNET-SHIRAZ BLEND (AUSTRALIAN PENFOLDS BIN 387)

SERVES 4

2 pounds hanger or skirt steak, cut into 2 × 2-inch pieces
Salt and freshly ground black pepper
2 tablespoons canola oil
2 large red onions, cut into ½-inch dice
2 large carrots, peeled and cut into ½-inch dice
2 celery stalks, cut into ½-inch dice
1 tablespoon fermented black beans, rinsed and drained
1 tablespoon finely chopped fresh ginger
Cloves from 2 heads of garlic, peeled
1 pound shiitake mushrooms, stems removed and quartered
1 cup Shaoxing wine or dry sherry
⅓ cup dark soy sauce
Garlic Mashers (page 214)

1. Season the meat with salt and pepper. Heat a medium Dutch oven or heavy pot over high heat, add 1 tablespoon of the oil, and swirl to coat the bottom of the pot. When the oil shimmers, add the meat and brown on all sides.

2. Remove the meat and wipe out the pot. Add the remaining 1 tablespoon of oil and when the oil shimmers, add the onions, carrots, celery, black beans, ginger, and garlic and sauté, stirring, until soft, about 8 to 10 minutes. Add the mushrooms and season with the salt and pepper to taste. Add the wine, stir, and cook to reduce it by 20 percent, 4 to 6 minutes. Add the soy sauce and correct the seasonings. Return the meat to the pot, add water to cover, and cook, covered, until the meat is tender, 2 hours.

3. Divide the mashers among 4 large pasta bowls. Cover with the stew and serve.

Garlic-Marinated Lamb Chops
with Yukon Gold Garlic Chive Mashers

Lamb with garlic is one of those great culinary combinations featured in almost every cuisine. I can never get enough garlic, so I've paired garlic-laced mashers—mashed potatoes—with the garlic-infused chops for a garlic double whammy. I confess that this dish is more West than East-Meets-West, but it's a personal favorite, and too good not to include.

BEVERAGE TIP: BORDEAUX BLEND (QUINTESSA, CHATEAU COMTESSE DE LALANDE)

SERVES 4

⅓ cup finely chopped garlic
⅓ cup canola oil
½ cup dry red wine
1 tablespoon coarsely ground and toasted black
  pepper
12 loin lamb chops, about 1 inch thick
Salt and freshly ground pepper
Yukon Gold Garlic Chive Mashers (page 216)
2 tablespoons Mustard Oil (page 228)

1. In a baking dish just large enough to hold the chops, combine the garlic, oil, wine, and coarsely ground pepper. Mix, add the chops, and turn to coat. Marinate in the refrigerator at least 4 hours and preferably overnight.

2. Prepare an outdoor grill or preheat the broiler. Season the chops with the salt and regular-grind pepper and grill them over high heat or broil, turning once, about 4 minutes per side for medium-rare.

3. Divide the potatoes among 4 plates and surround with 3 chops per plate. Season with the mustard oil and serve.

Grilled New Zealand Lamb Rack
with Wild Mushroom Ragout and
Basil Mashed Potatoes

This is paradise for all meat-and-potatoes people—and just about everyone else, too. The mustardy marinade for the lamb really enhances its flavor; the basil-flavored (and colored) potatoes and the earthy mushroom ragout complete the dish spectacularly.

I prefer New Zealand lamb racks; they're more tender and less fatty than domestic kinds, come from organically raised animals, and have a wonderful flavor. (But don't pass the dish by if you can't find them; domestic racks are also very good.)

This makes a marvelous winter dinner for family or friends.

BEVERAGE TIP: BORDEAUX BLEND (PAHLMEYER, CHATEAU LYNCH BAGES)

SERVES 4 TO 6

1 tablespoon black peppercorns, plus ground pepper
¼ cup Dijon mustard
¼ cup dark soy sauce
1 cup red wine
2 sprigs thyme, or ½ tablespoon dried
¼ cup finely chopped garlic
½ cup canola oil
4 lamb racks, about 1 pound each, chine bone removed
Salt
Basil Mashed Potatoes (page 218)
Wild Mushroom Ragout (page 211)
Basil Oil (page 231)
8 fresh basil leaves, for garnish
½ cup red wine

1. In a small dry skillet, heat the peppercorns over medium heat until fragrant, 4 to 6 minutes. Transfer to a pan large enough to hold the racks and add the mustard, soy sauce, red wine, thyme, garlic, and oil. Mix, add the racks, and turn to coat them. Marinate in the refrigerator, turning occasionally, at least 8 hours and preferably overnight.

2. Prepare an outdoor grill or preheat the broiler. Season the lamb with the salt and ground pepper and grill over high heat, or broil, turning once, until brown and crispy, 12 to 15 minutes.

3. Cut each rack in half and arrange so that the bones of the halves are interlaced. Alternatively, cut the racks into double chops. Place a mound of the potatoes on a large platter and stand the racks or chops against it. Sauce with the ragout and drizzle over the basil oil. Garnish with the basil leaves and serve.

MING'S TIP: DON'T BOTHER TRIMMING OR "FRENCHING" THE BONES, AS IS DONE TRADITIONALLY. SPEND TIME MAKING FOOD TASTE GOOD, I SAY, RATHER THAN ON DECORATIVE REFINEMENTS. THE RICH MEAT BETWEEN THE BONES IS GREAT, ANYWAY. BUT DO HAVE YOUR BUTCHER REMOVE THE LONG CHINE BONE.

Braised Curried Lamb Shanks
with Three-Onion Couscous

This dish began in Paris, where I first cooked lamb curry at the restaurant Natacha. There we used lamb stew meat; lamb shanks make a delicious and certainly more presentable replacement.

There's an interesting ingredient in the curry—banana. The banana melts into the sauce, thickening it somewhat and providing an elusive aroma. Hearty and delicious, this is a great dish to enjoy with friends. And should you be lucky enough to have leftovers, this makes an outstanding sandwich piled onto sourdough rolls and slathered with Dijon-Sambal Aïoli (page 237).

BEVERAGE TIP: JAMMY, PEPPERY ZINFANDEL (RIDGE LYTTON SPRINGS, RAVENSWOOD PICKBERRY)

SERVES 6

6 lamb shanks, about 1 pound each
Salt and freshly ground black pepper
¼ cup fennel seeds
½ cup coriander seeds
3 cups all-purpose flour
½ cup Madras curry powder
1 tablespoon ancho chile powder
3 tablespoons canola oil
2 large onions, cut into ½-inch dice
2 celery stalks, cut into ½-inch dice
2 large carrots, peeled and cut into ½-inch dice
¼ cup finely chopped fresh ginger
¼ cup finely chopped garlic
1 bottle dry red wine
1 cup dark soy sauce
2 bananas
4 Thai bird chiles
3 sprigs fresh thyme, or 1 tablespoon dried
Three-Onion Couscous (page 208)

1. Season the shanks well with salt and pepper. Grind the fennel and coriander coarsely in a spice grinder or clean coffee grinder and combine in a large baking dish with the flour, curry powder, and chile powder. Add the shanks and dredge well in the mixture.

2. Heat a heavy Dutch oven just large enough to accommodate the shanks over high heat, add 2 tablespoons of the oil, and swirl to coat. When the oil shimmers, add the shanks in batches and brown on all sides, 8 minutes. Remove the shanks, wipe out the Dutch oven, and add the remaining 1 tablespoon of oil. When hot, add the onions, celery, carrots, ginger, and garlic and sauté, stirring, until the vegetables are soft, 6 to 8 minutes. Season with salt and pepper, add the wine, turn down the heat, and simmer to reduce it by half, 6 to 8 minutes.

3. Add the soy sauce, bananas, chiles, and thyme. Return the shanks to the pot, add water to cover, and correct the seasonings; the liquid should have a good saltiness. Cover and braise until the meat falls from the bones, 3 to 4 hours. Remove the shanks and reduce the liquid over medium heat until thickened slightly, about 10 minutes. Remove the thyme sprigs, if used, and with a hand or standard blender, puree the sauce. Correct the seasonings and keep warm.

4. Mound the couscous in a large pasta bowl. Top with the shanks, ladle on the sauce, garnish with the scallion greens reserved when preparing the couscous, and serve.

MING'S TIP: YOU CAN SUBSTITUTE VEAL SHANKS FOR THE LAMB TO MAKE A THOROUGHLY UNORTHODOX BUT VERY GOOD OSSO BUCO. PROCEED AS DIRECTED, OR REPLACE THE SHANKS WITH ABOUT 4 POUNDS OF LAMB STEW MEAT. (THIS RETURNS THE DISH TO ITS CULINARY ROOTS.)

Spiced Venison
with Parsnip Puree and Parsley Oil

M
E
A
T

Tasting something like steak but with a heartier flavor, venison is one of my favorite game meats. It's most readily available farm- or ranch-raised, and is tender-fleshed and not overly gamy. All that's needed to cook the most popular cuts is a quick searing, the treatment the loin gets in this simple recipe.

The meat is spiced first to add flavor and also to balance its taste, then served with a honey-sweetened parsnip puree. The parsley oil adds color and a fresh herbiness that acts as a counterpoint to the richness of the meat and parsnips.

BEVERAGE TIP: TOASTED OAK, EUCALYPTUS-Y CABERNET SAUVIGNON (HONIG, PER SEMPRE)

SERVES 4

MING'S TIP: ONCE YOU TRY THIS, YOU'LL WANT TO FIND OTHER WAYS TO ENJOY VENISON. ONE OF MY FAVORITES IS TO SERVE IT RAW, IN A CARPACCIO WITH DEEP-FRIED SHIITAKE CAPS. ADD SPRINKLINGS OF SEA SALT AND BLACK PEPPER, DRIZZLES OF TRUFFLE OIL, AND A CHIVE GARNISH. THIS MAKES AN ELEGANT FIRST COURSE.

PARSNIPS
4 cups peeled parsnips cut into 1-inch dice (about 1½ pounds parsnips)
5 garlic cloves, peeled
Salt
1 tablespoon lychee honey or other honey
4 tablespoons (½ stick) unsalted butter
Freshly ground black pepper

VENISON
2 tablespoons ground fennel
2 tablespoons ground coriander
1 tablespoon ground cardamom
2 tablespoons freshly ground black pepper
2 venison tenderloins (about 8 ounces each), membrane removed
Salt
1 tablespoon canola oil
4 tablespoons Parsley Oil (page 232)

1. To make the parsnips, combine them and the garlic in a large saucepan, then add water to cover and a pinch of salt. Bring to a boil, reduce the heat, and simmer until the point of a knife inserted into the parsnips meets no resistance, about 25 minutes. Drain, transfer to a food processor, and puree. Add the honey and butter and season with salt and pepper to taste. Pulse to blend. Keep warm.

2. To make the venison, combine the fennel, coriander, cardamom, and black pepper on a large plate and mix. Season the venison with the salt to taste and roll it lightly in the spice mixture to coat it evenly.

3. Heat a large skillet over high heat. Add the oil and swirl to coat the pan. Add the venison and sear it, turning once, about 8 minutes for medium-rare. Allow the meat to rest for 5 minutes, then slice into 6 pieces each.

4. Divide the puree among 4 serving plates. Surround each portion with 3 upright pieces of the venison, drizzle over the parsley oil, and serve.

Chapter 7

Over the Top

THERE ARE TIMES IN YOUR COOKING LIFE WHEN YOU WANT TO PULL OUT ALL THE STOPS. FOR THESE OCCASIONS, OR FOR THE CHANCE TO FLEX YOUR COOKING MUSCLES, I OFFER THESE RECIPES. MANY TAKE TIME AND SOME TECHNICAL FACILITY TO PREPARE, AND SOME WILL PUT A DENT IN YOUR POCKETBOOK—BUT AREN'T LIFE'S SPECIAL MOMENTS WORTH SUCH INVESTMENTS? SERVE THE EXTRAORDINARY FOIE GRAS AND MOREL SHU MAI WITH CARAMELIZED SAUTERNES-SHALLOT BROTH AND TRUFFLED EDAMAME PUREE, FOR EXAMPLE, AND YOU'LL MAKE MEMORIES. AND YOU'LL FEEL THE PROWESS THAT COMES FROM PUTTING YOUR KITCHEN SKILLS TO THE TEST.

What makes these dishes so special? Uncommon ingredients, partly, like fresh foie gras. Velvety, rich, and voluptuous, foie gras is expensive, but easy to work with. I use it as I would butter (it's largely fat) to enrich sauces or to add a deep flavor finish. Alsatian Seared Duck Breast with Foie Gras Sauce benefits from the former technique; Rice Paper–Wrapped Halibut with Foie Gras Mousse and Gingered Spaghetti Squash, in which the foie gras melts into cooked halibut fillets, owes its extraordinary taste to the latter.

Other dishes call for truffles. When people tell me they don't "get" truffles, I say maybe they've never had really fresh ones. Truffles have an intoxicating aroma and taste that's only apparent when they're fresh. (See page 9 for truffle buying information.) Wild Mushroom Flan with Asparagus Truffle Sauce makes the fresh truffle point emphatically, as do the Shu Mai. I also exploit the special seasoning potency of truffle oil, which seasons most of the truffled recipes here. Less expensive and more readily obtainable than its fresh flavoring ingredient, truffle oil works beautifully to provide truffle aroma and taste.

Not all the dishes here call for foie gras and truffles. Asian Lacquered Poussin with Hoisin Lime Sauce, for example, uses more modest ingredients to its hearty but opulent result. Tea-Smoked Salmon with Wasabi Potato "Latkes" and Fuji Apple Salad uses tea to make their flavor points. Done in a wok, the Chinese tea-smoking technique gives the fish a wonderful perfume.

For a different over-the-top experience, you can't beat a Chinese fire pot feast. I've provided a complete blueprint for this communal cooking and eating event in which guests prepare their own food at table in simmering stock. Unlike all the other over-the-top meals, this one enlists your guests in the cooking. Like the others, however, it offers cooking pleasure and extravagantly good eating.

Wild Mushroom Flan
with Asparagus Truffle Sauce

Steamed savory custards are part of both Chinese and Japanese cuisines, but this woodsy dish is based on the flans I first made in France.

Serve the flan as an elegant first course or as an accompaniment to lobster medallions or seared sea scallops. It's most special with its truffle garnish, but you can omit it, if you like. The dish will still be excellent.

BEVERAGE TIP: EARTHY, SMOOTH MERLOT (SEAVY)

SERVES 8

SAUCE
5 tablespoons butter
2 medium white onions, thinly sliced
1 garlic clove, thinly sliced
2 teaspoons salt
Freshly ground black pepper
20 medium asparagus, trimmed,
    16 2-inch tops reserved for gar-
    nish, the rest cut into 2-inch
    pieces
1 cup spinach leaves, stems
    removed and well washed
Juice of $\frac{1}{2}$ lemon
1$\frac{1}{2}$ teaspoons white truffle oil,
    plus more for garnish

1 tablespoon canola oil
1 tablespoon finely chopped garlic
1 cup stemmed and quartered shiitake
    mushrooms
1 cup chanterelles cut into $\frac{1}{4}$-inch slices
1 cup roughly torn oyster mushrooms
1 cup fresh porcini mushrooms cut in
    $\frac{1}{4}$-inch slices, or dried porcini, soaked
    in warm water to cover until softened,
    about 20 minutes, drained and rinsed
Salt and freshly ground black pepper
$\frac{1}{2}$ cup dry white wine
8 eggs
2 cups heavy cream
2 tablespoons scallions, green parts only
    sliced $\frac{1}{8}$ inch thick
1$\frac{1}{2}$ tablespoons fresh lemon juice
1 small black truffle, cut into 16 thin slices

1. Set up a double boiler. Fill a medium bowl with water and add ice. To make the sauce, heat a medium saucepan over medium heat. Add 1 tablespoon of the butter and swirl to coat the bottom of the pan. Add the onions and garlic and sauté, stirring, until soft, about 5 minutes. Add 2 cups of water, the salt, and season with pepper to taste. Add the asparagus tops and pieces and cook until just tender, 3 to 5 minutes. Transfer just the asparagus tops to the bowl of ice water and when cold, drain and set aside for garnish. Continue cooking the remaining asparagus until soft, 3 minutes more. Add the spinach, stir, and cook until the leaves are wilted, about 30 seconds. Check the asparagus to be sure it's soft.

2. Using a hand or standard blender, puree the asparagus mixture. Add the remaining 4 tablespoons of butter and the lemon juice. Correct the seasonings, add the truffle oil, and transfer to the top of the double boiler. Keep warm.

3. Heat a medium skillet over medium heat. Add the oil and swirl to coat the pan. When the oil shimmers, add the garlic and sauté, stirring, until soft, about 3 minutes. Add the shiitakes, chanterelles, oyster, and porcini mushrooms and toss carefully. Season with the salt and pepper to taste, add the wine, and cook until it has evaporated completely, about 12 minutes. Correct the seasonings and transfer the mushrooms to a baking tray to cool completely.

4. Preheat the oven to 300°F. In a large bowl combine the eggs and cream and whisk to blend. Add the cooled mushrooms and scallions and mix.

5. Spray the interiors of eight 4-ounce ramekins with nonstick cooking spray. Bring a kettle of water to a boil and have ready a roasting pan just large enough to hold the ramekins.

6. Place the ramekins in the pan and fill them four-fifths full with the custard mixture, making sure the mushrooms are well distributed throughout the mixture. Place in the oven and carefully fill the pan with enough boiling water to come halfway up the sides of the ramekins. Bake the custards until just set, about 25 minutes.

7. Meanwhile, dress the reserved asparagus tops with the lemon juice and season with salt and pepper to taste. Set aside.

8. Ladle the asparagus sauce into 8 large pasta bowls. Invert 1 custard into each bowl and garnish the portions with the asparagus spears, truffle oil, and truffle slices, if using. Serve.

MING'S TIP: THE RESIDUAL HEAT OF THE FLAN WARMS THE BLACK TRUFFLE JUST ENOUGH TO RELEASE ITS WONDERFUL PERFUME. THIS IS AN IDEAL METHOD FOR "COOKING" TRUFFLES TO MAXIMIZE BOTH AROMA AND FLAVOR.

Ahi Tuna Parfait
with Two Caviars

Every cook should have a repertoire of show-off dishes as easy to make as this one. It consists of molded layers of silken ahi tuna and two caviars, the pungent wasabi-spiked tobiko, which is flavored flying fish roe, and osetra, the deliciously briny eggs of the like-named sturgeon. I don't advocate using deluxe ingredients just because they're deluxe, but this dish gives them a perfect showcase. Once you've made the vinaigrette, which gives the parfait a real finish, the dish is just minutes away from wowing your guests as a first course. I like to serve this on inverted martini glasses.

BEVERAGE TIP: TÊTE DU CUVÉE CHAMPAGNE (NICOLAS FEUILLATTE PALME D'OR, VEUVE CLICQUOT GRANDE DAME)

SERVES 4

VINAIGRETTE
½ tablespoon Dijon mustard
½ tablespoon rice wine vinegar
¼ cup canola oil
1 tablespoon wasabi tobiko
Salt and freshly ground black pepper

1 cup heavy cream
½ pound #1 grade ahi tuna, cut into very small dice
3 dashes Tabasco sauce
1 tablespoon finely chopped chives, plus 8 whole chives
1 tablespoon extra-virgin olive oil
Salt and freshly ground black pepper
2 ounces wasabi tobiko
2 ounces osetra caviar

1. To make the vinaigrette, combine the mustard, vinegar, oil, and tobiko in a small bowl. Season with the salt and pepper and whisk lightly.

2. In a small chilled bowl, whip the cream until stiff peaks form. Reserve.

3. Fill a large bowl with ice. Place a medium bowl in the ice and add the tuna, Tabasco sauce, chopped chives, and olive oil. Season with salt and pepper to taste and mix lightly.

4. Spray the insides of four 1- to 1½-inch ring molds, or tuna cans with tops and bottoms removed, with nonstick cooking spray. Layer the tuna mixture and caviars in the molds as follows: one-eighth of the tuna, one-fourth of the tobiko, one-eighth of the tuna, one-fourth of the osetra. Press down lightly on the parfaits after each layer with the bottom of a Tabasco bottle (it's the perfect size) or the butt end of a whisk. Top the layers with a thin layer of the cream, smooth to cover, and unmold cream side up onto white serving plates. Or use the Tabasco bottle to push the parfaits from the bottom, then carefully lift them onto a plate. Garnish each portion with 2 chives. Drizzle the vinaigrette around and serve with demitasse spoons.

MING'S TIP: YOU CAN MAKE INEXPENSIVE RING MOLDS FROM 1½-INCH PVC PIPE PURCHASED FROM A HARDWARE STORE. USE A HACKSAW TO CUT OFF 2-INCH LENGTHS. SAND THE CUT ENDS FIRST WITH COARSE AND THEN FINE-GRADE SANDPAPER.

O
V
E
R

T
H
E

T
O
P

Morel and Crab Tempura
with a Kaffir Lime Broth

This dish makes a great impression. The crab-stuffed morels, which are fried and then served in a fragrant broth, are greeted with delight.

For all its sophistication, this dish isn't difficult to make. You can and probably should prepare the broth beforehand, so everything comes together quickly.

The dish can also be dressed down by substituting large shiitake mushroom caps for the morels. Just pack the caps with the filling mixture (you don't need to pipe it), dip them in the batter, and fry. Or make a shiitake "hamburger" by enclosing the filling between two caps before dipping and frying.

BEVERAGE TIP: RICH, TANGY SAUVIGNON BLANC FROM POUILLY-FUMÉ (DAGUENEAU-SILEX)

SERVES 4

BROTH
1 tablespoon canola oil
2 cups thinly sliced red onions
1 jalapeño pepper, stemmed and chopped
10 kaffir lime leaves
Salt and freshly ground black pepper
2 tablespoons Thai fish sauce (nam pla)
4 cups Chicken Stock (page 14) or low-sodium canned broth

3 ounces skinless Chilean sea bass or other moderately fatty white fish
1 egg
$\frac{1}{4}$ cup heavy cream
Salt and freshly ground black pepper
$\frac{1}{2}$ pound lump crabmeat, picked over
$\frac{1}{4}$ cup chopped chervil, plus 4 sprigs for garnish
12 large fresh morels, cleaned
2 cups rice flour
1 to 1$\frac{1}{2}$ cups ice cold club soda
Canola oil, for frying
Juice of 1 lime

1. To make the broth, heat a large saucepan over medium heat. Add the oil and swirl to coat the bottom of the pan. When the oil shimmers, add the onions, jalapeño, and lime leaves and sauté, stirring, until the onions are golden, 8 to 10 minutes. Season with salt and pepper to taste, add the fish sauce, and reduce the liquid by three-fourths, about 1 minute. Add the stock and simmer until the broth is reduced by one-fourth, 15 to 20 minutes. Strain and correct the seasonings. Keep warm over very low heat.

2. In the food processor, combine the fish, egg, and cream and puree. Season the mixture with salt and pepper and transfer to a chilled bowl. Fold in the crab and chopped chervil and transfer the mixture to a resealable plastic bag (see Tip). Fill each morel with the mixture, piping it into the stem end. Leave a small mound of the puree at the stem tip.

3. Place the rice flour in a medium bowl and whisk in the club soda gradually until the mixture resembles pancake batter. Set aside.

4. Fill a large heavy-bottomed saucepan one-third full with the oil and heat until 375°F. Dip each morel in the tempura batter and add to the oil. Fry until golden brown, about 6 minutes. Keep the morels submerged in the oil while frying with a large-mesh spoon. Remove the mushrooms and drain on paper towels. Salt lightly.

5. Place 3 morels in each of 4 soup plates. Add the lime juice to the broth, ladle it around the morels, and serve.

MING'S TIP: A RESEALABLE PLASTIC BAG MAKES STUFFING THE MORELS EASY. JUST FILL THE BAG WITH THE CRAB MIXTURE AND SQUEEZE OUT ANY AIR. SEAL THE BAG, SNIP OFF ONE CORNER, AND PIPE AWAY. (YOU CAN ALSO USE A PASTRY BAG FITTED WITH A PLAIN ½-INCH TIP, IF YOU PREFER.)

OVER THE TOP

Seared Scallops
with Sweet Potato Risotto and Truffled Haricots Verts

This showstopping dish is as pretty to look at as it is good to eat. The green of the haricots verts, dressed with a truffle oil–based vinaigrette, contrasts beautifully with the orange of the sweet potato risotto, a unique dish. The ivory scallops, part golden from searing, and the deep yellow chanterelles complete the striking picture.

The risotto is time-consuming to prepare (the potatoes are cut into small cubes and cooked by the risotto method), but worth the effort. It's the soul of this dish, really, which would be a perfect culinary centerpiece for a stylish dinner.

BEVERAGE TIP: BIG, ROUNDED CHARDONNAY (NEWTON UNFILTERED, LOUIS LATOUR BATARD-MONTRACHET)

SERVES 4

SALAD
1 pound haricots verts or slender green beans, tips and strings removed
Juice of 1 lemon
1 tablespoon white truffle oil
¼ cup extra-virgin olive oil
Salt and freshly ground black pepper

2 pounds large sea scallops
Salt and freshly ground black pepper
3 tablespoons canola oil
1 tablespoon finely chopped garlic
1 tablespoon finely chopped fresh ginger
1 pound chanterelles, hedgehogs, or other wild mushrooms, or shiitakes, cleaned
Sweet Potato Risotto (page 220)
1 bunch chives, sliced 1 inch thick
Sweet Potato Crisps (page 219; optional)
White truffle oil

1. To make the salad, bring a large quantity of salted water to a boil. Fill a medium bowl with water and add ice cubes. Cook the haricots verts in the boiling water until tender-crisp, about 4 minutes. Drain and transfer to the ice water. When cold, drain. In a nonreactive bowl, combine the lemon juice, truffle oil, and olive oil. Season with the salt and pepper to taste. Ten minutes before serving, toss the beans with the vinaigrette and set aside.

2. Season the scallops with the salt and pepper. Heat a large skillet over high heat, add 2 tablespoons of the oil, and swirl to coat. When the oil shimmers, add the scallops and sauté, turning once, until golden brown and just cooked through, 3 to 4 minutes per side. Remove and set aside.

3. Wipe out the pan, add the remaining 1 tablespoon of oil, and swirl to coat the pan. When the oil shimmers, add the garlic and ginger, and sauté, stirring, until soft, about 1 minute. Add the mushrooms, season with the salt and pepper to taste, and sauté, stirring, until soft, 6 to 8 minutes. Transfer the mushrooms to a strainer to drain.

4. Place a 3-inch ring mold on each of 4 plates. Fill the bottom third of the rings with the sautéed mushrooms. Fill the rings with the risotto and unmold onto serving plates. Surround with the scallops and top with the haricots verts. Garnish with the chives and sweet potato crisps, if using, drizzle with truffle oil, and serve.

MING'S TIP: MAKE THIS DISH VEGETARIAN, IF YOU LIKE, BY OMITTING THE SCALLOPS AND SERVING THE HARICOTS VERTS AND RISOTTO ONLY. IN THAT CASE, SUBSTITUTE VEGETABLE STOCK (PAGE 15) FOR THE CHICKEN STOCK.

Scallops on the Half Shell
with Wasabi Lime Vinaigrette

If you are lucky enough to run across fresh scallops in the shell, try this simple dish, which is one of the best ways to enjoy them. Nestled in their shells on ice, drizzled with a pungent vinaigrette, and topped with a bit of wasabi tobiko (the spicy flying fish roe flavored with wasabi), the raw scallops make a royal first course. A half teaspoon of osetra caviar spooned onto each scallop would make this even more decadent.

The main requirement is, of course, fresh scallops in the shell. Ask your fish seller when he plans to have unshucked scallops on hand. If you can't get absolutely fresh scallops, choose another recipe.

BEVERAGE TIP: DRY, TART MUSCADET FROM MUSCADET DE SEVRE ET MAINE

SERVES 2 TO 4

1 shallot, finely chopped
1 teaspoon finely chopped fresh ginger
¼ cup fresh lime juice
1 tablespoon wasabi tobiko, plus additional for garnish
20 fresh bay or Nantucket scallops, shucked and returned to their half-shells

1. In a small bowl, combine the shallot, ginger, lime juice, and tobiko. Mix well.

2. Set the scallops on 1 or more platters in cracked ice. Immediately spoon the vinaigrette over the scallops. Garnish with the additional tobiko and serve.

MING'S TIP: BAY SCALLOPS ARE RELATIVELY EASY TO SHUCK BECAUSE THEIR SHELLS AREN'T TIGHTLY CLOSED. JUST SLIDE A SHARP PARING KNIFE ALONG THE INSIDE OF THE TOP SHELL; REMOVE AND DISCARD IT. REPEAT WITH THE BOTTOM SHELL, DETACH THE SCALLOP, AND PULL OFF THE SURROUNDING VISCERA, MEMBRANES, AND TOUGH WHITE MUSCLE.

Foie Gras and Morel Shu Mai
with Caramelized Sauternes-Shallot Broth and Truffled Edamame Puree

If I were asked for a single recipe that epitomizes East-West cuisine, this would be it. Shu mai are, of course, usually filled with a pork and shrimp mixture. Here, they're filled with foie gras and morels, a deluxe stuffing that makes a fine introduction to foie gras for those unfamiliar with it.

Foie gras and Sauternes are also a classic pairing, thus the Sauternes-infused version here. Edamame—fresh soybeans in the pod—make a wonderful puree, especially when spiked with truffles. I think of edamame as Japanese fava beans, but they're ever so much easier to prepare and are just as sweet.

BEVERAGE TIP: ELEGANT PINOT NOIR FROM GEVREY-CHAMBERTIN OR CHAMBOLLE-MUSIGNY

SERVES 6

BROTH
1 teaspoon canola oil
2 cups thinly sliced shallots
1 cup Sauternes or late harvest
   Sémillon or Barsac
4 cups Chicken Stock (page 14) or
   low-sodium canned broth
2 bay leaves
1 thyme sprig, or ½ teaspoon dried
Salt and freshly ground black pepper

SHU MAI
2 teaspoons canola oil
1 cup cleaned and chopped fresh
   morels, chanterelles, hedgehogs, or
   shiitakes
4 ounces boneless and skinless chicken
   breast, julienned and frozen
2 eggs
½ cup heavy cream
1 teaspoon white truffle oil
12 ounces fresh foie gras, B or C grade,
   cleaned and cut into chunks
Salt and freshly ground black pepper
1 tablespoon finely chopped chives
18 square wonton wrappers

(recipe continues)

PUREE

1 tablespoon canola oil

½ cup thinly sliced shallots

Salt and freshly ground white pepper

2 cups Chicken Stock (page 14) or low-sodium canned broth

2 cups shelled fresh or thawed frozen edamame (soybeans in the pod)

2 cups spinach leaves

1 tablespoon white truffle oil

1 tablespoon cold butter

2 tablespoons finely chopped black truffle

¼ cup chives cut into ½-inch lengths

Truffle oil, for garnish

1. To make the broth, heat a large saucepan over high heat. Add the oil and swirl to coat the bottom of the pan. When the oil shimmers, add the shallots and sauté, stirring, until brown, about 6 to 8 minutes. Add the wine and reduce by three-fourths, 6 to 8 minutes. Add the stock, bay leaves, and thyme. Season with the salt and pepper to taste, turn down the heat, and simmer until the broth is reduced by one-fourth, about 30 minutes. Keep warm.

2. To make the shu mai, heat the oil in a skillet over medium heat. Add the mushrooms and sauté lightly until softened, 4 to 6 minutes. Transfer to a bowl and refrigerate until cold.

3. Fill a large bowl with ice. In a food processor, combine the frozen chicken, eggs, cream, and truffle oil and puree until smooth. Add the foie gras and puree. Do not over-process. Season with the salt and pepper to taste, transfer the mixture to a chilled medium bowl, and fold in the morels and chives. Heat a small nonstick skillet over medium heat, add ½ teaspoon of the filling, and cook through, about 30 seconds. Taste and correct the filling seasonings, if necessary.

4. Hold 1 wonton wrapper in your hand as shown. Place about 1 tablespoon of the filling in the center of the wrapper. Bring the wrapper up around the filling, pressing it to adhere to the filling and pleating as you go. Continue around the filling. There will be 6 to 8 pleats. Tap the dumpling against the work surface to flatten it. The filling should be level with the top of the dumpling. Repeat with the remaining wrappers and filling. Cover the dumplings lightly with plastic and refrigerate.

5. Set up a double boiler. To make the puree, heat a medium saucepan over medium heat. Add the oil and swirl to coat the bottom of the pan. When the oil shimmers, add the shallots and sauté, stirring, until soft, 3 to 5 minutes. Season with the salt and pepper to taste. Add the stock, raise the heat, and bring to a boil. Correct the seasonings; the stock should be well flavored. Add $1\frac{3}{4}$ cups of the edamame, reduce the heat, and simmer until the edamame are very soft, 25 to 30 minutes. During the last 2 minutes, add the spinach and allow the leaves to wilt. Transfer to a food processor and puree. Add the truffle oil and butter and pulse to incorporate fully. Remove to a small bowl and fold in the truffles; the heat from the puree will release the fragrance of the truffles. Keep warm in the double boiler.

6. Set up a steamer. If using a stainless-steel steamer, spray with nonstick cooking spray; if using a bamboo basket, line with red leaf lettuce or Chinese cabbage leaves. When the water boils, add the dumplings to the steamer tray and place 2 of the remaining edamame on top of each; some edamame will be left. Steam until the filling is cooked through, about 8 minutes.

7. Place small mounds of the edamame puree in 6 large soup bowls. Surround with 3 of the shu mai, ladle in the broth, and sprinkle with the chives. Garnish with the truffle oil and the remaining edamames and serve.

MING'S TIP: TO MAKE THE SHU MAI FILLING, FOIE GRAS IS PUREED WITH OTHER INGREDIENTS IN A PROCESSOR. ONCE IT'S ADDED, BE CAREFUL NOT TO OVERPROCESS IT; HEAT FROM THE MACHINE'S ACTION CAN CAUSE IT TO BREAK.

Tea-Smoked Salmon
with Wasabi Potato "Latkes" and Fuji Apple Salad

I'm a huge fan of tea-smoking, a traditional Chinese technique that gives wonderful flavor to foods like duck and chicken. Equally rich-fleshed salmon makes a perfect candidate for tea-smoking, which can be accomplished without mess in a wok.

I team the fish with wasabi potato "latkes" (everyone calls them that), a nod to the classic combination of salmon and potatoes. Devised to balance the rich elements, the fuji apple salad—a jolt of crisp apple in a cider emulsion—completes the feast.

This dish, which was created with Adam Ross, one of my line cooks, makes good weekend cooking. If you're pressed for time, though, you can stagger the preparation by smoking the salmon a day ahead. Just wrap and refrigerate it and when you're ready, steam it until it's warm. The salad and potatoes can, of course, stand on their own; they make great appetizers.

BEVERAGE TIP: ROSE CHAMPAGNE (BILLECART SALMON, VEUVE CLICQUOT GRANDE DAME)

SERVES 4

SALMON
1 pound skinless salmon fillet, preferably
    center cut, cut into 4 equal pieces
1 cup plus 1 tablespoon sugar
$\frac{1}{2}$ cup mirin (Japanese sweet sake)
$\frac{1}{2}$ cup water
4-inch piece fresh ginger, julienned
1 tablespoon salt
1 teaspoon toasted Szechwan
    peppercorns
1 cup long-grain rice
1 cup oolong tea or black lychee tea leaves

LATKES
3 large Idaho potatoes
Salt
1 tablespoon butter
$\frac{1}{4}$ cup scallions, green parts only,
    sliced $\frac{1}{8}$ inch thick
1 tablespoon prepared horseradish
1 tablespoon wasabi powder mixed
    with $\frac{1}{2}$ teaspoon water
Freshly ground black pepper

TERIYAKI SALMON WITH MIRIN CUCUMBER SALAD (PAGE 112).

OPPOSITE: CRISPY SCALLOPS WITH CARROT-STAR ANISE SYRUP (PAGE 106). ABOVE: WOK-FLASHED SALT AND PEPPER SHRIMP WITH LEMON BASMATI RICE (PAGE 102). LEFT: MOREL AND CRAB TEMPURA WITH A KAFFIR LIME BROTH (PAGE 172).

LEFT: SEARED SCALLOPS WITH SWEET POTATO RISOTTO AND TRUFFLED HARICOTS VERTS (PAGE 174). THIS PAGE: LOBSTER IN LEMONGRASS BROTH WITH TRUFFLED SHIITAKE FLANS (PAGE 188).

OPPOSITE: BLUE GINGER SEA BASS WITH SOBA
NOODLE SUSHI (PAGE 186). ABOVE: WHOLE CRISPY
RED SNAPPER WITH MANGO PINEAPPLE SAUCE AND
SPICY CHINESE LONG BEANS (PAGE 114). LEFT:
SEARED ARCTIC CHAR WITH WILD MUSHROOM
RAGOUT AND TRUFFLE OIL (PAGE 121).

LEFT: POMEGRANATE-MARINATED SQUAB
WITH THAI QUINCE CHUTNEY (PAGE 132) AND
ROASTED GARLIC AND SWEET POTATO HASH
(PAGE 215). ABOVE: ASIAN LACQUERED
POUSSIN WITH HOISIN-LIME SAUCE (PAGE
196) AND BRAISED TRIPLE CABBAGE LASAGNA
(PAGE 210).

LEFT: ACHIOTE DUCK BREASTS WITH SWEET POTATO PUREE, ASIAN PEAR CHUTNEY, AND SPICED PECANS (PAGE 194). THIS PAGE: ASIAN-MARINATED PORK LOIN WITH GINGERED SWEET POTATOES AND FIVE-SPICE APPLES (PAGE 144).

ABOVE: BRAISED CURRIED LAMB SHANKS WITH
THREE-ONION COUSCOUS (PAGE 160). RIGHT:
SAVORY BRAISED OXTAIL WITH PRESERVED LEMON
POLENTA (PAGE 153).

ABOVE: BITTERSWEET CHOCOLATE CAKE WITH
CARDAMOM ICE CREAM AND CHOCOLATE SAUCE
(PAGE 264). RIGHT: GREEN TEA MOUSSE WITH
SAKE-MARINATED DRIED CHERRIES (PAGE 248)
AND HONEY SESAME TUILES (PAGE 256).
OPPOSITE: HOMEMADE GINGER ALE FLOAT WITH
LEMONGRASS ICE CREAM AND GINGER CANDY
(PAGE 263).

LEMONGRASS PARFAIT WITH PINEAPPLE SALSA (PAGE 246).

SALAD
2 cups apple cider
1/2 cup rice wine vinegar
1 star anise
1 3-inch cinnamon stick
1 3-inch piece fresh ginger
1/2 cup canola oil
Salt and freshly ground black pepper
3 Fuji apples (Granny Smiths may be
    substituted)
1 tablespoon chopped chives

2 cups canola oil, for frying
1 cup all-purpose flour
1 cup panko or bread crumbs
3 eggs
Salt

1. To prepare the salmon, place the fillets in a baking dish. In a medium bowl, combine the 1 tablespoon sugar, mirin, water, ginger, salt, and peppercorns. Stir until the salt and sugar have dissolved, pour over the salmon, cover, and allow to brine, refrigerated, about 1 hour.

2. Line the wok with foil, fitting it closely against the wok's interior. Add the rice, remaining cup of sugar, and tea. Remove the salmon from the brining mixture and place it in a bamboo steamer basket. Heat the wok over medium heat until the rice mixture begins to smoke. Dampen 2 dishcloths. Fit the steamer into the wok and fold and wrap the towels around the juncture of the wok and the steamer to make a seal. Cover the wok, turn the heat to low, and smoke the salmon for 15 minutes. Turn off the heat and smoke the salmon for 15 minutes more. The salmon will be cooked medium-rare to medium. Keep the salmon warm in the wok.

3. Meanwhile, begin the latkes. Bring a large pot of salted water to a boil. Add the potatoes and cook until they can be pierced easily with the tip of a knife, about 30 minutes. Drain the potatoes and pass through a ricer into a medium bowl. Add the butter, scallions, horseradish, and wasabi, and season with the salt and pepper. Keep warm.

4. To make the salad, combine the cider, vinegar, star anise, cinnamon, and ginger in a medium nonreactive saucepan, and cook over low heat until the liquid is reduced by half, about 15 minutes. Strain the mixture into a blender and turn it on. Drizzle in the oil to form a light emulsion and season the dressing with the salt and pepper to taste.

5. Peel and julienne the apples. Transfer them to a medium bowl, and immediately toss with half of the dressing. Correct the seasonings, add the chives, and toss. Set aside.

6. To complete the latkes, half-fill a large, heavy skillet with the oil and heat over high heat to 375°F. Meanwhile, using your hands, form the potatoes into 8 latkes about 3 inches in diameter and ½ inch thick.

7. Place the flour and panko on separate plates, and beat the eggs in a small bowl. Dredge the cakes in the flour, followed by the eggs and the panko. You can make these up to 4 hours in advance. Add the latkes to the oil and fry until golden brown, turning once, about 5 minutes. Remove with a slotted spoon and drain on paper towels. Season lightly with the salt to taste.

8. To assemble, divide half of the salad equally among 4 serving plates. Place a latke on each portion and top with the remaining salad. Add the remaining latkes and top with a piece of salmon. Drizzle with the remaining dressing

Rice Paper–Wrapped Halibut
with Foie Gras Mousse and Gingered Spaghetti Squash

You'd never think of serving duck or goose with seafood, but foie gras—duck or goose liver—is a great fish and shellfish accompaniment.

In this recipe the buttery liver is the basis of a mousse used to coat halibut fillets, which are then wrapped in rice paper. The packages are seared, oven-roasted, and accompanied by the squash and mushroom ragout. The wrapped fish is deliciously moist and the ragout ties all the flavors together.

This is stellar eating, yet not that difficult to prepare.

BEVERAGE TIP: DELICATE, BALANCED PINOT NOIR FROM CHAMBOLLE-MUSIGNY OR MOREY-ST-DENIS

SERVES 4

MOUSSE
2 ounces boneless and skinless
   chicken breast, cut into
   small dice, frozen
1 egg
1/4 cup heavy cream
1 teaspoon white truffle oil
8 ounces fresh foie gras, B or C
   grade, cut into 1/2-inch cubes and
   chilled
1/2 bunch chives, finely chopped, plus
   4 chives cut into 1/2-inch lengths for
   garnish
Salt and freshly ground black pepper

SQUASH
1 medium spaghetti squash, halved and
   seeded
2 tablespoons butter
1 tablespoon honey
1/2 tablespoon finely chopped fresh
   ginger
Salt and freshly ground black pepper

4 halibut fillets, about 6 ounces each
Salt and freshly ground black pepper
4 12-inch round rice paper wrappers
2 tablespoons canola oil
Wild Mushroom Ragout (page 211)
White truffle oil, for garnish

1. Preheat the oven to 375°F. To make the mousse, combine the chicken, egg, cream, and truffle oil in a food processor and puree until smooth. Add the foie gras and pulse to incorporate. Do not overmix (see Tip, page 179). Transfer the mousse to a medium bowl, fold in the $\frac{1}{8}$-inch chive pieces, and season with the salt and pepper to taste. Reserve refrigerated.

2. To make the squash, place it on a baking sheet and distribute the butter, honey, and ginger evenly over each half. Season with the salt and pepper to taste and bake the squash until tender-firm, 45 to 60 minutes. Do not overcook. With a fork, scrape the squash strands into a bowl and correct the seasonings. Keep warm. Increase the oven temperature to 400°F.

3. Place the fillets on a work surface and season with the salt and pepper. Spread each fillet with one quarter of the mousse. Fill a baking dish with warm water, add the wrappers, and soak until softened, 2 to 3 minutes. Remove and place on a kitchen towel to drain and dry. Place a sheet of rice paper on a work surface. Lay a halibut fillet, mousse side down, in the middle of the wrapper. To form, bring the bottom of the wrapper over the halibut, fold in the sides, and continue to flip the package over itself to make a rectangular enclosure. Repeat with the remaining rice paper and fillets. Allow the packages to rest seam side down, about 2 minutes.

4. Heat a medium ovenproof nonstick skillet over medium heat. Add the oil and swirl to coat the pan. When the oil shimmers, add the packages seam side down and cook until lightly browned and the package is sealed, about 2 minutes. Turn and cook until browned, 3 minutes more. Turn once again and transfer the skillet to the oven. Roast the packages for 6 minutes.

5. Divide the squash among 4 plates and top with 1 package per plate, mousse side up. Surround with the mushrooms and drizzle the plate with the truffle oil. Garnish with the chives.

MING'S TIP: THE PACKAGES CAN BE HELD UP TO 4 HOURS IN ADVANCE. WRAP THEM INDIVIDUALLY IN PLASTIC FILM AND REFRIGERATE.

Blue Ginger Sea Bass
with Soba Noodle Sushi

I consider this my signature dish—it's been on the menu at Blue Ginger since day one, and people can't seem to get enough of it. It's evolved along the way and it's definitely a keeper.

You might say it is a synthesis of two great dishes I ate and admired: the miso-brushed yakitoris I enjoyed in Osaka, and miso black cod, a great dish created by Nobu Matsuhisa. My dish is a real flavor-texture revelation—unusual and truly satisfying. I'm going on about this dish, but it truly kicks bass!

BEVERAGE TIP: TOASTED OAK, VANILLAN CHARDONNAY (MIRIMAR TORRES, ANY LE MONTRACHET)

SERVES 4

1 cup light miso *(shiro-miso)*
½ cup mirin (sweet Japanese rice wine)
½ cup sake
1 tablespoon finely chopped fresh ginger
½ cup canola oil
¼ cup sugar
4 5 × 3-inch pieces skinless and boneless Chilean
   sea bass (cut from the fillet), about 7 ounces each

SUSHI
½ pound dried soba noodles
¼ cup chopped fresh cilantro
¼ cup chopped scallions, green parts only
2 tablespoons soy sauce
1 tablespoon finely chopped fresh ginger
2 tablespoons rice wine vinegar
2 tablespoons Wasabi Oil (page 228)
4 tablespoons chopped Pickled Ginger (page 238) or gari
Salt and freshly ground black pepper
4 sheets toasted nori
1 cucumber, peeled, seeded, and julienned

MING'S TIP: MISO, THE FERMENTED SOYBEAN PASTE, IS ONE OF THE WORLD'S GREAT FLAVORINGS. I USE THIS JAPANESE PRODUCT OFTEN—IN SOUPS, MARINADES, MAIN DISHES, AND VINAIGRETTES. EXPERIMENT WITH DIFFERENT TYPES UNTIL YOU HAVE A "MISO SENSE" OF YOUR OWN.

1 red bell pepper, cored, seeded, and julienned
1 yellow bell pepper, cored, seeded, and julienned
10 ounces Wakame Salad (see Variation, page 213)
Freshly ground black pepper
Soy Syrup (page 236)
Wasabi Oil (page 228)
¼ cup toasted sesame seeds

1. In a medium nonreactive bowl, combine the miso, mirin, sake, ginger, oil, and sugar and stir to blend. Add the bass, turn to coat, and marinate, covered and refrigerated, overnight.

2. To make the sushi, bring a large quantity of salted water to a boil. Fill a medium bowl with water and add ice. Add the noodles to the boiling water and cook until slightly softer than al dente, about 8 minutes. Drain and transfer the noodles to the ice water. When cold, drain well. In a large bowl combine the noodles, cilantro, scallions, soy sauce, chopped ginger, vinegar, wasabi oil, and 2 tablespoons of the pickled ginger and toss to blend. Season with salt and pepper to taste.

3. Have a small bowl of water handy. Place a sheet of nori shiny side down on the rolling mat with a long edge toward you. Evenly spread a ¼-inch layer of the noodle mixture on the bottom half of the nori and top the upper third of the mixture with 3 to 4 strips of the cucumber and 2 pieces of each of the peppers. Roll as illustrated on page 79. Gently but firmly press the mat to seal. Allow the roll to rest, seam side down, for 2 minutes. Repeat with the remaining nori and filling ingredients. Cover the rolls lightly with plastic wrap and set aside.

4. Prepare an outdoor grill or preheat the broiler. Wipe the marinade from the fish and season it with pepper to taste. Grill or broil the fish, turning it once, until just cooked through, 10 to 12 minutes. Meanwhile, cut each roll into 5 pieces, 3 straight across and 2 diagonally.

5. Divide the sushi pieces among 4 plates. Add a small mound of the salad, if using, to each and top each with a piece of the fish. Drizzle over the soy syrup and wasabi oil, garnish with the sesame seeds and remaining pickled ginger, and serve.

Lobster in Lemongrass Broth
with Truffled Shiitake Flans

Developed at Blue Ginger with Tom Berry, one of my sous chefs, this celebratory dish is an East-West spectacular. One look at the ingredients—lobster with lemongrass, shiitakes with truffles—reveals its multicultural pedigree; to me, however, it's just great eating.

I'm inclined to enjoy scallops more than lobster—scallops are so flavorful and not as costly or fussy to prepare as lobster—but when it's served this way, with a broth, I'm a convert. I love the truffled shiitake flans, too; their subtle taste and trembling texture mate perfectly with the other ingredients.

This is serious cooking, no doubt about it, but really rewarding to prepare. It would make a perfect East-West holiday dinner or intimate New Year's supper.

BEVERAGE TIP: HUGE, FATTY CHARDONNAY (PETER MICHAELS, UNFILTERED NEWTON)

SERVES 4

4 live lobsters, 1¹⁄₂ pounds each

BROTH

1 tablespoon canola oil

1 tablespoon tomato paste

1 fennel bulb, cut into ¹⁄₄-inch slices

1 medium red onion, cut into ¹⁄₄-inch slices

1 carrot, cut on the diagonal into ¹⁄₄-inch slices

1 celery stalk, chopped

6 lemongrass stalks, white parts only, pounded to flatten and sliced ¹⁄₄ inch thick

2 ¹⁄₄-inch-thick slices fresh ginger

1 cup Chardonnay or other dry, full-bodied white wine

1 bay leaf

¹⁄₂ teaspoon green peppercorns

FONDUE

2 tablespoons butter

1 tablespoon finely chopped garlic

1 teaspoon finely chopped fresh ginger

1 large bok choy, sliced ¹⁄₄ inch thick

Salt and freshly ground black pepper

FLANS

1 tablespoon canola oil

1 tablespoon finely chopped shallots

1½ cups shiitake mushroom caps sliced ¼ inch thick

4 eggs

1 cup heavy cream

2 tablespoons scallions, green parts only, sliced ⅛ inch thick

2 teaspoons white truffle oil, plus more for garnish

Salt and freshly ground white pepper

Salt and freshly ground white pepper

2 tablespoons canola oil

1½ tablespoons fresh lemon juice

⅓ cup scallions, green parts only, sliced diagonally ⅛ inch thick

1. Fill the sink with cold water and add ice cubes. Bring a medium pot of salted water to a boil.

2. Meanwhile, numb the lobsters by placing them in the freezer for 30 minutes. Transfer them to a heavy cutting board, insert the tip of a large, heavy knife at the base of the heads, and cut completely through. Remove the claws, knuckles (the sections beneath the claws), and tails. Set the bodies aside for the broth. Cut the tails in half lengthwise up to the flat feathery appendages at the base of the tails (these remain intact) and reserve.

3. Transfer the claws to a large heatproof bowl, pour the boiling water over them to cover, and allow them to cook, about 5 minutes. After 3 minutes, add the knuckles. Remove the lobster parts and plunge into the ice water. When the lobster is cold, remove the meat and reserve.

4. To make the broth, split the reserved lobster bodies. Heat a large, heavy pot over high heat. Add the oil and swirl to coat the bottom of the pot. When the oil shimmers, add the lobster bodies and sauté, stirring, until the shells turn red, about 10 minutes. Add the tomato paste, fennel, onion, carrot, celery, lemongrass, and ginger and sauté, stirring, until the vegetables are soft, about 8 minutes. Add the wine, stir, and reduce the liquid by half, 10 to 15 minutes. Do not boil; it will cloud the broth. Add the bay leaf, peppercorns, and about 8 cups of water to cover the bodies. Reduce the heat and simmer for 2 hours, strain, and keep hot.

5. To make the fondue, heat a large skillet over medium heat. Add 1 tablespoon of the butter and swirl to coat the pan. Add the garlic and ginger and sauté, stirring, until soft, about 5 minutes. Add the bok choy and $\frac{1}{2}$ cup of the reserved lobster broth. Season with the salt and pepper to taste and cook until the bok choy is soft, about 5 minutes. Fold in the remaining 1 tablespoon of butter, correct the seasonings, and keep warm. Add the knuckles right before serving to warm.

6. Preheat the oven to 300°F. To make the flans, heat a medium skillet over high heat. Add the oil and swirl to coat the pan. When the oil shimmers, add the shallots and sauté, stirring, until soft, about 5 minutes. Add the mushrooms and sauté, stirring, until softened, about 8 minutes. Transfer the mixture to a large bowl and place in the freezer to chill quickly, about 15 minutes. When cold, add the eggs, cream, scallions, and truffle oil and mix.

7. Fill a kettle with water and bring to a boil. Spray four 4-ounce ramekins lightly with nonstick cooking spray and have ready a baking dish large enough to hold them. Fill the ramekins four-fifths full with the flan mixture and transfer them to the pan. Add sufficient boiling water to the pan to come halfway up the sides of the ramekins and transfer to the oven. Bake just until the flans are set, about 25 minutes.

8. Meanwhile, season the reserved lobster tails with the salt and pepper to taste. Heat a large skillet over high heat. Add the canola oil and swirl to coat the pan. When the oil shimmers, add the tails, feeler sides down. Cook, turning once, until the shells turn red, about 5 minutes. Add the claws, stir, and add 3 cups of the broth. Add the lemon juice and season with the salt and pepper to taste.

9. Divide the fondue among 4 large pasta bowls. Carefully invert a flan onto each portion. Top with the lobster tail and claws and ladle the broth around. Garnish with the scallions and serve.

> MING'S TIP: THE LOBSTER CLAWS AND KNUCKLES USED FOR THIS ARE COOKED QUICKLY TO PERFECT DONENESS—STILL RARE, BUT REMOVABLE FROM THE SHELLS—BY POURING BOILING WATER OVER THEM (SEE STEP 3). THANKS GO TO MY HEAD PREP COOK, LUIS PAREDES, FOR THIS FOOLPROOF TECHNIQUE.

Alsatian Seared Duck Breast
with Foie Gras Sauce

My inspiration for this suavely hearty dish was food I enjoyed while in Strasbourg, France. The region is noted for its choucroute garni, which contains sausage, cabbage, and potatoes, and for duck and foie gras. For this dish, foie gras is used to enrich a luscious sauce; a tart slaw and sautéed potato salad, brightened by a Chinese vinegar emulsion, add excitement and balance the richer elements perfectly.

This is deluxe dining but surprisingly straightforward and easy to prepare. You can do some of the work ahead. The slaw can be prepared (though not dressed) in advance, and the breasts can be held after their preliminary cooking.

BEVERAGE TIP: BORDEAUX BLEND (CAIN FIVE, CHATEAU MARGAUX)

SERVES 4

SLAW
1 tablespoon Dijon mustard
Juice of 1 lemon
$1/4$ cup canola oil
Salt and freshly ground black pepper
2 cups shredded red cabbage
$1/2$ cup scallions, green parts only,
    diagonally sliced $1/16$ inch thick

EMULSION
2 cups balsamic vinegar
$1/2$ cup Chinese black vinegar
1 cup canola oil
Salt and freshly ground black pepper

DUCK
4 duck breasts with skin, about 6
    ounces each, trimmed
Salt and freshly ground black pepper

1 tablespoon canola oil
4 shallots, sliced $1/8$ inch thick
Salt and freshly ground black pepper
$1/2$ cup cognac
2 cups Chicken Stock (page 14) or low-
    sodium canned broth
4 ounces fresh foie gras, cleaned (see
    Tip), cut into $1/2$-inch cubes and
    chilled

4 tablespoons canola oil
2 large red onions, thinly sliced
6 medium Yukon Gold potatoes,
    unpeeled, sliced $1/8$ inch thick
Salt and freshly ground black pepper

1. To make the slaw, combine the mustard and lemon juice in a small bowl and blend. Whisk in the oil and season with salt and pepper to taste. In a medium bowl, combine the cabbage and scallions and toss. Set aside. Ten minutes before serving, add the dressing and toss again.

2. To make the emulsion, combine the vinegars in a medium nonreactive saucepan, and bring to a boil over high heat. When the mixture boils, turn down the heat and simmer to reduce by three-fourths, or until syrupy, about 20 to 30 minutes. Immediately transfer to a blender and blend, drizzling in the oil gradually until an emulsion is formed. Season with the salt and pepper to taste. Set aside.

3. To make the duck, score the skin sides of the breasts down to the meat with the point of a small sharp knife, making diamond-shaped patterns. Season the breasts with the salt and pepper. Heat a heavy medium skillet over medium-low heat and add the breasts, skin side down. Allow to sear until brown and crispy and the fat has rendered, 12 to 15 minutes. Do not turn. Set aside.

4. Set up a double boiler. Heat a small saucepan over high heat. Add the oil and swirl to coat the bottom of the pan. When the oil shimmers, add the shallots, season with salt and pepper to taste, and sauté, stirring, until brown, about 4 to 6 minutes. Avert your face, add the cognac, and deglaze the pan. Reduce by three-fourths, about 3 minutes, add the stock, and reduce by half, about 10 minutes. Transfer to a blender and puree. With the motor running, add the foie gras 2 pieces at a time. Correct the seasonings. Transfer to the double boiler and keep warm.

5. Heat a medium nonstick skillet over medium heat. Add 1 tablespoon of the oil and swirl to coat the bottom of the pan. When the oil shimmers, add the onions and sauté, stirring, until very brown, about 12 to 15 minutes. Set aside.

6. Wipe out the pan with a paper towel and reheat it over high heat. Add the remaining 3 tablespoons of oil and swirl to coat the bottom of the pan. When the oil shimmers, add the potatoes, distributing them evenly. Season the potatoes with the salt and pepper to taste, press down on them with a spatula, and cook until the underside is golden brown, about 10 minutes. Turn the potatoes (they needn't cohere) and brown the second side,

about 10 minutes. Transfer to a medium bowl, add the reserved onions and enough of the emulsion to coat, toss, and correct the seasonings. Keep warm.

7. Wipe out the pan and heat over high heat. Add the reserved breasts, meat side down, and sear 3 minutes then flip to re-crisp the skin for 3 minutes. The breasts should be medium-rare. Allow to rest for 3 minutes, then cut diagonally in 6 to 8 slices each.

8. Divide the potato salad among 4 large plates and surround each portion with 1 sliced breast, fanned out in a semicircle. Top the salad with some of the slaw and pour the foie gras sauce around the duck. Drizzle the remaining emulsion on the plate and serve.

MING'S TIP: TO PREPARE FOIE GRAS FOR COOKING, MAKE SURE THAT IT IS COLD BUT PLIABLE. WITH YOUR HANDS, CAREFULLY PULL APART THE TWO LOBES AND PUSH OUT AND REMOVE AS MANY BLOOD VESSELS AS YOU CAN; TRY TO AVOID BREAKING UP THE LIVER. RETURN THE FOIE GRAS TO THE REFRIGERATOR TO CHILL BEFORE USING.

Achiote Duck Breasts
with Sweet Potato Puree, Asian Pear Chutney, and Spiced Pecans

I first became acquainted with fresh achiote, the musky-tasting seasoning, in the Southwest. Since then, I've often used the cube or powdered forms in marinades, as I do in this dish. Achiote adds fascinating flavor and color to the duck breasts, which are pan-seared and accompanied by an Asian pear chutney—my bow to classic duck and fruit combinations like *caneton à l'orange*. The pecans are a new spin on a traditional Chinese sweet made with walnuts. Both can be made ahead of time. The dish is a great East-West play of flavors and textures—and a perfect cool-weather meal.

BEVERAGE TIP: RED MERITAGE (CLOS DU BOIS MARLESTONE)

SERVES 6

¼ cup compressed achiote or powder
¼ cup finely chopped garlic
¼ cup finely chopped fresh ginger
½ cup dry red wine
½ cup canola oil
5 scallions, white and green parts, sliced ⅛ inch thick and reserved separately
6 duck breasts with skin, about 6 ounces each, trimmed

CHUTNEY

2 tablespoons canola oil
2 cups diced onions, in ⅛-inch pieces
1 tablespoon sambal oelek
½ cup finely chopped fresh ginger
5 Asian pears, or 3 Granny Smith or other tart apples and 2 pears, peeled, cored, and cut into ¼-inch dice
1 cup rice wine vinegar
Salt and freshly ground black pepper
1 cup apple juice

PECANS

4 cups sugar
1 cup rice wine vinegar
¼ cup five-spice powder
¼ cup ground cinnamon
¼ cup ancho chile powder
¼ cup salt
1 cup egg whites (5 large eggs)
1 pound pecans
Canola oil for deep frying

Gingered Sweet Potatoes (page 217), hot
Chile Oil (page 14)

1. Combine the achiote, garlic, ginger, wine, oil, and scallion whites in a medium nonreactive bowl and stir. With the point of a sharp knife, score the skin sides of the breasts down to the meat in a diamond pattern. Add to the marinade, and turn to coat. Marinate in the refrigerator, covered, for at least 8 hours and preferably overnight.

2. To make the chutney, heat a medium saucepan over high heat. Add the oil and swirl to coat the bottom of the pan. When the oil shimmers, add the onions, sambal oelek, and ginger and sauté, stirring, until brown, about 8 to 10 minutes. Add the Asian pears (or apples and pears) and vinegar, stir, and cook to reduce the vinegar by one-half, 8 to 10 minutes. Season with salt and pepper to taste, add the apple juice, reduce the heat, and simmer until the fruit is soft but still holding its shape, about 20 minutes. Cool and set aside. (This can be refrigerated for a week or two.)

3. To make the pecans, preheat the oven to 375°F. In a medium saucepan, combine the sugar, vinegar, five-spice powder, cinnamon, chile powder, and salt and heat over high heat until the mixture boils. Reduce the heat and simmer until the mixture has thickened into a caramel-colored syrup, 15 to 20 minutes.

4. Meanwhile, line a medium baking tray with parchment paper. Whisk the egg whites lightly until foamy. Fill a fryer or heavy medium pot one-third full with the oil and heat over high heat to 375°F. Working in batches, add the nuts to the egg whites, remove with a slotted spoon, and fry until slightly brown, stirring, 3 to 4 minutes. Remove with a large-mesh spoon, drain on paper towels, and transfer to a medium bowl. Pour the hot syrup over the nuts, stir to coat evenly, and transfer to the prepared baking tray. Make sure the nuts are separated. Bake until brown, about 20 minutes, and cool. Store at room temperature in a covered container.

5. Prepare an outdoor grill. Grill the breasts skin side down over medium-low heat until brown and crispy and the fat is rendered, 10 to 12 minutes. Turn and cook the meat side, about 3 minutes for medium rare. Alternatively, heat a heavy medium skillet over medium-low heat. Add the breasts skin side down and cook as above, 12 to 15 minutes. Turn and cook on the meat side, about 4 minutes. Allow the breasts to rest for 3 minutes, then cut each diagonally into 4 to 6 slices.

6. Divide equal portions of the sweet potato puree and chutney among 6 plates and fan the breasts beside them. Garnish with the chile oil and pecans and serve.

MING'S TIP: IF YOU CAN'T FIND ACHIOTE, SUBSTITUTE 2 TABLESPOONS PAPRIKA MIXED WITH 2 TABLESPOONS CAYENNE FOR THE 1/4 CUP ACHIOTE INDICATED.

Asian Lacquered Poussin
with Hoisin Lime Sauce

I love Peking duck—but not the time and effort it takes to get that crackling skin and luscious meat. This is an easier way that's spectacular in itself—poussins are given a dip in a sweet-sour bath and allowed to dry, roasted briefly, then fried to achieve a perfect lacquerlike crispness. My version of the traditional hoisin-sauce accompaniment is lighter and, with the addition of fresh lime juice, better balanced; it also contains candied ginger for an intriguing spicy sweetness. I often serve the poussins with lasagna-like cabbage napoleons.

BEVERAGE TIP: VELVETY SMOOTH, PLUMY MERLOT (LEWIS)

SERVES 4

¼ cup five-spice powder

2 cups salt

3 cups Chinese black vinegar

1 cup dark soy sauce

1 cup molasses

1 cup honey

4 poussins or Cornish game hens

SAUCE

½ cup plus 2 tablespoons canola oil

½ cup finely chopped shallots

¼ cup finely chopped garlic

1 cup hoisin sauce

½ cup fresh lime juice

½ cup chopped candied ginger

1 teaspoon freshly ground white pepper

½ teaspoon salt

Canola oil, for deep frying

Braised Triple Cabbage Lasagna (page 210)

8 scallions, green parts only, sliced ⅛ inch thick

1. A day in advance, combine the five-spice powder and salt in a small bowl and mix. In a large pot, combine the vinegar, soy sauce, molasses, and honey and bring to a boil over high heat.

2. Meanwhile, bring a large quantity of water to a boil. Season the poussins inside and out with the five-spice mixture. (There will be extra; set aside.) Using a large-mesh spoon, dip each poussin into the boiling water, remove, and dip again. Drain each poussin in the spoon and dip each 3 times in the boiling vinegar mixture, pausing for about 3 seconds between dips. Transfer them breast sides up to a roasting pan fitted with a rack. Refrigerate uncovered overnight.

3. The following day, preheat the oven to 300°F. To make the sauce, heat a medium skillet over medium heat. Add the 2 tablespoons oil and swirl to coat the pan. Add the shallots and garlic and sauté, stirring, until soft, about 2 minutes. Add the hoisin sauce and cook, stirring, about 3 minutes. Add the lime juice, ginger, white pepper and salt, heat thoroughly, and transfer to a blender. Blend to puree and with the machine running, slowly add the ½ cup canola oil to make an emulsion. Correct the seasonings and set aside.

4. Season the poussins inside and out with some of the remaining five-spice mixture and arrange in a roasting pan with a rack. Roast to rare (a thermometer inserted next to the thigh joint will read 120° to 130°F), about 25 minutes. The skin will have tightened somewhat and still be pale. Meanwhile, fill a fryer or large, heavy pot half full with the oil and heat over high heat to 375°F. Lower the poussins into the oil 2 at a time and fry until golden, about 10 minutes. Remove with the mesh spoon and drain on paper towels. Check for doneness by piercing the poussins at the joint between the thigh and the body. If the juices run clear, the poussins are done; if not, return the poussins to the oil and cook a few minutes longer. Season with a sprinkle of the five-spice mixture.

5. Divide the lasagna among 4 plates and top each portion with a poussin. Spoon the hoisin sauce over the plate in a zigzag design, garnish with the scallions, and serve.

MING'S TIP: WHEN INCORPORATING HOISIN SAUCE INTO A DISH, ALWAYS COOK IT FOR A FEW MINUTES. THIS REMOVES ITS RAW BEAN FLAVOR AND MAKES IT MORE COMPATIBLE WITH OTHER INGREDIENTS.

OVER THE TOP

Chinese Fire Pot

Almost every culture has a special dish that is cooked and eaten communally, whether it's Swiss fondue, Korean barbecue, Japanese shabu-shabu, or French raclette. Here's the Chinese version, named after the traditional cooking vessel, a kind of chafing dish fueled originally by charcoal.

The pot—or more usually nowadays an electric wok or burner-pot arrangement—arrives at table filled with boiling stock. It's surrounded by platters of thinly sliced raw meats, poultry, seafood, noodles, and vegetables plus condiments and seasonings for dip making. Guests prepare their own dips, then help themselves to the various raw ingredients. They cook these in the broth, flavor them with the dips, and enjoy wonderful eating. At the end of the meal, everyone receives bowls of the now richly flavored broth for a final satisfying "bite."

This is one of my favorite ways to entertain hungry guests and, once your prep is done, it involves little work. The ingredients below, which include spicy fish balls, will feed eight to twelve people depending on appetite. (Though fire pot diners usually eat like there's no tomorrow!) You can improvise, if you like, substituting your own ingredient choices; just follow the steps below, tell your guests how to proceed, relax, and have fun.

EQUIPMENT

An *electric wok, propane-fueled burner with a large casserole,* or, for high-tech types, a *portable induction burner with a conductive casserole.* Most electric woks are 14 inches in diameter and can accommodate 6 to 8 people for hot-pot dining. Woks or casseroles are most easily used if guests are seated at a round table. For more than 8, or at long tables, use one or more additional heat sources strategically placed so all guests have access to a cooker.

Small rice bowls and plates. For mixing dips and for eating. For the most informal occasions, the condiments can be brought to the table in their containers.

Platters. These should be large enough to display the meats and other ingredients without crowding.

Chopsticks. For cooking and eating.

Small Chinese mesh spoons. These are the most efficient tools for dipping ingredients into the stock and retrieving them without mess or conflict.

Large ladle, soup bowls, and Chinese spoons. For serving and eating the final soup.

At-Table Ingredients for Dip Making

You can subtract items from the following list, as you like. I prefer to use raw eggs to enrich dips; this Japanese technique (much favored by my father) is optional. If you do use raw eggs, take steps to minimize the possibility of health risks, which in fact are few: Buy refrigerated eggs only and transfer them to your own refrigerator as quickly as possible. Never use a cracked or otherwise suspect egg. When cracking an egg, make sure the egg and its shell do not touch. Before and after handling an egg, wash your hands.

BEVERAGE TIP: CLEAN, EXOTIC MULLER-THURGAU (SOKOL BLOSSER) AND/OR SLIGHTLY CHILLED CABERNET FRANC FROM CHINON OR BOURGUEIL

CONDIMENTS
2 cups creamy peanut butter
2 cups Chinese sesame paste
1 cup toasted sesame oil
1 cup oyster sauce
1 cup rice wine vinegar
1 cup Shaoxing wine
1 cup soy sauce
2 cups chopped scallions
2 cups chopped fresh cilantro
1 egg per diner (optional)
½ cup sambal oelek

FOR COOKING
2 pounds soft tofu, cut into ¼-inch slices
2 Shanghai cabbages or bok choy, roughly chopped
2 bok choy, roughly chopped
4 packages (4 ounces each) bean threads, soaked in warm water to cover until soft, about 30 minutes
1 pound shiitake mushrooms, stems removed
2 pounds flank steak, cut across the grain into ⅛-inch slices
2 pounds boneless and skinless chicken breasts, sliced across the grain into ¼ × 2-inch strips
1 pound large shrimp, peeled and deveined
2 pounds bay scallops
Spicy Fish balls (recipe follows)
2 quarts Chicken Stock (page 14) or low-sodium canned broth

1. Divide the condiments among bowls or plates and bring these to table with spoons for serving. Arrange the tofu, vegetables, bean threads, mushrooms, steak, chicken, seafood, and fish balls attractively on the platters and bring these to the table also.

2. Heat the stock in a large pot on the stove and when boiling, carefully transfer the stock to the wok(s) or casserole(s). Bring these to the table and place on your heat source. Return to a boil. Before guests begin to cook, put a few large handfuls of the vegetables, some bean threads, mushrooms, tofu, and the fish balls into the stock. Allow the vegetables to cook until softened, about 6 minutes.

3. Invite your guests to take whatever condiments they wish with spoons and prepare their own dipping sauces in their bowls. They should then select whatever they want from the meat, chicken, and seafood platters and cook it in the boiling stock. Nothing requires more than 3 minutes' cooking time. As the diners retrieve their cooked meat and seafood they should also help themselves to the cooked vegetables, bean threads, mushrooms, tofu, and fish balls. After everyone has been served, replenish the wok or casserole with vegetables, tofu, and bean threads as necessary. The stock must be kept boiling throughout the meal, so don't add too much of any of these ingredients at one time, allowing the stock to return to a boil after each addition. If the stock level becomes low, replenish it with the boiling water.

4. When all the ingredients have been cooked and eaten, or whenever guests are ready, ladle the cooking broth into soup bowls and pass.

Spicy Fish Balls

These savory mouthfuls can be bought but are best homemade. Prepare them up to six hours in advance and store them, covered, in the fridge, or freeze them in plastic containers for up to two weeks. Frozen fish balls can be added directly to the hot stock at table.

MAKES ABOUT 24 FISH BALLS

2 pounds Chilean sea bass or other fatty white-fleshed fish
4 eggs, separated
1 teaspoon kosher salt
1 teaspoon freshly ground white pepper
1 teaspoon toasted sesame oil
1 tablespoon Thai fish sauce *(nam pla)*
3 Thai bird chiles, finely chopped
6 scallions, green and white parts, sliced $1/16$ inch thick

1. Bring a large quantity of water to a boil. In a food processor, combine the bass and egg yolks and puree. Add the salt, pepper, sesame oil, fish sauce, and chiles and pulse to blend. Transfer the mixture to a bowl and fold in the scallions.

2. Beat the egg whites until stiff peaks form. Gently fold the whites into the fish mixture and cook a very small portion in the boiling water. Taste and correct seasonings if necessary.

3. With 2 tablespoons, form 1-inch balls from the fish mixture and add 10 at a time to the boiling water. Poach until just cooked through, about 3 minutes. Using a large-mesh spoon, remove and drain the balls on paper towels. Allow to cool and store refrigerated.

Chapter 8

Sides

WHEN I CREATE A DISH, I ALWAYS THINK ABOUT ITS ACCOMPA-
NIMENTS. ONCE I'VE DEVISED THEM, THESE SIDES BECOME
"PART" OF THE DISH, PROVIDING FLAVOR, TEXTURE, AND SOME-
TIMES TEMPERATURE CONTRAST. THIS WAY I'M ASSURED THAT
THE DISHES I SERVE TOUCH EVERY BASE.

Crispy Napa Slaw illustrates the point. I serve this delightful side with hoisin-marinated chicken (see page 127) among other dishes. Likewise, creamy Yukon Gold Garlic Chive Mashers was created to partner garlic-marinated lamb chops (see page 157). You should, however, feel free to use these sides as you wish in your own menus. The Napa Slaw works beautifully in sandwiches.

The Yukon Gold Mashers are fantastic with grilled beef or birds. Lemon Basmati Rice, paired with wok-flashed salt and pepper shrimp (see page 102), is also superior with scallops or fish. Spicy Chinese Long Beans, joined with crispy red snapper (page 114), is excellent, too, with roasted duck or pork.

Some of the sides included here can stand beautifully on their own. Braised Triple Cabbage Lasagna, a partner of Asian Lacquered Poussin with Hoisin Lime Sauce (page 196), and Sweet Potato Risotto, served with seared scallops and truffled haricots verts (see page 174), make savory but elegant first courses, and would get any important dinner going spectacularly.

Put these sides to work in your own cooking. Packed with savory flavor, they're sure to become favorites for everyday and special-occasion enjoyment.

Spicy Chinese Long Beans

An Asian native, long beans can grow up to three feet in length and are sometimes sold in looped bunches. They're delicious and excel in simple stir-frys. I like them best, however, when they're quickly deep-fried and seasoned. These make a great partner for fried whole fish.

SERVES 3 TO 4

Canola oil, for deep-frying
3 cups long beans cut into 3-inch lengths
Salt
2 tablespoons sambal oelek
½ tablespoon toasted sesame oil

1. Fill a large wok one-third full with the oil and heat over high heat to 350°F. Add the beans and fry until softened and wrinkled, about 2 minutes. Using a large-mesh spoon, transfer the beans to paper towels to drain.

2. Remove the beans to a medium bowl and season with the salt to taste. Add the sambal oelek and sesame oil, toss, and serve.

Napa Slaw

My East-West take on the traditional favorite makes a great addition to sandwiches or wraps where its crunch and mild heat give other fillings a real boost. Try it also with cold cuts of all kinds.

SERVES 4

$1/2$ cup Thai fish sauce *(nam pla)*
$1/2$ cup rice wine vinegar
$1/2$ tablespoon red pepper flakes
8 large basil leaves, cut lengthwise into $1/4$-inch ribbons
$1 1/2$ teaspoons sugar
3 cups napa cabbage cut into $1/8$-inch ribbons (1 medium head)
1 cup shredded carrots
1 cup bean sprouts
$1/2$ cup scallions, green parts only, cut $1/8$ inch thick
Salt and freshly ground black pepper

1. In a large bowl, combine the fish sauce, vinegar, pepper flakes, basil, and sugar and whisk to blend.

2. Add the cabbage, carrots, bean sprouts, and scallions and toss well. Season with the salt and pepper to taste and allow to rest to flavor, about 3 minutes. Serve.

Three-Onion Couscous

I'm always looking for interesting ways to use couscous and this recipe, which features scallions and red and yellow onions, is one of the best. A perfect accompaniment to stewy dishes like Braised Curried Lamb Shanks (page 160), it's a great alternative to the usual starch dishes. It's easy to prepare, too—it "cooks" in a covered bowl while you go about your business.

SERVES 4

1 tablespoon canola oil
1 medium red onion, cut into $\frac{1}{8}$-inch dice
1 medium yellow onion, cut into $\frac{1}{8}$-inch dice
1 bunch scallions, white and green parts, sliced $\frac{1}{8}$ inch thick and
    reserved separately
Salt and freshly ground black pepper
3 cups couscous
2 tablespoons extra-virgin olive oil
$\frac{1}{3}$ cup dried currants

1. Heat a medium skillet over high heat. Add the oil and swirl to coat the pan. When the oil shimmers, add the onions and scallion whites and sauté, stirring, until golden, about 10 minutes. Season with salt and pepper to taste.

2. Bring a kettle of water to a boil. In a large bowl, combine the couscous, olive oil, currants, and the cooked onion mixture. Add $3\frac{1}{4}$ cups of boiling water to the mixture and stir quickly to blend. Immediately cover the bowl with plastic wrap, sealing it tightly against the bowl, and allow to stand until the couscous is tender, about 30 minutes. Fluff the couscous with a fork and correct the seasonings. Sprinkle with the scallion greens and serve.

Five-Spice Apples

These fragrant caramelized apples are flavored with five-spice powder, a mixture containing cinnamon (or the stronger cassia). Cinnamon is, of course, a classic accompaniment to cooked apples, and this dish benefits from its warm sweetish taste, as well as that of the other five-spice ingredients. A natural with pork dishes, the apples would also be wonderful with any game dish.

These can be prepared ahead and warmed over low heat just before serving.

SERVES 4

2 tablespoons canola oil
1 small red onion, cut into $\frac{1}{4}$-inch dice
$1\frac{1}{2}$ teaspoons five-spice powder
1 tablespoon brown sugar, packed
2 Granny Smith apples, peeled, cored, and cut into $\frac{1}{4}$-inch dice
1 cup apple juice
Salt and freshly ground black pepper
1 tablespoon butter

1. Heat a medium skillet over medium heat. Add the oil and swirl to coat the bottom of the pan. When the oil shimmers, add the onion and sauté, stirring, until brown, about 8 to 10 minutes.

2. Add the five-spice powder, brown sugar, apples, and juice. Stir, season with salt and pepper to taste, and cook until the liquid is reduced by half, about 12 minutes. The apples should retain their shape and some liquid should remain in the pan; do not overcook. Stir in the butter and correct the seasonings. Serve warm.

Braised Triple Cabbage Lasagna

It's believed pasta originated in the East, so I'm retrieving lasagna for the home team, so to speak, with this luscious Asian-inspired pasta and cabbage cake. Unbaked, free-form, and prepared without binders, this lasagna is deliciously savory. Whenever you think mashed potatoes, or wonder what starch and which vegetables to serve—remember this lasagna. Or serve it as an appetizer with grilled sausage or portobellos.

SERVES 4

2 tablespoons canola oil
2 tablespoons finely chopped garlic
2 tablespoons finely chopped fresh ginger
2 cups green cabbage cut into $\frac{1}{4}$-inch ribbons
2 cups napa cabbage cut into $\frac{1}{4}$-inch ribbons
2 cups bok choy or choy sum cut into $\frac{1}{4}$-inch ribbons
$\frac{1}{2}$ cup Chicken Stock (page 14) or low-sodium canned broth
$\frac{1}{4}$ cup Shaoxing wine or dry sherry
6 tablespoons butter
Salt and freshly ground black pepper
8 3 × 3-inch squares cut from fresh pasta sheets, or 8 wonton wrappers

1. Heat a medium skillet over high heat. Add the oil and swirl to coat the pan. When the oil shimmers, add the garlic and ginger and sauté, stirring, until soft, about 2 minutes.

2. Add the cabbages and bok choy, stir, and add the stock and wine. Reduce the heat and simmer until the vegetables are soft, about 15 minutes. Add the butter, swirl the pan until melted, and season with the salt and pepper to taste. Keep warm.

3. Meanwhile, bring a large quantity of salted water to a boil. Add the pasta sheets and cook until al dente, 4 to 6 minutes. Drain well.

4. To serve, spoon 1 heaping tablespoon of the cabbage mixture onto each of 4 serving plates. Top with a pasta square and another spoonful of cabbage. Place one more pasta square on each serving and top with a final layer of cabbage. Serve immediately.

Wild Mushroom Ragout

This woodsy dish, with its deep flavor notes, is one of my favorite sides. I use it often—as an accompaniment to arctic char (page 121), lamb rack (page 158), even as a soup garnish (page 26). The truth is, it's wonderful with virtually any meat, poultry, or fish dish that isn't saucy. You can even use it as a dip with bread!

Feel free to vary the kinds of mushrooms called for or follow the suggestions in the ingredients listing below. What you want to use, in any case, are the freshest, best looking mushrooms your market has to offer.

SERVES 4

3 tablespoons butter
1 tablespoon finely chopped garlic
4 large shallots, thinly sliced
1 cup chanterelle, hedgehog, or lobster mushrooms
1 cup small fresh shiitake caps
1 cup quartered button or cremini mushrooms
$1/3$ cup Chinese dried black mushrooms, soaked in a small bowl of warm water to soften, about 20 minutes, stemmed and quartered
Salt and freshly ground black pepper
$1/2$ cup dry red wine
$1/2$ cup Chicken Stock (page 14) or low-sodium canned broth
$1/2$ cup veal demi-glace, or $1/2$ cup Chicken Stock mixed with 1 tablespoon soy sauce
1 tablespoon dark soy sauce
$1/2$ tablespoon chopped fresh thyme, or $1/2$ tablespoon dried

1. Heat a heavy medium saucepan over medium heat. Add 1 tablespoon of the butter and swirl to coat the bottom of the pan. Add the garlic and shallots and sauté, stirring, until soft, 3 to 5 minutes. Add all the mushrooms and sauté until soft, 8 to 10 minutes. Season with salt and pepper to taste.

2. Add the wine, stir, and cook until the wine is reduced by half, about 5 minutes. Add the stock, demi-glace, dark soy sauce, and thyme, and simmer until reduced by half, about 25 to 30 minutes. Stir in the remaining 2 tablespoons of butter and correct the seasonings. Serve.

Crispy Onions

Once cooked, these addictive onions stay as crisp as potato chips. I use them as a garnish for dishes including Five-Peppercorn Grilled Rib-Eye Steaks (page 154); they're also great for snacking. For a party, make a big bowlful—they won't last long. They're a natural with sandwiches, too.

MAKES 2 CUPS

Canola oil, for deep-frying
2 cups rice flour
1 large red onion, sliced paper thin
Salt

1. Fill a fryer or medium heavy pot one-third full with the oil and heat over high heat to 350°F.

2. Place the flour in a paper bag, add the onion, and shake well to coat. Shake off excess flour, add the onion to the oil and fry until golden brown, about 3 to 5 minutes. Drain on paper towels, sprinkle with the salt, and serve.

Hijiki Salad

This delightful salad, a natural partner to seared or grilled seafood, features hijiki, the Japanese dried seaweed. High in protein and low in fat, and with a flavor reminiscent of the sea, hijiki is not only tasty but also extremely good for you. I pair it simply with cucumbers and scallions for a refreshing salad.

The salad can be prepared and held for about thirty minutes before serving.

SERVES 4

1 cup dried hijiki seaweed
1 cup peeled, seeded, and finely diced cucumber
2 tablespoons rice wine vinegar
2 teaspoons toasted sesame oil
2 tablespoons scallions, green parts only, sliced $\frac{1}{4}$ inch thick
1 teaspoon sugar
Salt and freshly ground white pepper

1. Bring 4 cups of water to a boil. In a small bowl, combine the hijiki with enough of the water to cover it. Allow the hijiki to soften, about 30 minutes. Drain well.

2. In a medium bowl, combine the hijiki with the cucumber, vinegar, sesame oil, scallions, and sugar. Season with salt and pepper to taste and toss well.

VARIATION: WAKAME SALAD. For a very different taste and texture, substitute an equal amount of dried wakame seaweed for the hijiki and prepare as above.

Garlic Mashers

The smell of garlic cooking is right up there with bread baking in my hall of favorite culinary scents. Then comes the pleasure of actually tasting that aromatic seasoning, a delight amply provided by these creamy garlic-infused potatoes. These are just the thing for any hearty meat dish, like Beef and Shiitake Stew (page 156). Infusing the cream with sautéed garlic before adding it to the potatoes ensures deliciously pungent mashers.

SERVES 4

5 large Russet potatoes, peeled and quartered
1 tablespoon canola oil
3 tablespoons finely chopped garlic
2 cups heavy cream
6 tablespoons butter
Salt and freshly ground pepper

1. In a large saucepan, combine the potatoes with enough water to cover and salt lightly. Bring to a boil over high heat and cook until the tip of a knife inserted into the potatoes meets no resistance, 30 to 40 minutes.

2. Meanwhile, heat a medium saucepan over medium heat. Add the oil and swirl to coat the bottom of the pan. When the oil shimmers, add the garlic and sauté, stirring, until golden, about 2 minutes. Add the cream and reduce by one-third over low heat, about 12 minutes.

3. Transfer the potatoes to a large bowl or the bowl of a mixer and add the cream mixture. Using a hand masher and wooden spoon or a mixer with a paddle attachment, whip the potatoes until smooth. Fold in the butter, season with salt and pepper, and serve immediately.

MING'S TIP: AN IMPORTANT BUT OFTEN OVERLOOKED "TRICK" TO MAKING CREAMY MASHERS IS TO BUY POTATOES OF UNIFORM SIZE AND TO QUARTER THEM PRECISELY TO ENSURE EVEN COOKING.

Roasted Garlic and Sweet Potato Hash

This quick, skin-on-potatoes hash departs from more traditional recipes in interesting ways. First, you heat the pan before adding the potatoes to give them a nice leg up on crusting. Second, the hash is made in the oven, producing crispiness and flavor depth. This isn't one of those hashes you have to stand over, either. A few tosses of the potatoes while they bake is all that's needed.

These are wonderful with just about anything you'd serve potatoes with, especially grilled or seared meats or poultry.

SERVES 4

3 large sweet potatoes, unpeeled, washed, and cut into $\frac{1}{2}$-inch dice
12 garlic cloves, peeled
$1\frac{1}{2}$ teaspoons finely chopped fresh thyme, or 1 teaspoon dried
1 tablespoon extra-virgin olive oil
1 tablespoon canola oil
Salt and freshly ground black pepper

1. Preheat the oven to 375°F. Place a large, heavy, heatproof skillet in the oven and allow to heat thoroughly, about 20 minutes.

2. In a medium bowl, combine the potatoes, garlic, thyme, and olive and canola oils, and mix well. Season to taste with salt and pepper.

3. Using an oven mitt, remove the skillet from the oven and add the potato mixture; the potatoes should sizzle. Return the skillet to the oven and roast the potatoes, tossing them from time to time for even cooking, until the potatoes are brown and crusty, 30 to 45 minutes. Remove, correct the seasonings, and serve.

Yukon Gold Garlic Chive Mashers

I consider these my "down-home" garlic mashers. Made with yellow-fleshed Yukon Gold potatoes and laced with chives, these potatoes are an indispensable partner to lamb and are also great with roasted chicken.

Don't peel the potatoes when making these for extra vitamins and for flavor, and mash them coarsely, country-style. This recipe is lighter on the fat than other mashers, so you can eat more.

SERVES 4

8 medium Yukon Gold potatoes, washed
2 tablespoons butter
8 garlic cloves, roughly chopped
1 cup roughly chopped garlic or Chinese chives or scallion greens
1 cup heavy cream
Salt and freshly ground black pepper

1. Preheat the oven to 350°F. Bake the potatoes until the tip of a knife inserted into them meets no resistance, about 45 minutes.

2. Heat a medium saucepan over medium heat. Add 1 tablespoon of the butter and swirl to coat the bottom of the pan. Add the garlic and half the chives and sauté, stirring, until the garlic softens, 3 to 5 minutes. Add the cream and allow the mixture to reduce by half, about 10 minutes. With a hand or standard blender, blend the ingredients until pureed and season with salt and pepper to taste. Add the remaining chives and mix.

3. Using a hand masher, mash the potatoes coarsely. Add the cream and fold in the remaining tablespoon of butter. Correct the seasonings and serve.

Gingered Sweet Potatoes

These creamy potatoes, fragrant with ginger and garlic, are a natural accompaniment to roasted pork dishes. They're also great with poultry roasts—try them for Thanksgiving dinner in place of the usual spuds.

SERVES 4

6 tablespoons butter
6 garlic cloves, peeled
2 tablespoons finely chopped fresh ginger
1$\frac{1}{2}$ cups heavy cream
4 medium sweet potatoes, peeled and roughly
   chopped
Salt and freshly ground black pepper

1. Heat a small saucepan over medium heat. Add 1 tablespoon of the butter and swirl to coat the bottom of the pan. Add the garlic and ginger and sauté, stirring occasionally, until the garlic is brown, 3 to 4 minutes. Add the cream and reduce by one-third over low heat, about 10 minutes. Keep warm.

2. Meanwhile, combine the sweet potatoes in a large saucepan with enough water to cover them completely. Bring to a boil over high heat and cook until they can be pierced easily with the tip of a knife, 20 to 30 minutes. Drain and transfer to a food processor. Add the cream and process until well blended. Add the remaining butter, season with salt and pepper, and puree until smooth. Transfer the potatoes to a bowl, correct the seasonings, and serve.

Basil Mashed Potatoes

Perfect with grilled lamb rack, these herby potatoes are also outstanding with roast chicken, seared mahi-mahi, and other meaty fish. I love the delicate basil color of these mashers as well as their taste; they make a great presentation.

The potatoes are rich, but the butter and cream used to make them are necessary for superior taste and texture. Eat less of them, if you must, rather than deprive yourself of a special treat.

SERVES 4 TO 6

2 cups heavy cream, or more as needed
8 Russet potatoes, peeled and quartered
1/2 cup peeled garlic cloves (about 2 heads)
1 cup Basil Oil (page 231)
1/4 pound (1 stick) butter
Salt and freshly ground black pepper

1. Preheat the oven to 250°F. In a small saucepan, heat the cream over medium heat. When it comes to a boil, turn down the heat and reduce by one-fourth, about 15 minutes.

2. Meanwhile, place the potatoes in a large pot and add cold water to cover them by 3 inches. Add the garlic and bring to a boil over high heat, reduce the heat, and simmer until the potatoes can be pierced easily with the tip of a knife, 30 to 45 minutes. Drain the potatoes and garlic well, and transfer both to a pan fitted with a rack. Dry them in the oven, about 15 minutes.

3. Rice the potatoes and the reserved garlic into a mixing bowl and whip using a mixer with a paddle attachment. Add half of the cream, mix to incorporate, and add the basil oil. Mix, add the butter, and whip until the potatoes are fluffy. Add more cream if the potatoes seem dry. Season with salt and pepper to taste and serve immediately.

MING'S TIP: OVEN-DRYING THE SPUDS ALLOWS THEM TO ABSORB MORE OF THE CREAM AND BUTTER WITHOUT GETTING RUNNY.

Sweet Potato Crisps

Though extra-crunchy julienned crisps are good on their own, I like to use them as a garnish for soft-textured dishes that need a bit of snap, like risottos or purees. There's no trick to making these, other than cutting the potatoes to uniform thinness. A mandoline does this beautifully, but a good sharp knife will also get the job done.

SERVES 4 AS A GARNISH

1 large sweet potato
Canola oil, for deep-frying
Salt

1. Using a mandoline, cut the potato into a $\frac{1}{8}$-inch julienne. Alternatively, with a thin-bladed knife, cut the potato into $\frac{1}{8}$-inch slices; stack one-third of the slices and cut into a julienne. Repeat with the remaining slices.

2. Fill a small heavy pot one-third full with the oil and heat to 275°F. Dry the potatoes well, add to the oil, and fry until golden brown, about 4 minutes. Use a large-mesh spoon to spread the potatoes evenly over the surface of the oil. As they cook, the potato pieces will form a large sheet. Cook until the crisp is lightly golden; turn to cook the second side. Watch carefully to prevent the potatoes from burning.

3. Remove the crisp with the spoon and drain on paper towels. Season with the salt to taste while hot and serve or store at room temperature, uncovered; it will hold for about 8 hours. To serve, break the crisp into 4 abstract pieces.

VARIATION: RUSSET CRISPS. Prepare exactly as above, substituting a Russet potato for the sweet potato. You can cut the potato with a turning slicer to make spaghetti-like strands or on a mandoline to make a neat julienne.

Sweet Potato Risotto

The idea behind this dish is to treat potatoes like rice and to cook them using the risotto technique. The result is a marvelously textured dish, part creamy, part chewy, that almost always stops the show. It goes wonderfully with sweet-fleshed seafood like lobster or scallops.

I won't kid you—cutting the potatoes is work, but fully worth the effort. I strongly recommend using a mandoline to julienne the potatoes, which are then cut into rice-size pieces. You don't need one of those expensive battle-ax cutters; the Japanese make a small but thoroughly functional plastic mandoline that's sold in Asian markets. Once the potatoes are cut (which can be done ahead of time), you're almost home free. If you've ever made a risotto, you know the drill.

SERVES 4

4 large sweet potatoes
2 tablespoons butter
4 shallots, cut into very small dice
3 to 4 cups hot Chicken Stock (page 14) or
  low-sodium canned broth
Salt and freshly ground black pepper

1. Fill a medium bowl with cold water. Using a mandoline or by hand, cut the potatoes into ⅛-inch julienne. Working in batches, stack the strips, align the edges, and cut into cubes a little larger than rice grains. Transfer the cubes to the cold water as you work.

2. Heat a medium saucepan over medium heat. Add 1 tablespoon of the butter and swirl to coat the bottom of the pan. Add the shallots and sauté, stirring, until soft, about 3 minutes.

3. Drain the potatoes and dry on paper towels. Add the potatoes to the saucepan and sauté, stirring, until tender-crisp, about 4 minutes. Add a ladleful of the stock and continue to cook, stirring, until the liquid is absorbed. Add more stock and continue to cook and stir, allowing each addition of stock to be absorbed before adding the next, until the potatoes are cooked through and creamy, 15 to 20 minutes. Do not allow the potatoes to become mushy. Season with salt and pepper to taste and stir in the remaining butter.

Potato, Spinach, and Shiitake Gratin

Based on the traditional French *gratin dauphinoise,* this luscious casserole is melt-in-your-mouth savory. It's perfect with grilled steak or any simply prepared meat dish, and can be served in its baking dish, family style, or cut into attractive portions with a ring mold for fancier presentations.

SERVES 4

1 tablespoon canola oil
2 cups shiitake caps, cut into $1/4$-inch slices
Salt and freshly ground black pepper
8 large Russet potatoes, peeled, cut lengthwise into $1/8$-inch slices, and held in a
    large bowl of cold water
2 tablespoons finely chopped garlic
1 teaspoon freshly grated nutmeg
1 pound spinach, well washed and tough stems removed
1 quart heavy cream

1. Preheat the oven to 325° F. Heat a medium skillet over medium heat, add the oil, and swirl to coat the bottom of the pan. When the oil shimmers, add the shiitakes and sauté, stirring occasionally, until soft, about 6 minutes. Season with salt and pepper, allow to cool, and set aside.

2. Drain the potatoes. In a large bowl, combine the potatoes, garlic, nutmeg, spinach, cream, and the reserved shiitakes and season with salt and pepper to taste. Transfer to a 6 × 10 × 2-inch baking dish; the cream should cover the potatoes; if it doesn't, add more.

3. Place the dish on a cookie sheet to catch any spills, transfer both to the oven, and bake for 30 minutes. With a spatula, turn the potatoes so the browned slices are on the bottom and bake until the cream has thickened and the potatoes are soft, about $1\frac{1}{2}$ hours more; do not stir during this time. Serve.

> MING'S TIP: THE GRATIN REQUIRES AMPLE TIME TO BAKE. DON'T
> RUSH IT BY INCREASING THE HEAT, WHICH WILL CAUSE THE CREAM
> TO BREAK.

Preserved Lemon Polenta

I didn't invent polenta, but I was, as far as I know, the first to make it with preserved lemon, the North African pickle that so enlivens many dishes. This creamy polenta makes an awesome accompaniment to a wide variety of dishes, and is particularly nice with braises and stews.

Like most people, I'd always prepared polenta on the stove. Then Budi Kazali, my executive sous chef, showed me how to make it in the oven. This effort-saving method is virtually foolproof—you bake the polenta, fold in some butter, and that's it.

SERVES 4

5 tablespoons butter
¼ cup finely chopped shallots
2 tablespoons finely chopped fresh ginger
1 cup medium-grain polenta or yellow cornmeal
¼ cup diced Preserved Lemons (page 239), pulp and rinds
4 cups Chicken Stock (page 14) or low-sodium canned broth
Salt and freshly ground black pepper

1. Preheat the oven to 325°F. Heat a large ovenproof saucepan over medium heat. Add 1 tablespoon of the butter and swirl to coat the bottom of the pan. Add the shallots and ginger and sauté, stirring, until soft, about 6 minutes.

2. Add the polenta, preserved lemon, and stock. Season with salt and pepper, stir well, fold in the remaining butter, and cover tightly with foil. Transfer to the oven and bake until the liquid is absorbed, 45 minutes to 1 hour. Correct the seasonings and serve.

MING'S TIP: BE SURE TO USE MEDIUM-GRAIN POLENTA WHEN FOLLOWING THIS TECHNIQUE— NOT THE COARSE-GRAINED OR INSTANT!

Lemon Basmati Rice

This fragrant rice is a natural partner to Wok-Flashed Salt and Pepper Shrimp (page 102), but complements virtually any fish or poultry dish. Because of its fresh lemon tartness, it's a particularly good counterpoint to rich cooking.

SERVES 4

2 cups basmati rice
1 tablespoon canola oil
4 scallions, white and green parts finely chopped and reserved separately
Zest of 2 lemons plus the juice of 1
2 $\frac{1}{4}$-inch-thick slices fresh ginger
$\frac{1}{2}$ teaspoon salt
Pinch of freshly ground white pepper
3 cups Chicken Stock (page 14) or low-sodium canned broth, or water

1. Place the rice in a large bowl, add water to cover, and swish the rice to wash. Pour off the water and repeat washing until the water is clear. Drain well.

2. Heat a medium saucepan over medium heat. Add the oil and swirl to coat the bottom of the pan. When the oil shimmers, add the white scallion pieces and the lemon zest and sauté, stirring, until soft, about 2 minutes. Add the rice and ginger and cook, stirring, until the rice is opaque, about 5 minutes.

3. Add the lemon juice, salt, pepper, and stock, cover, and bring to a boil. Reduce the heat to low and simmer until the stock is absorbed and the rice is tender-firm, 20 to 25 minutes. Remove the rice from the heat and allow to rest, covered, 25 minutes more. Fluff the rice with a fork, correct the seasonings, sprinkle with the scallion greens and serve.

MING'S TIP: I ALWAYS WASH IMPORTED BASMATI RICE BEFORE COOK-
ING IT. IT'S USUALLY TRAVELED FAR TO REACH OUR MARKETS,
RUBBED AGAINST ITSELF, AND CONSEQUENTLY HAS A STARCHY
RESIDUE. TO ENSURE SEPARATE GRAINS, WASH THIS POWDER AWAY.

Chapter 9

Oils, Dips, and Seasonings

FLAVORED OILS AND DIPS ARE ESSENTIAL TO THE FOOD AT BLUE GINGER. THEY ADD DEPTH AND FINISH TO MY DISHES, AND WILL DO THE SAME FOR YOURS. THOUGH IN MANY CASES THEY FUNCTION AS "SAUCES," THEY ARE MUCH LIGHTER AND MORE INTENSELY FLAVORED THAN THOSE ACCOMPANIMENTS USUALLY ARE.

In wok cooking, a dish often begins with hot oil that is flavored with aromatics like garlic and ginger. The Chinese also season with flavored oils. These practices plus seasoning experimentation with my friend chef Ken Oringer at Silks in San Francisco inspired the palette of oils I rely upon so frequently.

Keep a pantry of these oils and you open the door to easy flavor making. For example, Mustard Oil, which I pair with peppered steak (page 154), enhances all grilled meats it's drizzled on; it can also be used to make superior vinaigrettes. Basil Oil adds herby freshness to risottos and can also be turned into a marvelous aïoli. Wasabi oil, which imparts the flavor of that powerful seasoning in a temptingly tamed form, makes a wonderful drizzle for grilled fish or a piquant mayonnaise.

Some of the oils can also be used for cooking. Curry Oil, which is terrific in vinaigrettes, can also be heated to sauté scallops or used as a frying medium to make potato sticks. I rely on this oil also to flash-cook hamachi sashimi, a process in which the hot oil sears the fish partially for intriguing taste and texture.

The dipping sauces derive from traditional Asian soy sauce, vinegar, and sambal table condiments. Flavored variously with mint, ginger, and citrus fruit, among other ingredients, these dips are perfect with pot stickers, spring rolls, and other "small eats." And they can't be beat as a dunk for fish and chips and similar fried dishes. Soy Syrup makes a perfect seasoning and garnish for fish; Soy Ginger Glaze does wonders brushed onto grilled chicken or salmon, or sprinkled onto vegetables. These flavorings invite improvisation, but before using them think about the foods their ingredients would normally accompany. (I wouldn't, for example, pair the Wasabi Oil with chicken.) Follow your own good sense, and enjoy their flavor-making power often.

Most of these seasonings can be stored, refrigerated. (Avoid returning used dips to their containers, which could introduce bacteria to them and shorten shelf life.) Keep the oils in squeeze bottles so the seasonings can be drizzled onto foods conveniently.

Wasabi Oil

This delightfully pungent oil is a wonderful way to enjoy wasabi flavor without what I call "wasabi blast." It's delicious drizzled on grilled fish or added to mayonnaise (in the proportion of 1 part oil to 4 parts mayo) for sandwiches. The oil will keep in an airtight container, refrigerated, for about two weeks, though it loses its zip over time. For extra pungency, reduce the quantity of canola to $\frac{1}{3}$ cup oil.

MAKES ABOUT 1 CUP

$\frac{1}{2}$ cup wasabi powder
2 tablespoons mirin (Japanese sweet sake)
2 teaspoons sugar
$\frac{1}{2}$ cup canola oil

In a small stainless-steel bowl, combine the wasabi powder, mirin, and sugar and whisk to blend. Add a little less than $\frac{1}{2}$ cup of water gradually, whisking, until a pancake batter–like puree is formed. Whisk in the oil. Let stand for 10 minutes before using.

Mustard Oil

This is excellent on grilled meats or as a basis for vinaigrettes. Or try making a large quantity of the oil and cooking *frites* in it. The oil gives them a pleasing mustardy flavor.
    This lasts for about a month in the fridge.

MAKES 2 CUPS

2 tablespoons dry mustard
1 teaspoon ground turmeric
1 teaspoon salt
2 cups canola oil

In a small bowl, combine the mustard, turmeric, and salt. Stir in 2 to 3 tablespoons water to form a paste. Whisk in the oil and allow to stand overnight to develop flavor. The mixture will separate; use the oil only.

Scallion Oil

Anything that benefits from the flavor of scallions will profit from a drizzle of this oil. I use it with Classic Roast Chicken with Sticky Rice Stuffing (page 130), among other dishes in this book; it's also good in Thai salads, as a garnish for roasted butternut squash, or in leek and potato soup. You can use the same technique to make Shiso Oil, a delicately flavored oil that is sensational drizzled on grilled fish, chicken, or as a garnish for soup.

Store the oil in an airtight container in the fridge, where it will last for at least a week. The oil's green color will fade as time passes, but its flavor will intensify.

MAKES 2½ CUPS

2 bunches scallions, green parts only
1 cup spinach leaves, well washed
1 teaspoon salt
1 teaspoon sugar
2 cups canola oil

1. Fill a large bowl with cold water and add ice cubes. Bring a large pot of salted water to a boil. Add the scallions and the spinach to the boiling water and blanch for 2 minutes. Drain and transfer the vegetables to the ice water.

2. Squeeze the vegetables to extract most of their water and transfer to a blender. Add the salt and sugar and blend. With the machine running, add the oil in a steady stream and continue to blend until completely pureed, about 3 minutes. Transfer the oil to a container and use or refrigerate.

VARIATION: SHISO OIL. Substitute 1 cup shiso leaves for the scallions and prepare as above.

Chile Oil

This may be my most-used seasoning oil; it adds fire and color to a wide range of meat, poultry, seafood, and game dishes, and is also good in soups.

Store it in a tall, fairly wide-mouthed glass container in the fridge, where it will keep for about two months. For easiest use, bend an old teaspoon and use it as a dipper.

MAKES ABOUT 3 CUPS

½ cup chile powder, such as ancho, chimayo, or pasilla
½ tablespoon ground cumin
1 teaspoon salt
3 cups canola oil

1. In a medium skillet, combine the chile powder, cumin, and salt, and heat over medium heat just until the mixture begins to smoke. Whisk in the oil and remove from the stove.

2. Allow the chile oil to cool, transfer it to a glass jar, and let stand overnight. Cover and use or store. The oil will separate from the solids; use the red oil only.

Curry Oil

I use this pungent oil to flash-cook hamachi sashimi (page 64) and Crispy Scallops with Carrot–Star Anise Syrup (page 106). Use it also for sautéing scallops or in a vinaigrette, or make a large quantity and fry potato sticks with it.

Store the oil for up to one month, refrigerated, in an airtight container.

MAKES ½ CUP

½ cup curry powder
Pinch of salt
2 cups canola oil

In a small bowl, combine the curry powder and salt with ⅛ to ¼ cup water to make a loose paste. Whisk in the oil slowly, stirring. Allow the oil to stand for 1 hour to settle. Use the clear oil only.

Basil Oil

This fragrant oil adds herby flavor to Grilled New Zealand Lamb Rack with Wild Mushroom Ragout and Basil Mashed Potatoes (page 158). Use it with other grilled dishes or for superior vinaigrettes and aïolis.

Store it tightly covered in the fridge, where it will last for about one week. It will darken in time, but the flavor remains excellent. Shake it before using.

MAKES ABOUT 2 CUPS

2 cups basil leaves
1 cup spinach leaves
1 cup canola oil
$\frac{1}{2}$ teaspoon salt

1. Bring a large quantity of highly salted water to a boil. Fill a large bowl with water and add ice.

2. Add the basil and spinach leaves to the boiling water and cook until very soft but still green, about 2 minutes. Drain and transfer the greens to the cold water. When cold, remove and squeeze as much water as possible from the greens.

3. Transfer the vegetables to a blender. Add the oil and salt and blend until smooth, about 3 minutes. Remove the oil and use or store.

Parsley Oil

This herby oil is well matched with venison and other game. It can also be combined with chopped and sautéed garlic to make an almost instant sauce for pasta. For the most intense flavor, stir the oil before using it.

The oil will last, refrigerated, for at least a week

MAKES ABOUT 2 CUPS

1 cup flat-leaf parsley leaves
1 teaspoon salt
1 teaspoon sugar
2 cups canola oil

1. Bring a large quantity of salted water to a boil. Fill a bowl with water and add ice.

2. Add the parsley to the boiling water and blanch until softened, about 2 minutes. Transfer to the ice water. When cold, drain and squeeze the parsley well to remove as much water as possible. Transfer to a blender and add the salt and sugar. Start the machine, and add the oil in a thin, steady stream. Blend until the blender jar feels slightly warm, 3 to 5 minutes. Remove and use or store.

Spicy Soy Dipping Sauce

This is my version of the classic vinegar and soy sauce dim sum dip that's a natural accompaniment to Pork and Ginger Pot Stickers (page 46) and other dumplings. I've added sambal oelek for spiciness—a bow to my Hunan roots. Refrigerated, this lasts for two weeks. Try it also with spring rolls and tempura.

MAKES ABOUT 1 CUP

$\frac{1}{3}$ cup soy sauce
$\frac{1}{3}$ cup rice wine vinegar
$\frac{1}{3}$ cup scallions, green parts only, sliced $\frac{1}{8}$ inch thick
1 tablespoon toasted sesame oil
1 tablespoon sambal oelek

In a medium bowl combine the soy sauce, vinegar, scallions, sesame oil, and sambal oelek. Stir to blend and use or store.

Mint Dipping Sauce

The Vietnamese serve the spring rolls called *cha gio* with lettuce and fresh mint. I've used the idea of a refreshing mint accompaniment to create this dipping sauce. It makes a perfect companion to Mushroom and Leek Spring Rolls (page 52), and is also good with vegetable tempura.

MAKES ABOUT $\frac{1}{4}$ CUP

$\frac{1}{4}$ cup fresh mint leaves cut into thin ribbons
1 teaspoon sugar
$\frac{1}{4}$ cup soy sauce
Juice of 1 lemon

In a small bowl, combine the mint, sugar, soy sauce, and lemon juice. Stir to dissolve the sugar and serve.

Ginger Dipping Sauce

This sprightly sauce is good with dumplings or any other dim sum. It will last, refrigerated, for about one week.

MAKES ABOUT 1$\frac{1}{2}$ CUPS

$\frac{1}{4}$ cup soy sauce
$\frac{1}{4}$ cup Chinese black vinegar
1$\frac{1}{4}$ cups scallions, green parts only, sliced $\frac{1}{8}$ inch thick
1 teaspoon finely chopped fresh ginger
1 teaspoon red pepper flakes
1 teaspoon sugar

In a small bowl, combine the soy sauce, vinegar, scallions, ginger, red pepper flakes, and sugar. Stir to blend until the sugar is dissolved, then use or store.

Citrus Dipping Sauce

Containing lemon, lime, and orange juices, this tart-savory dip is marvelous with Seafood Spring Roll Sticks (page 56). It also doubles as a sauce for seafood tempura and as a glaze for grilled or broiled fish.

Make sure to use fresh-squeezed juices for this; canned or bottled varieties lose their flavor when reduced and get an "off" flavor. The dip will last for one week, refrigerated.

MAKES ABOUT 1 CUP

1 tablespoon soy sauce
Juice of 1 orange
Juice of 1 lemon
Juice of 1 lime
1 tablespoon Dijon mustard
¼ cup fresh mint leaves
¼ cup canola oil
Salt and freshly ground black pepper

1. In a medium nonreactive saucepan, combine the soy sauce and orange, lemon, and lime juices and bring to a boil over medium heat. Turn down the heat and cook until reduced by half, 10 to 12 minutes. Cool to room temperature.

2. Transfer the soy mixture to a blender, add the mustard, and blend. Add the mint, blend, and add the oil slowly to emulsify. Season with salt and pepper to taste and use or store.

OILS DIPS AND SEASONINGS

Soy Ginger Glaze

A savory addition to Grilled Sushi Rice (page 76), this is similar to teriyaki sauce, but more delicate. It has many uses—brush it on grilled chicken or salmon or sprinkle it on vegetables. It will last, refrigerated, for two to three months. If chilled, bring the glaze to room temperature before using it.

MAKES 1½ CUPS

1 cup soy sauce
Juice and zest of 2 oranges
3 tablespoons brown sugar
1 tablespoon finely chopped fresh ginger

In a small bowl, combine the soy sauce, orange juice and zest, brown sugar, and ginger. Stir to dissolve the sugar and blend well. Use or store.

Soy Syrup

This thickish flavoring is a perfect seasoning or garnish for fish and all types of sushi. Store it, tightly covered, in the fridge, where it will last for a month. (In a pinch, you can substitute kechap manis, the Indonesian sweet soy sauce, for soy syrup.)

MAKES 2 CUPS

2 cups soy sauce
½ cup brown sugar
Juice of 1 lime

In a medium saucepan, combine the soy sauce, brown sugar, and lime juice. Bring to a boil slowly over medium heat, turn down the heat, and reduce the mixture by three-fourths or until syrupy, about 30 minutes. Strain, cool, and use or store.

Dijon-Sambal Aïoli

I love this garlicky-hot mayonnaise. It works equally well with a wide range of sandwich fillings, from turkey to baloney. Try it, too, mixed with diced cucumber as a tzatziki-like dip for pita or other bread.

Store this in an airtight container in the fridge, where it will keep for two weeks.

MAKES 2 CUPS

2 egg yolks
1 tablespoon sambal oelek
1 tablespoon Dijon mustard
2 cups canola oil
1 tablespoon fresh lemon juice
Salt and freshly ground black pepper

In a food processor, combine the yolks, sambal oelek, and mustard and process. With the machine running, add the oil slowly at first through the feed tube. When the mixture emulsifies, add the oil more quickly until the mixture is mayonnaise-like. Add the lemon juice, season with salt and pepper, and use or store.

MING'S TIP: SHOULD THE AÏOLI BREAK AS YOU'RE MAKING IT, STOP THE PROCESSOR, THEN ADD THE JUICE OF $1/2$ LEMON AND A FEW SMALL ICE CUBES TO THE MIXTURE. RESTART THE MACHINE AND CONTINUE. THE SAUCE SHOULD RE-EMULSIFY. IF IT DOESN'T, TRANSFER THE BROKEN AÏOLI TO A BOWL. CLEAN AND DRY THE PROCESSOR BOWL WELL, ADD AN EGG YOLK TO IT, AND PROCESS, DRIZZLING IN THE BROKEN AÏOLI GRADUALLY.

Pickled Ginger

O
I
L
S

D
I
P
S

A
N
D

S
E
A
S
O
N
I
N
G
S

Called *gari* or *sushōga* in Japanese, pickled ginger is an obligatory accompaniment to sushi. I like to use it also in vinaigrettes or in sandwiches, as you might use a cucumber pickle. A little Thai pepper gives this a pleasing kick.

The pickled ginger can be stored, refrigerated, for about one month.

MAKES ABOUT 2 CUPS

2 cups rice wine vinegar

1 tablespoon salt

$\frac{1}{2}$ cup sugar

1 small red beet, peeled and halved

2 bay leaves

$\frac{1}{2}$ tablespoon white peppercorns

2 Thai bird chiles

8 ounces ginger, peeled and cut into $\frac{1}{8}$-inch slices

In a medium saucepan, combine the vinegar, salt, sugar, beet, bay leaves, peppercorns, and chiles. Bring to a boil over high heat and add the ginger. Reduce the heat and simmer for about 30 minutes. Remove from the heat and cool, about $\frac{1}{2}$ hour. Transfer to a jar and refrigerate overnight.

MING'S TIP: THOUGH PICKLED GINGER WILL TURN A NICE PINK COLOR OVER TIME, I OFTEN USE BEETS OR RED SHISO LEAVES TO TINT THE PICKLE DELICATELY. THOUGH HARD TO COME BY, THE RED SHISO PROVIDES SUPERIOR COLOR AND AN HERBY FLAVOR.

Preserved Lemons

This is my take on the traditional North African ingredient and condiment, which is used in many Moroccan lamb and vegetable tagines. I feature it in Preserved Lemon Polenta (page 222) and also like its pungent flavor in meat sandwiches.

There's no trick to making the lemons, and once the pickling process is completed—a matter of one week—they last indefinitely in the refrigerator. (Be careful, though, not to use your fingers when removing the pickles, as they can introduce bacteria to the brine.) I slice the lemons into wedges to speed the process.

Though many recipes that call for preserved lemons specify that you use the peel only, I like to use both pulp and peel—why throw away the tasty lemon interior?

MAKES 1 QUART

10 lemons
1 quart freshly squeezed lemon juice
6 ⅛-inch-thick slices fresh ginger
6 Thai bird chiles
1 cup salt
1 cup sugar

1. Halve the lemons widthwise and cut each half into 4 wedges; remove the seeds.

2. In a clean, dry, wide-mouth 1-quart canning jar, combine the lemons, lemon juice, ginger, chiles, salt, and sugar. With a long-handled wooden spoon, stir well. Make sure the lemons are covered with liquid and the jar completely filled; add more juice if necessary.

3. Place the jar in the refrigerator for 1 week. Shake the jar every other day.

Curry Paste

This curry paste is really versatile. Use it to flavor curry dishes, or add it to mayonnaise for a superior sandwich spread. You can also combine it with chicken stock in the proportion of 1 tablespoon of paste for every 2 cups stock for a quick, flavorful soup.

Make extra of this; you'll use it. Store the paste in an airtight container, refrigerated, for up to two months.

MAKES 4 CUPS

⅓ cup Thai bird chiles

2 tablespoons cumin seeds

5 tablespoons coriander seeds

2 tablespoons black peppercorns, plus additional
    freshly ground

2 tablespoons ground turmeric

¼ cup peeled chopped galangal or fresh ginger

1 cup cilantro leaves and stems

½ cup chopped garlic

3 lemongrass stalks, white parts only, chopped

½ cup fresh lime juice

½ cup Thai fish sauce *(nam pla)*

1 cup medium shallots

2 tablespoons kosher salt, plus additional as needed

2 cups Asian peanut oil

1. In a small, heavy skillet, combine the chiles, cumin seeds, coriander seeds, and peppercorns and heat over medium heat, stirring occasionally, just until the spices start to smoke, about 6 minutes. Using a spice grinder, grind the spices finely and reserve.

2. In a food processor, combine the turmeric, galangal, cilantro, garlic, lemongrass, lime juice, and fish sauce and process to make a smooth puree. Add the shallots, reserved spices, and salt and puree again. With the machine running, drizzle in the oil to make a paste. Season with salt and pepper to taste, and use or store.

Thai Quince Chutney

Quince, with its penetrating perfume, makes a wonderful chutney. This sweet-tart accompaniment, fired by Thai chiles, is perfect with poultry of all kinds, or as a sandwich condiment. I particularly like to couple it with squab (page 132).

MAKES 3 CUPS

1 tablespoon canola oil
1 large red onion, cut into $\frac{1}{4}$-inch dice
4 Thai bird chiles, finely chopped
Salt and freshly ground black pepper
3 medium quinces, peeled, cored, and cut into $\frac{1}{4}$-inch dice
Juice of 1 lime

1. Heat a small skillet over medium heat. Add the oil and swirl to coat the bottom of the pan. When the oil shimmers, add the onion and the chiles and sauté, stirring, until brown, about 8 minutes. Season with the salt and pepper to taste.

2. Add the quinces and lime juice, reduce the heat to low, and cook, stirring occasionally, until the quinces are soft, about 20 minutes. Correct the seasonings, cool, and use or store.

MING'S TIP: WHEN SHOPPING FOR QUINCES, LOOK FOR RELATIVELY LARGE AROMATIC FRUIT, WHICH CAN BE PEELED MORE EASILY THAN SMALLER SPECIMENS. REMOVE THE HARD CENTERS WITH A SMALL, SHARP KNIFE.

Chapter 10

Desserts

THE ASIAN TABLE HAS MANY GLORIES BUT, WITHOUT THE BEN-
EFIT OF BUTTER, CREAM, AND OVENS FOR BAKING, LACKS
DESSERTS AS WE KNOW THEM. SOUFFLES, TARTS, PARFAITS,
MOUSSES—THERE'S NOTHING LIKE THEM IN THE ASIAN
REPERTOIRE.

My challenge, therefore, was to bring the Western dessert approach together
with Asian flavoring ingredients, and to make such a marriage really work. The
results have been gratifying. Better still, they've yielded fabulous finales like
Green Tea Mousse with Sake-Marinated Dried Cherries or Lemongrass Parfait—dishes that strike just the right East-West note while delivering dessert
thrills. Jasmine Tea Soufflés, for example, are served with scoops of fragrant ice
cream that's allowed to melt in the soufflés. It's an awesome combination of hot
and cold, airy and creamy and represents the tea's subtle perfume beautifully.

Not all these desserts are full-dress. Honey Sesame Tuiles—meltingly thin cookies you can make in their traditional roof-tile shape, as little bowls to hold ice cream or sorbet, as thin rolls or as "fortune cookies"—are a simple but sophisticated nibble. And the Homemade Ginger Ale Float is a perfect summer dessert featuring ginger ale you make yourself. Once you've prepared your own ginger ale, a simple process, you'll find it hard to drink the bottled kind.

I haven't abandoned Eastern sweets entirely. Glutinous Rice with Coconut and Mango is my take on a traditional Asian snack, enhanced with vanilla and tangy mango. Prepared in a banana leaf for its subtle perfume, the dish is the East's answer to rice pudding—and also makes an intriguing accompaniment to spicy foods.

For a gala meal ending with surprisingly little work, Tropical Fruit Granité with a Champagne Splash definitely fills the bill. Served in tuile bowls or champagne glasses, this suave but remarkably easy-to-make sweet is another example of true East-West dessert making.

Lemongrass Parfait
with Pineapple Salsa

A parfait flavored with the fresh tang of lemongrass represents the best of two culinary worlds: French and Southeast Asian.

I developed this exploration of taste and textural contrast—cold and hot, mild and pungent—after some experimentation with a lemongrass ice cream. The parfait is close to ice cream, but doesn't have to be churned; it's also lighter, thanks to the inclusion of whipped cream (a typical parfait ingredient). The addition of warm pineapple salsa, heated with a little pepper, raises the multicultural stakes and adds zip. You'll need eight 3×2-inch dessert rings or eight 5- to 6-ounce ramekins for the parfaits.

BEVERAGE TIP: LATE HARVEST SEMILLON (CHALK HILL)

SERVES 8

3 cups heavy cream
10 lemongrass stalks, white parts only, thinly sliced
3 tablespoons pure vanilla extract
4 vanilla beans, preferably Tahitian
12 egg yolks plus 6 eggs
1¾ cups confectioners' sugar

PINEAPPLE SALSA
1 pineapple, peeled, cored, and cut into ¼-inch dice
Juice of 1 orange
½ teaspoon freshly ground white pepper
1 tablespoon pink peppercorns

1. In a medium nonreactive saucepan, combine the cream, lemongrass, and vanilla extract. Halve the vanilla beans and scrape the seeds into the cream. Add the beans and bring just to a boil over high heat. Immediately reduce the heat to low and simmer, uncovered, until the mixture has reduced by one-fourth, about 30 minutes. Remove from the heat and cool, then refrigerate, covered, for at least 6 hours and preferably overnight.

2. Chill a medium bowl. Strain the cream into the bowl, discarding the lemongrass. Beat until stiff peaks form.

3. In the top of a double boiler over barely simmering water, combine the egg yolks and confectioners' sugar and cook, whisking constantly, until the mixture forms a ribbon when the whisk is lifted from the pan, 12 to 15 minutes. Transfer to a mixer bowl and beat at high speed until lightened and pale in color, about 10 minutes. Fold in the whipped cream. If using the dessert rings, place them on a parchment-lined baking sheet that will fit into your freezer. Pour the mixture into the molds and freeze until firm, at least 8 hours and preferably overnight.

4. While the parfaits chill, prepare the salsa. Heat a medium nonstick saucepan over high heat. Add the pineapple and sear, stirring, about 1 minute. Reduce the heat to medium, add the orange juice and white pepper, and cook until the pineapple is tender-firm, 3 to 5 minutes. Keep warm.

5. To unmold the parfaits, place each on a serving dish, warm the sides of the rings with your hands, and lift off the rings. If using ramekins, dip them in hot water for no more than 5 seconds and invert the parfaits onto plates. Surround with the warm pineapple salsa, garnish with the pink peppercorns, and serve.

MING'S TIP: MAKE THESE IN ADVANCE—THEY NEED TO BE STARTED AT LEAST A DAY AHEAD TO BE WELL FLAVORED AND TO FREEZE.

Green Tea Mousse
with Sake-Marinated Dried Cherries

This creamy yet light mousse is flavored with green tea. Unlike other tea-flavored desserts you may have tried, this one really delivers the subtle flavor of the tea. The mousse is presented in a marble sponge cake "case," and is accompanied by a tart cherry garnish. This delightful dessert is especially nice in warm weather or after a rich meal. Thanks are due to my pastry chef, Marina Brancely, who came up with this winner.

Use six $2\frac{1}{2} \times 2$-inch dessert molds for the mousse.

BEVERAGE TIP: JAPANESE GREEN TEA

SERVES 6

1 cup water
8 green tea bags

CHERRIES
½ cup sake
½ cup sugar
2 ounces dried
    cherries
¼ cup water

MOUSSE
¾ cup milk
4 tablespoons sugar
3 eggs, separated
1 cup heavy cream
2 teaspoons powdered
    unflavored gelatin

Marble Sponge Cake
(page 250)

1. To make the tea for the mousse, bring the water to a boil. Steep 6 of the tea bags in the water 10 to 15 minutes; the tea should be very strong. Cool to room temperature and chill.

2. To make the cherry accompaniment, combine the sake, sugar, cherries, and water in a small saucepan and bring to a boil over medium heat. Remove from the heat, cool to room temperature, and chill, about 30 minutes.

3. To make the mousse, combine the milk with the contents of the remaining 2 tea bags in a medium saucepan and bring to a simmer over medium heat. Remove from the stove and allow the mixture to steep about 20 minutes.

4. Return the milk mixture to the stove and bring to a simmer over low heat. Meanwhile, in a medium bowl, whisk together 2 tablespoons of the sugar and the egg yolks. Whisk the milk mixture gradually into the egg mixture. Transfer this mixture to the saucepan and heat over medium-low heat, stirring, until the mixture thickens slightly, 3 to 5 minutes. Transfer to a medium bowl and cool to room temperature.

5. Whip the cream until it holds medium-soft peaks and reserve, refrigerated. Add the remaining 2 tablespoons of sugar to the egg whites and whip until medium-stiff peaks form.

6. Set up a double boiler. In the top, combine the gelatin with 3 tablespoons of the chilled tea (discard the rest); the mixture will become thick. Cook, stirring, until the gelatin has become liquid, 3 to 5 minutes.

7. Add the gelatin mixture to the milk mixture and stir to combine. Gently fold in the whipped whites, and then fold in the whipped cream just until combined.

8. Using a dessert mold, cut 6 circles from the sponge cake. From the remaining cake, use a paring knife to cut six 1 × 5-inch strips. Spray the molds with nonstick cooking spray and place them on a cookie sheet. Line the sides of each mold with a cake strip and fit a sponge cake circle into each. It will be a tight fit; trim the sponge as necessary. Spoon about 5 cherries onto the sponge bases and spoon on some of the syrup to moisten them. Fill the molds with the mousse and chill at least 3 hours and preferably overnight.

9. To serve the mousse, warm the sides of the molds with your hands. Release the mousse by pushing the bottoms up through the molds with your hands, or rest the bottoms against a soup can and press the rings down. Transfer each serving to a plate and surround with the remaining marinated cherries.

MING'S TIP: IF YOU PREFER NOT TO USE THE SPONGE CAKE, SPOON THE UNCHILLED MOUSSE ONTO ATTRACTIVE DESSERT DISHES OR INTO MARTINI GLASSES (ADD A FEW OF THE CHERRIES FIRST IF USING THE GLASSES) AND SPOON THE CHERRY ACCOMPANIMENT OVER EACH SERVING.

Marble Sponge Cake

MAKES A 12 × 18 × 1-INCH SHEET CAKE

1⅓ cups cake flour
6 large eggs
¾ cup sugar
¼ cup canola oil
1 tablespoon unsweetened cocoa powder

1. Preheat the oven to 350°F and set up a double boiler. Grease a 12 × 18-inch sheet pan and line it with parchment paper.

2. Sift the flour twice onto a sheet of parchment or waxed paper and set aside.

3. In the top of the double boiler, combine the eggs and sugar. Place over, but not touching, simmering water and heat, whisking constantly, until the mixture is very warm to the touch (about 110°F). Transfer the mixture to a medium bowl and, using a mixer set at high speed, beat the mixture until it has tripled in volume and is no longer warm, about 15 minutes. Fold in the flour and then the oil.

4. Transfer ½ cup of the batter to a small bowl, add the cocoa powder, and blend. Using a finger, spread the chocolate batter over the sheet pan in a marbleized pattern. Pour the remaining batter over the chocolate batter and spread it evenly with a spatula to cover the chocolate batter completely.

5. Bake until a cake tester inserted into the cake comes out clean, 7 to 10 minutes. Invert the cake onto a large rack, allow to cool, and peel off the parchment.

Glutinous Rice with Coconut and Mango

This refreshing dessert is based on a traditional Southeast Asian dish that appears at many festive occasions, both familial and religious. To enhance the original, I've added vanilla to the rice and mango, which accentuates the sweetness.

The recipe calls for steaming the rice on a large banana leaf, the customary cooking method. I urge you to prepare the rice this way for the subtle flavor the leaf imparts. You can, however, steam the rice on cheesecloth and the results will be almost as tasty.

BEVERAGE TIP: MUSCAT FROM BEAUMES DE VENISE

SERVES 4

2¼ cups glutinous rice
1 teaspoon pure vanilla extract
½ cup unsweetened flaked coconut
½ teaspoon freshly ground white pepper
1 large ripe mango, peeled and cut into ¼-inch dice
½ cup unsweetened coconut milk

1. A day in advance, place the rice in a bowl, add water, and swish the rice to wash it. Pour off the water, replace it, and swish the rice again. Repeat as necessary until the water runs clear. Cover with water and add the vanilla. Refrigerate overnight to flavor the rice.

2. Preheat the oven to 350°F. Spread the coconut on a baking sheet and toast until golden, 6 to 8 minutes. Toss occasionally and watch carefully to prevent burning. Set aside.

3. Rinse a banana leaf with water and fold it in quarters. With a scissors, snip the folded point to make a 2- to 3-inch circle when the leaf is opened. Set up a bamboo steamer and line the steaming tray with the leaf. Alternatively, line the steamer basket with cheesecloth. Drain the rice and arrange it on the leaf in a ½-inch-thick ring around the central hole. If steaming in cheesecloth, distribute the rice evenly over the cheesecloth. Steam the rice until fully cooked but not mushy, about 45 minutes. The rice will be sticky.

4. Transfer the rice to a large serving bowl and add the pepper and mango. Add the coconut milk and toss lightly. Garnish with the toasted coconut and serve hot.

MING'S TIP: I SOMETIMES SERVE THE RICE AS AN ENTREE ACCOMPA-
NIMENT—IT GOES BEAUTIFULLY WITH SPICY SHRIMP. IF YOU PAIR THE
TWO, JUST MAKE SURE THAT THE SHRIMP ARE VERY WELL SEASONED.

East-West Spice Cake
with Cardamom Cream

While working in France I discovered a fruitcake at Fauchon, the famous food emporium. The cake was spicy and good, but the candied fruit was too sweet for my taste. When I tried my hand at re-creating the cake I replaced the fruit with candied ginger, and ended up with a truly delicious confection. A cardamom-flavored cream gives a fragrant finish. The result has zip and a fine spice balance.

   I could have called this "cakes"—it's baked in eight individual ramekins (though you can also use a cake pan). Any unused cakes can be frozen. You can also make the cream ahead and store it, refrigerated, in an airtight container.

BEVERAGE TIP: BLACK LYCHEE TEA

SERVES 8

$\frac{2}{3}$ cup cake flour
$\frac{2}{3}$ cup all-purpose flour
1 teaspoon baking soda
$\frac{1}{4}$ teaspoon ground cinnamon
$\frac{1}{3}$ teaspoon ground cloves
$\frac{1}{8}$ teaspoon freshly ground black pepper
$\frac{1}{2}$ cup granulated sugar
1 egg
$\frac{1}{2}$ cup canola oil
$\frac{1}{2}$ cup molasses
$\frac{1}{4}$ cup minced candied ginger,
   or 2 tablespoons finely chopped fresh
   ginger plus 1 tablespoon sugar
$\frac{1}{2}$ cup water

CREAM
1 cup heavy cream
$\frac{1}{4}$ cup brown sugar
1 teaspoon ground cardamom

Mint leaves, for garnish

1. Preheat the oven to 300°F. In a medium bowl, combine the flours, baking soda, cinnamon, cloves, and black pepper and stir to blend.

2. In a large mixing bowl, combine the sugar, egg, oil, molasses, and ginger. Using an electric mixer set at medium speed, beat the mixture until well blended. With the machine running, add the water and mix to incorporate.

3. Remove the bowl from the machine and fold in the dry ingredients by hand until well incorporated. Spray eight 4-ounce ramekins or a round 8- to 10-inch cake pan with non-stick cooking spray and fill with the batter. Bake until a cake tester inserted into the middle of the individual cake(s) comes out clean, 20 to 25 minutes. If using the cake pan, bake 30 to 35 minutes.

4. Meanwhile, prepare the cream. In a chilled bowl, combine the cream, brown sugar, and cardamom and whip until stiff peaks form. Refrigerate.

5. To serve, allow the cakes to cool to room temperature (or serve them warm) and unmold onto 8 serving plates or a plate. Garnish each cake with a dollop of the cream and the mint leaves.

Tahitian Vanilla Crème Brûlée

Few eating pleasures are greater than a mouthful of this creamy custard with its crackling caramel topping. Everyone loves the combo. There are many flavored crème brûlées around—I've seen them spiked with tea, with lemongrass, with ginger, with coffee, and with fruit. When it comes to this incomparable dessert, however, I'm a purist: classic is best. And this version is classic classic.

I'd be lying if I said that this is a true East-West dish; the vanilla beans from the South Pacific are as close to Asia as this dessert gets. In any case, try to get Tahitian beans—they're particularly plump and fragrant—though any fresh vanilla beans will do.

BEVERAGE TIP: SNIFTER OF MYERS'S DARK RUM

SERVES 8

1 cup half-and-half
1 vanilla bean, preferably Tahitian
½ teaspoon pure vanilla extract
1 egg plus 8 egg yolks
⅔ cup granulated sugar
1½ cups heavy cream, cold
4 tablespoons superfine sugar
  (see Tip)

1. Preheat the oven to 325°F. In a small saucepan, combine the half-and-half, vanilla bean, and vanilla extract. Heat over medium heat just until scalded; do not allow the mixture to boil.

2. Fill a large bowl with water and add ice. In a medium mixing bowl, combine the egg, egg yolks, and granulated sugar and mix. Gradually stir in the scalded half-and-half mixture and place the smaller bowl in the bowl of ice water to cool completely. Stir in the heavy cream and divide among eight 4-ounce ramekins. Place in a baking dish just large enough to hold them and add enough hot water to the pan to come halfway up the sides of the ramekins. Cover the baking dish tightly with foil and bake until the custard is set but still quivers in the center, about 35 minutes. Remove the ramekins from the water and refrigerate to cool completely.

3. Preheat the broiler, if using. Sprinkle 1 tablespoon of the sugar on top of each custard, spread over the surface, and tap out any excess. Place the ramekins on a broiling tray and broil until the top is melted and caramelized, about 30 seconds. Watch carefully; the sugar can burn easily. If using a torch (see Tip), pass the flame about 2 inches over the surface of the custards until the sugar is completely caramelized. Serve while the sugar is still warm.

MING'S TIP: TO CARAMELIZE THE SUGAR COATING, USE EITHER A BROILER OR PROPANE TORCH. WORKING WITH THE LATTER MAY SEEM SCARY, BUT TORCHES ARE EASILY HANDLED AND ARE BEAUTIFULLY EFFICIENT. LOOK FOR A SMALL VERSION, OFTEN CALLED A KITCHEN TORCH. IF USING A TORCH, REPLACE THE SUPERFINE SUGAR WITH RAW SUGAR, WHICH CARAMELIZES MORE SUCCESSFULLY UNDER A TORCH FLAME.

Honey Sesame Tuiles

Tuiles—those delicate, roof tile–shaped cookies—are a delicious staple of the French pâtisserie. Substituting sesame seeds for the usual almonds is my new spin. The addition of lychee honey to the batter provides a deeper, more fragrant sweetness than sugar alone.

These tuiles are versatile, too. You can form them in many ways: over a rolling pin to make the classic curved shape; draped over ramekins to produce pretty cookie bowls for ice cream or fruit; rolled into thin cylinders for garnishing; or folded to produce tuile "fortune cookies"—definitely the East-West favorite.

MAKES 20

½ pound (2 sticks) butter, at room temperature
2 cups confectioners' sugar
½ cup lychee honey or any pure honey
1 cup egg whites (about 8 eggs)
2 cups sifted all-purpose flour
¼ cup white sesame seeds

1. Preheat the oven to 300°F. In a mixing bowl, combine the butter and sugar and beat until creamy. Add the honey and beat until blended. Add the egg whites and mix. Add the flour all at once and mix until the batter is smooth.

2. Line a medium baking sheet with parchment paper or spray it lightly with nonstick cooking spray. Have a small bowl of water handy. Working in batches, drop the batter by measuring tablespoons about 3 inches apart. Wet a finger in the water and spread the cookies using a circular motion to a diameter of 4 to 5 inches and a thickness of about $\frac{1}{16}$ inch. Sprinkle the tuiles with the sesame seeds and bake until golden brown, 8 to 10 minutes. Watch the tuiles carefully because they can brown quickly.

3. Remove from the oven, and as soon as you can touch them comfortably, use a wide thin-bladed metal spatula to drape them over a rolling pin. Once the tuiles are firm, remove them to racks to cool. To make cookie bowls, drape the tuiles over inverted 3-inch ramekins, and transfer the cookies to racks when firm. To make cookie cylinders, roll the tuiles around a round wooden spoon handle. For fortune cookies, fold the still-pliable cookies in half and in half again, bring the 2 points at opposite ends of the curved side together, and tuck the cookies into egg-carton cavities. Allow to firm.

MING'S TIPS: DON'T WORRY IF THE TUILES HARDEN BEFORE YOU CAN FORM THEM. JUST REHEAT THEM BRIEFLY IN THE OVEN, WHERE THEY WILL RESOFTEN, AND FORM THEM AS DESIRED.

FOR A MORE TROPICAL FLAVOR YOU CAN SUBSTITUTE UNSWEETENED COCONUT FOR THE SESAME SEEDS.

Tropical Fruit Granité
with a Champagne Splash

This simple granité, fragrant with mango and passion fruit, is perfect for people who like frozen desserts but don't have, or don't want to bother with, an ice cream machine. To make it, you prepare a puree, freeze it overnight on a tray, scrape it into tuile bowls (page 256) or pretty dishes, and that's it. The secret ingredient in this, if there is one, is Champagne; it provides a burst of sophisticated flavor that people really love. (You could, however, omit it, in which case the granité will freeze a bit harder.) Serve this to end a meal of rich dishes, or between courses as a palate cleanser—it's light and refreshing.

BEVERAGE TIP: ANY BLANC DE BLANC CHAMPAGNE

SERVES 8

8 passion fruits or the juice of 3 limes
2 mangoes, peeled, 1½ chopped roughly, ½ sliced thinly, for garnish
2 cups fresh orange juice
½ cup Blanc de Blanc or other Champagne
Zest of 2 oranges, 1 tablespoon reserved for garnish
4 tuile bowls (page 256; optional)

1. Cut the shell tip from each passion fruit and scrape the pulp into a sieve placed over a bowl. Using a rubber spatula, press down on the pulp to extract the juice in the bowl. Discard the pulp and seeds.

2. Place the chopped mango in a food processor and puree until very smooth. Add the passion fruit juice (or lime juice), orange juice, wine, and orange zest, and pulse twice to incorporate. Transfer the mixture to a 10×10-inch pan. Freeze overnight.

3. If using tuile bowls, with the side of a fork, scrape a small amount of the granité onto the centers of 4 plates and top with the bowls (the granité will anchor them). Scrape additional granité into the bowls. Alternatively, scrape granité into serving dishes. Garnish with the mango slices and reserved orange zest and serve.

MING'S TIP: PASSION FRUIT IS AVAILABLE YEAR-ROUND. LOOK FOR SPECIMENS THAT ARE LARGE AND HEAVY, A SIGN THAT THEY'RE FILLED WITH PULP. THE FRUIT SHOULD BE RELATIVELY SOFT AND SOUND SLOSHY WHEN SHAKEN. PASSION FRUIT SYRUP OR PUREE WILL ALSO WORK QUITE WELL.

Jasmine Tea Soufflés

Subtly flavored with Chinese tea, this is a celebratory dessert—and a good exercise in soufflé making. It's not difficult to prepare, however; just follow the detailed instructions. The contrast of hot and cold, airy and dense, makes this a memorable meal conclusion.

BEVERAGE TIP: ANY WINE FROM SAUTERNES (CHATEAU RIEUSSEC OR CHATEAU D'YQUEM)

SERVES 6

½ cup jasmine tea leaves
¼ cup oolong tea leaves
3 cups heavy cream
1 cup milk
2 vanilla beans, preferably Tahitian,
    split lengthwise and scraped
½ cup pure honey
10 eggs, separated
½ cup cornstarch
½ cup granulated sugar
Confectioners' sugar
Lemongrass Ice Cream
    (page 262)

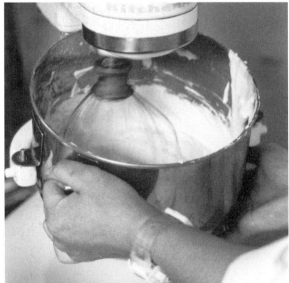

1. Heat the oven to 375°F. Butter six 4- to 5-inch ramekins and sprinkle lightly with sugar to coat. In a medium nonreactive saucepan, combine the teas, cream, milk, and vanilla beans and heat over low heat. Simmer to flavor, about 20 minutes. Remove from the heat and allow to steep for an hour or so.

2. Strain the mixture, return it to the saucepan, and add the honey. Scald over medium heat. Meanwhile, in a nonreactive bowl, combine the egg yolks, cornstarch, and $\frac{1}{4}$ cup of the granulated sugar and mix well. Add a ladleful of the tea mixture to the yolks, stir to temper, and stir the yolk mixture back into the saucepan. Cook, whisking constantly, until the mixture thickens to the consistency of thick custard, 6 to 8 minutes. Transfer to a shallow baking pan, cover the surface of the mixture with plastic film, and refrigerate to cool. The mixture can be held overnight.

3. Place a heavy cookie sheet in the oven. Using a mixer, beat the egg whites at low speed with 1 tablespoon of the sugar until soft peaks form. Add the remaining 3 tablespoons of sugar, increase the speed to high, and whip the egg whites in two 3-second bursts.

4. Transfer the cooled tea mixture to a large nonreactive bowl and whisk until smooth. You should have an equal volume of the tea mixture and the egg whites; if not, discard enough of whichever is in excess to make the quantities equal. Add the whites to the tea mixture and, using a spatula, fold until completely blended. Fill the ramekins to the top with the mixture and tap them on a work surface to disperse any air bubbles. Wipe away any mixture that splatters on the sides of the molds. Place the ramekins on the heated sheet and bake until the sides of the soufflés, which will have risen above the edges of the ramekins, are golden brown, about 12 minutes. After 6 minutes check to make sure that the soufflés have not adhered to the sides of the ramekins, which will cause uneven rising; use the tip of a sharp paring knife to free any stuck portions.

5. Sprinkle the soufflés with the confectioners' sugar and serve. Scoop the ice cream into the soufflés at table.

MING'S TIPS: NOTE THAT WHEN MAKING THE SOUFFLÉS, AIR IS BEATEN INTO THE EGG WHITES SLOWLY AND IN TWO STAGES. THIS AVOIDS INCORPORATING TOO MUCH AIR TOO QUICKLY AND HELPS TO ENSURE A LIGHT RESULT.

WHEN CHECKING THE PROGRESS OF THE SOUFFLÉS HALFWAY THROUGH THEIR BAKING, DO IT QUICKLY AND AVOID BANGING THE OVEN DOOR.

Lemongrass Ice Cream

This tempting dessert can also be flavored with cardamom (see Variation).

BEVERAGE TIP: NIVOLE MOSCATO D'ASTI (BANYLUS)

SERVES 6

3 cups milk
8 lemongrass stalks, white parts only, sliced $1/4$ inch thick
1 vanilla bean, preferably Tahitian, split lengthwise and scraped
$3/4$ cup egg yolks (5 to 6 large eggs)
1 cup plus 2 tablespoons sugar
2 cups heavy cream

1. In a nonreactive medium saucepan, combine the milk, lemongrass, and vanilla bean and heat over medium heat until scalded. Turn the heat to low and simmer until the mixture is reduced by one-third, about 15 minutes. Remove from the heat and allow to steep at least 1 hour and preferably overnight; the longer it steeps, the more flavor will develop. Strain the mixture, return the milk to the saucepan, and bring just to the point of boiling.

2. Meanwhile, fill a medium bowl with cold water and add ice. In a nonreactive medium bowl, combine the yolks and the sugar and whisk to blend. Add a ladleful of the scalded milk mixture to the yolk mixture, mix well, and transfer the tempered yolk mixture to the saucepan. Cook over medium heat, whisking, until thickened, about 5 minutes. Do not overcook or the eggs will scramble.

3. Strain the mixture into a medium bowl, and place it in the bowl of ice water to cool. When cool, add the cream, and stir to blend. Freeze in an ice cream maker following the manufacturer's instructions. Do not overharden; the ice cream should have a soft consistency. Transfer to the freezer.

VARIATION: CARDAMOM ICE CREAM. Use 8 crushed cardamom pods or $1/2$ tablespoon toasted ground cardamom in place of the lemongrass. Steep the cardamom in the milk and proceed as above.

Homemade Ginger Ale Float
with Lemongrass Ice Cream and Ginger Candy

This float is an awesome summer dessert, fragrant and cooling. And to gild the lily there's a chewy ginger candy accompaniment.

As a kid, I'd visit soda fountains and see the countermen concocting drinks from flavored syrups and carbonated water. Years later I learned to prepare sugar syrups for desserts. Put these memories together, add the recollection of my mom making ginger tea (great for upset stomachs and sore throats), and you now know how this dessert came into being.

The ginger ale and candy are, of course, delicious on their own.

SERVES 4

2 cups fresh ginger cut into $\frac{1}{8}$-inch slices (about 2 large "hands")
4 cups sugar
2 cups water
1 quart club soda, well chilled
1 lime, quartered
Lemongrass Ice Cream (page 262)
4 mint sprigs

1. To make the syrup, combine the ginger, 2 cups of the sugar, and the water in a medium saucepan and bring to a boil over high heat. Reduce the heat and simmer until syrupy or reduced by half, 40 to 45 minutes. The syrup will thicken as it cools so don't overreduce it. Strain the syrup and reserve the ginger.

2. Preheat the oven to 225°F. To make the candy, place the remaining 2 cups sugar in a large bowl, add the reserved ginger, and toss to coat on all sides. Place the ginger on a baking sheet and bake until dried but still chewy, about 3 hours.

3. To make the floats, fill four 8-ounce glasses with the club soda. Pour 2 tablespoons of the ginger syrup down the side of each glass (4 if you prefer a sweeter float). Squeeze a lime wedge into each drink, add a scoop of the ice cream, and garnish with a mint sprig. Serve with the candy.

MING'S TIP: WHEN ADDING THE GINGER SYRUP TO THE SODA WATER, GO SLOWLY, EASING THE SYRUP DOWN THE SIDE OF THE GLASSES. THE SYRUP WILL FORM AN ATTRACTIVE LAYER AT THE BOTTOM OF THE GLASSES. REMIND GUESTS TO STIR THEIR FLOATS BEFORE PARTAKING.

Bittersweet Chocolate Cake
with Cardamom Ice Cream and Chocolate Sauce

I think every chef has made a version of flourless chocolate cake, but the one I offer here is the best, guaranteed. Credit for the recipe goes to master pastry chef Bo Friberg, who passed it on to my pastry chef, Marina Brancely, before she came to Blue Ginger. The dessert got Marina her job!

As good as the cake is, it's even better when served with cardamom ice cream and a rich chocolate sauce. This is the kind of dessert that everyone loves, kids to grown-ups.

BEVERAGE TIP: BLACK GRENACHES (BANYULS)

SERVES 6

CAKE
½ cup sugar plus 1½ tablespoons
⅓ cup water
3 ounces bittersweet chocolate, roughly chopped
3½ ounces unsweetened chocolate, roughly chopped
9 tablespoons (1 stick plus 1 tablespoon) butter, cubed
3 large eggs, at room temperature

SAUCE
3 ounces bittersweet chocolate
½ cup heavy cream

Cocoa powder, for garnish
Cardamom Ice Cream (see Variation, page 262)
Chocolate curls, for garnish
   (optional; see Tip)

1. To make the cake, preheat the oven to 300°F. In a medium saucepan, combine the ½ cup of the sugar with the water and bring to a boil, stirring, over high heat.

2. Meanwhile, combine the chocolates and the butter in a medium bowl. When the sugar mixture boils, pour it over the chocolates and stir until blended. Set aside.

3. In a large mixing bowl, combine the 1½ tablespoons sugar and the eggs. Using a mixer set at high speed, whip the eggs and sugar until the mixture falls back onto itself in a slowly dissolving ribbonlike pattern when the beater is lifted. Add one-third of the egg mixture to the chocolate mixture and fold in with a spatula to lighten. Fold in the remaining egg mixture.

4. Bring a kettle of water to a boil. Spray six 6-ounce ramekins or six 2 × 3-inch loaf pans with nonstick cooking spray and place them in a roasting pan just large enough to hold them. Divide the batter among the ramekins or pans, place the roasting pan in the oven, and add enough water to the pan to come three-fourths of the way up the sides of the ramekins. Bake until a cake tester inserted in the middle of the cakes comes out with just a few crumbs sticking to it, about 30 minutes. Allow the cakes to cool to room temperature, about 30 minutes.

5. While the cakes bake, make the sauce. In a small saucepan, combine the chocolate and cream and heat over low heat, stirring constantly, until the chocolate is melted. Cool for at least 30 minutes.

6. To serve, dust the serving plates with the cocoa. Invert the ramekins onto the plates and add a scoop of the ice cream to each. Drizzle the chocolate sauce over the cake and ice cream, sprinkle with the chocolate curls, if using, and serve.

MING'S TIP: TO MAKE THE CHOCOLATE CURLS, USE 1 LARGE BAR OF SEMISWEET CHOCOLATE. HOLD A LARGE KNIFE WITH TWO HANDS, ONE ON THE HANDLE AND THE OTHER ON THE TIP. TILT THE KNIFE SO THAT IT IS AT A 60° ANGLE TO THE SURFACE OF THE CHOCOLATE AND SCRAPE IT TOWARD YOU. AS THEY ARE MADE, TRANSFER THE CURLS TO A LARGE SHEET OF PLASTIC FILM. WRAP THE CURLS LOOSELY IN THE FILM AND STORE AT ROOM TEMPERATURE.

Mail Order Sources

D'Artagnan
280 Wilson Avenue
Newark, NJ 07105
800-327-8246 ext. 118
fax: (973) 465-1870
www.dartagnan.com
Foie gras and game birds

Hudson Valley Foie Gras
80 Brooks Road
New York, NY 12734
(516) 773-4400
fax: (516) 773-4434
Foie gras

Kalustyan's
123 Lexington Avenue
New York, NY 10016
(212) 685-3451
fax: (212) 683-8458
www.kalustyans.com
Rices and grains, spices,
seasonings, vinegars, and
more

Kan Man Foods
200 Canal Street
New York, NY 10013
(212) 571-0330
fax: (212) 766-9085
Chinese and Japanese
products

Katagiri
224 East 59th Street
New York, NY 10022
(212) 755-3566
fax: (212) 752-4197
www.katagiri.com
Japanese noodles,
seasonings, spices, and
pickles

Kyocera America, Inc.
8611 Balboa Ave.
San Diego, CA
800-537-0294
fax: (858) 569-9412
www.kyocera.com

Oriental Food Market and
   Cooking School, Inc.
2801 West Howard Street
Chicago, IL 60645
(773) 274-2826
Chinese products and
spices

Penzeys Spices
W19362 Apollo Drive
Muskego, WI 53150
800-741-7787
fax: (414) 574-0278
www.penzeys.com
Spices and flavorings

Professional Cutlery
   Direct
242 Branford Road
North Branford, CT 06471
800-859-6994
fax: (203) 871-1010
www.cutlery.com
Ming Tsai's signature
series of ceramic knives
and other cooking
accessories

Urbani U.S.A.
29-24 40th Avenue
Long Island City, NY
   11101
or 5851 West Washington
   Blvd.
Culver City, CA 90232
800-281-2330
www.urbani.com
Truffles and truffle
products

For more information, you
can visit these web sites:
www.blueginger.net and
www.mingtsai.com.

Afterword

How many Yale graduates with engineering degrees and professional squash careers go on to win an Emmy Award? Then again, how many of them have their own award-winning restaurants?

We first met Ming Tsai when he made a memorable appearance on Food Network's *In Food Today,* and we instantly recognized a distinct personality who appealed to novice and expert cooks alike.

But then Ming Tsai's always been ahead of the curve.

In an era when Asian cooking was popular, Ming broke new culinary ground at his restaurant, Blue Ginger, by uniting Asian and Western cuisines. Blue Ginger then ran away with a "Best New Restaurant" award from *Boston Magazine* and a Chef of the Year award from *Esquire*. A National Association of Minorities in Cable award soon followed, and then the Emmy, the ultimate recognition of television achievement.

We consider ourselves fortunate and, of course, very smart, to have Ming Tsai's groundbreaking television show *East Meets West with Ming Tsai* on Food Network.

Every episode showcases the reach of his imagination and the breadth of his culinary prowess. In watching his show and preparing his recipes, people all over the world discover that great food happens when east meets west under the guidance of the masterful Ming Tsai.

Eric Ober,
President and General Manager,
Food Network

Acknowledgments

Both authors would like to thank their superlative editor, Pam Krauss, for her keen eye and ready ear, for her commitment to the book—and for keeping us on schedule! Thanks also to other Potter family members: Barbara Marks, Amy Boorstein, Joy Sikorski, Marysarah Quinn, Maggie Hinders, and Chloe Smith, whose attention to so many details, large and small, was greatly appreciated.

My thanks to the Food Network family: Eric Ober, Eileen Opatut, Heidi Diamond, Lesia Figueira, Bill Calamita, Sheila Feren, and Kelli Stitch. Deepest appreciation to Georgia Downard and Susan Stockton and the entire culinary team, and most importantly, my fabulous producer, Julia Harrison.

To co-author Arthur Boehm, who put me and my cooking on paper with patience and persistence and who constantly kept us on time—a big thank you.

Much appreciation to photographer extraordinaire Alan Richardson and his macchiato-drinking assistants, Alessandra Mortola and Brad Paris, who made my food come alive on the page. Thanks also to Subtitle, who gave the pages their clean look, and to Douglas Lew, who designed the sun and moon chop, the literal translation of my name.

Thanks to my agents Jon Rosen, Larry Kramer, and especially Michael Carlisle, assisted by Mary Beth Brown, who believed in the book from the start and helped bring it into the world.

To all my investors in Blue Ginger, especially my parents, Steve and Iris Tsai, Dr. Tom Olsen, Ming-Hsi and Linda Tsai, all of whom had faith in the project, my deepest thanks.

Last, but not least, to my entire Blue Ginger team, including most notably Budi Kazali, Amy Trujillo, Tom Berry, Marina Brancely, and Marco Hunter-Melo, my thanks and appreciation.
—M.T.

My love and thanks, as ever, to Judy Fireman and Judy Gingold for their sweet support. Thanks, too, to Nick Malgieri, master baker and friend, for his ever-thoughtful attention.

To Ming Tsai, for his wonderful food and the pleasure of writing about it, much appreciation.

Love and thanks, of course, to Leonore Boehm and to Richard Getke, still the best of all dining partners.
—A.B.

Index

Accompaniments. *See also* Chutney; Oils; Sauce
Black Bean Aïoli, 148–49
Chile Paste, 116–17
Curry Paste, 240
Dijon-Sambal Aïoli, 237
Ginger Candy, 263
Pickled Ginger, 238
Preserved Lemons, 239
Sake-Marinated Dried Cherries, 248–49
Achiote Duck Breasts with Sweet Potato Puree, Asian Pear Chutney, and Spiced Pecans, 194–95
Ahi Tuna, Asparagus-Crusted, with Asparagus Vinaigrette, 66–67
Ahi Tuna Parfait with Two Caviars, 170–71
Aïoli, Black Bean, 148–49
Aïoli, Dijon-Sambal, 237
Almond Sauce, Spicy, 68–69
Alsatian Seared Duck Breast with Foie Gras Sauce, 191–93
Appetizers. *See also* Dim Sum
Asparagus-Crusted Ahi Tuna with Asparagus Vinaigrette, 66–67
Braised Triple Cabbage Lasagna, 210
Grilled Sushi Rice with Soy Ginger Glaze, 76
New Hamachi Sashimi with Curry Oil, 64
Shrimp Toast, 24–25
Spinach Tofu Napoleons with Spicy Miso Dressing, 49
Tempura Shrimp Cocktail with Two Purees, 62–63
Wasabi Potato "Latkes," 180–82
Apple, Fuji, Salad, 180–82
Apples, Five-Spice, 209
Arctic Char, Seared, with Wild Mushroom Ragout and Truffle Oil, 121

Aromatics, types of, 3–5
Asian Gazpacho with Cilantro-Jicama Cream, 20–21
Asian Lacquered Poussin with Hoisin Lime Sauce, 196–97
Asian Pear Chutney, 194–95
Asian Pear "Maki," Prosciutto and, 55
Asian Pesto Grilled Shrimp, 100
Asian-Marinated Pork Loin with Gingered Sweet Potatoes and Five-Spice Apples, 144–45
Asparagus, Gingered Beef with Leeks and, 147
Asparagus Truffle Sauce, 168–69
Asparagus-Crusted Ahi Tuna with Asparagus Vinaigrette, 66–67
Avocado Puree, 62–63

Basil Mashed Potatoes, 218
Basil Oil, 231
Beans, green. *See* Haricots Verts
Beans, Long, Spicy Chinese, 206
Beef
Aromatic Braised Short Ribs with Napa Cabbage-Orzo Stew, 150–51
Five-Peppercorn Grilled Rib-Eye Steaks, 154–55
Gingered, with Leeks and Asparagus, 147
Ming's Pho, 16–17
Noodles, Sweet and Spicy, 90–91
Sandwiches, Mongolian, with Black Bean Aïoli, 148–49
Savory Braised Oxtail with Preserved Lemon Polenta, 152–53
and Shiitake Stew with Garlic Mashers, 156
Bell Pepper-Bacon Salsa, 22–23

Bittersweet Chocolate Cake with Cardamom Ice Cream and Chocolate Sauce, 264–65
Black Bean Aïoli, 148–49
Black Bean Mussels, Spicy, with Rice Stick Noodles, 108–9
Blue Ginger Sea Bass with Soba Noodle Sushi, 186–87
Bok Choy, Baby, Red-Roast Duck with, 136–37
Braised Chicken Curry with Yams, 126
Braised Chicken with Shiitakes and Snap Peas, 128–29
Braised Curried Lamb Shanks with Three-Onion Couscous, 160–61
Braised Triple Cabbage Lasagna, 210
Broth
Caramelized Sauternes Shallot, 177–79
Lemongrass, 188–90
Miso, with Tatsoi-Enoki Salad, 18–19
Sweet Pea, 50–51
Buns, Pan-Fried Chive and Shrimp, 44–45
Buns, Steamed Chicken and Shiitake, 42–43

Cabbage. *See also* Bok Choy; Napa
Alsatian Seared Duck Breast with Foie Gras Sauce, 191–93
Braised Triple, Lasagna, 210
Cake, Bittersweet Chocolate, with Cardamom Ice Cream and Chocolate Sauce, 264–65
Cake, East-West Spice, with Cardamom Cream, 252–53
Cake, Marble Sponge, 250
Candy, Ginger, 263
Cardamom Cream, 252–53

Cardamom Ice Cream, 262
Carrot Garlic Soup with Curry Potato Hash, 30–31
Carrot-Star Anise Syrup, 106–7
Caviars, Ahi Tuna Parfait with Two, 170–71
Celeriac and Roasted Garlic Soup with Wild Mushroom Ragout, 26–27
Cherries, Dried, Sake-Marinated, 248–49
Chicken
    Braised, Curry with Yams, 126
    Braised, with Shiitakes and Snap Peas, 128–29
    Chow Mein My Way, 92–93
    Classic Roast, with Sticky Rice Stuffing, 130–31
    Hoisin-Marinated, with Napa Slaw, 127
    and Shiitake Buns, Steamed, 42–43
    Stock, 14
Chile Oil, 230
Chile Paste, 116–17
Chile Skate Wings in Banana Leaves, 116–17
Chilean Sea Bass
    Blue Ginger, with Soba Noodle Sushi, 186–87
    Seafood Spring Roll Sticks, 56–57
    Spicy Fish Balls, 201
Chiles, types of, 6
Chili ingredients, 6
Chinese Fire Pot, 198–201
Chipotle Sweet Potato Soup with Bell Pepper-Bacon Salsa, 22–23
Chocolate Cake, Bittersweet, with Cardamom Ice Cream and Chocolate Sauce, 264–65
Chow Mein, Chicken, My Way, 92–93
Chutney, Asian Pear, 194–95
Chutney, Thai Quince, 241
Cilantro-Jicama Cream, 20–21
Citrus Brown Butter Vinaigrette, 118–19
Citrus Dipping Sauce, 235
Clam Broth, Lemongrass, Udon Noodles with, 88
Coconut and Mango, Glutinous Rice with, 251
Condiments, 3–5. See also Accompaniments

Corn Fritters, Oyster, with Two-Vinegar Emulsion, 60–61
Corn Lemongrass Soup with Lobster Salad, 28–29
Cornmeal-Crusted Skate and Pea Sprout Salad with Citrus Brown Butter Vinaigrette, 118–19
Couscous, Three-Onion, 208
Crab
    and Fennel Wontons with Mango-Lime Puree, 58–59
    Handrolls, Spicy, 80–81
    and Herb Salad Maki, 82
    Lemongrass Tartlettes, 40
    Tempura, Morel and, with a Kaffir Lime Broth, 172–73
    Wasabi Seafood Salad, 104–5
Cream, Cardamom, 252–53
Cream, Cilantro-Jicama, 20–21
Crème Brûlée, Tahitian Vanilla, 254–55
Crispy Onions, 212
Crispy Scallops with Carrot-Star Anise Syrup, 106–7
Cucumber Salad, Mirin, 112–13
Curried Lamb Shanks, Braised, with Three-Onion Couscous, 160–61
Curried Noodles, Shrimp, 89
Curry, Braised Chicken, with Yams, 126
Curry Oil, 230
Curry Paste, 240
Curry Potato Hash, 30–31

Dashi, 18–19
Desserts, 244–65
    Bittersweet Chocolate Cake with Cardamom Ice Cream and Chocolate Sauce, 264–65
    Cardamom Ice Cream (variation), 262
    East-West Spice Cake with Cardamom Cream, 252–53
    Glutinous Rice with Coconut and Mango, 251
    Green Tea Mousse with Sake-Marinated Dried Cherries, 248–49
    Homemade Ginger Ale Float with Lemongrass Ice Cream and Ginger Candy, 263
    Honey Sesame Tuiles, 256–57
    Jasmine Tea Soufflés, 260–61
    Lemongrass Ice Cream, 262

Lemongrass Parfait with Pineapple Salsa, 246–47
    Marble Sponge Cake, 250
    Tahitian Vanilla Crème Brûlée, 254–55
    Tropical Fruit Granité, with a Champagne Splash, 258–59
Dijon-Sambal Aïoli, 237
Dim Sum, 38–69
    Crab and Fennel Wontons with Mango-Lime Puree, 58–59
    Crab Lemongrass Tartlettes, 40
    Lobster and Mango Summer Rolls, 41
    Mushroom and Leek Spring Rolls with Mint Dipping Sauce, 52–53
    Oyster Corn Fritters with Two-Vinegar Emulsion, 60–61
    Pan-Fried Chive and Shrimp Buns, 44–45
    Pork and Ginger Pot Stickers with Spicy Soy Dipping Sauce, 46–48
    Prosciutto and Asian Pear "Maki," 55
    Rock Shrimp Lollipops with Spicy Almond Sauce, 68–69
    Salmon Roll Tempura, 54
    Seafood Spring Roll Sticks, 56–57
    Smoky Turkey Shu Mai in a Sweet Pea Broth, 50–51
    Steamed Chicken and Shiitake Buns, 42–43
Dipping Sauce, Citrus, 235
Dipping Sauce, Ginger, 234
Dipping Sauce, Mint, 234
Dipping Sauce, Spicy Soy, 233
Dressing, Spicy Miso, 49
Dried seaweed. See also Nori
    Dashi, 18–19
    Hijiki Salad, 213
    types of, 2
Duck, Red-Roast, with Baby Bok Choy, 136–37
Duck Breast, Alsatian Seared, with Foie Gras Sauce, 191–93
Duck Breasts, Achiote, with Sweet Potato Puree, Asian Pear Chutney, and Spiced Pecans, 194–95
Dumplings. See Buns; Pot Stickers; Shu Mai

East-West Spice Cake with Cardamom Cream, 252–53
Edamame Puree, Truffled, 177–79
Enoki Salad, Miso Broth with Tatsoi-, 18–19

Fennel Wontons, Crab and, with Mango-Lime Puree, 58–59
Fire Pot, Chinese, 198–201
First courses. *See also* Dim Sum; Soup
    Ahi Tuna Parfait with Two Caviars, 170–71
    Scallops on the Half Shell with Wasabi Lime Vinaigrette, 176
    Sticky Rice Pouches with Garlic-Flashed Scallops, 84–85
    Wild Mushroom Flan with Asparagus Truffle Sauce, 168–69
Fish. *See also specific fish*
    Balls, Spicy, 201
Five-Peppercorn Grilled Rib-Eye Steaks, 154–55
Five-Spice Apples, 209
Flan, Wild Mushroom, with Asparagus Truffle Sauce, 168–69
Flans, Truffled Shiitake, 188–90
Foie Gras and Morel Shu Mai with Caramelized Sauternes-Shallot Broth and Truffled Edamame Puree, 177–79
Foie Gras Mousse, 183–85
Foie Gras Sauce, 191–93
Fried rice. *See* Rice
Fritters, Oyster Corn, with Two-Vinegar Emulsion, 60–61
Fuji Apple Salad, 180–82

Garlic
    Basil Mashed Potatoes, 218
    Chive Mashers, Yukon Gold, 216
    -Flashed Scallops, Sticky Rice Pouches with, 84–85
    -Marinated Lamb Chops with Yukon Gold Garlic Chive Mashers, 157
    Mashers, 214
    Roasted, and Celeriac Soup with Wild Mushroom Ragout, 26–27

Roasted, and Sweet Potato Hash, 215
Soup, Carrot, with Curry Potato Hash, 30–31
Gazpacho, Asian, with Cilantro-Jicama Cream, 20–21
Ginger, Pickled, 238
Ginger Ale Float, Homemade, with Lemongrass Ice Cream and Ginger Candy, 263
Ginger Candy, 263
Ginger Dipping Sauce, 234
Gingered Beef with Leeks and Asparagus, 147
Gingered Spaghetti Squash, 183–85
Gingered Sweet Potatoes, 217
Glaze, Soy Ginger, 236
Glutinous Rice with Coconut and Mango, 251
Green beans. *See* Haricots Verts
Green Tea Mousse with Sake-Marinated Dried Cherries, 248–49
Grilled New Zealand Lamb Rack with Wild Mushroom Ragout and Basil Mashed Potatoes, 158–59
Grilled Ponzu-Marinated Snapper with Ginger Pea Sprout Salad, 110–11
Grilled Quail with Sambal and Braised Green Papaya, 134–35
Grilled Sushi Rice with Soy Ginger Glaze, 76

Halibut, Rice Paper-Wrapped, with Foie Gras Mousse and Gingered Spaghetti Squash, 183–85
Hamachi Sashimi, New, with Curry Oil, 64
Haricots Verts Chow Fun, Shrimp and, 86–87
Haricots Verts, Truffled, Seared Scallops with Sweet Potato Risotto and, 174–75
Hash, Curry Potato, 30–31
Hash, Roasted Garlic and Sweet Potato, 215
Herb-Crusted Trout with Shiitake Sticky Rice and Shiso Oil, 120
Hijiki Salad, 213

Hoisin Lime Sauce, 196–97
Hoisin Pork Tenderloin Sandwiches with Napa Slaw, 146
Hoisin-Marinated Chicken with Napa Slaw, 127
Honey Sesame Tuiles, 256–57
Hors d'oeuvres. *See* Appetizers
Hot and Sour Soup, Thai, with Shrimp Toast, 24–25

Ice Cream, Cardamom, 262
Ice Cream, Lemongrass, 262
Ingredients, pantry, 1–10

Jasmine Tea Soufflés, 260–61
Jicama Cream, Cilantro-, 20–21
Jicama Maki Sushi, Smoked Salmon and, 78–79

Lamb Chops, Garlic-Marinated, with Yukon Gold Garlic Chive Mashers, 157
Lamb Rack, Grilled New Zealand, with Wild Mushroom Ragout and Basil Mashed Potatoes, 158–59
Lamb Shanks, Braised Curried, with Three-Onion Couscous, 160–61
Lasagna, Braised Triple Cabbage, 210
"Latkes," Wasabi Potato, 180–82
Leek(s)
    and Asparagus, Gingered Beef with, 147
    and Mushroom Spring Rolls with Mint Dipping Sauce, 52–53
    Salmon Roll Tempura, 54
Lemon Basmati Rice, 223
Lemongrass
    Broth, 188–90
    Ice Cream, 262
    Parfait with Pineapple Salsa, 246–47
    Tartlettes, Crab, 40
Lemons, Preserved, 239
Lobster
    in Lemongrass Broth with Truffled Shiitake Flans, 188–90
    and Mango Summer Rolls, 41
    Salad, 28–29
    Wasabi Seafood Salad, 104–5
Long Beans, Spicy Chinese, 206

INDEX

Maki. *See* Rolls
Mango(es)
   Glutinous Rice with Coconut and, 251
   -Lime Puree, 58–59
   and Lobster Summer Rolls, 41
   Pineapple Sauce, 114–15
   Spicy Shrimp with, and Snow Pea Salad, 101
Marble Sponge Cake, 250
Meat. *See specific types*
Ming's Pho, 16–17
Mint Dipping Sauce, 234
Mirin Cucumber Salad, 112–13
Miso Broth with Tatsoi-Enoki Salad, 18–19
Miso Dressing, Spicy, 49
Mongolian Beef Sandwiches with Black Bean Aïoli, 148–49
Morel and Crab Tempura with a Kaffir Lime Broth, 172–73
Morel Shu Mai, Foie Gras and, with Caramelized Sauternes-Shallot Broth and Truffled Edamame Puree, 177–79
Mousse, Foie Gras, 183–85
Mousse, Green Tea, with Sake-Marinated Dried Cherries, 248–49
Mushroom(s). *See also* Morel; Shiitake(s); Truffle(d)
   and Leek Spring Rolls with Mint Dipping Sauce, 52–53
   Miso Broth with Tatsoi-Enoki Salad, 18–19
   Wild, Flan with Asparagus Truffle Sauce, 168–69
   Wild, Ragout, 211
Mussel Soup, Thai-Spiced, with Leeks and Carrot Spaghetti, 34–35
Mussels, Spicy Black Bean, with Rice Stick Noodles, 108–9
Mustard Oil, 228
Mustard Sauce, 154–55

Napa Cabbage-Orzo Stew, Aromatic Braised Short Ribs with, 150–51
Napa Slaw, 207
Napoleons, Spinach Tofu, with Spicy Miso Dressing, 49

Noodle(s)
   Beef, Sweet and Spicy, 90–91
   Chicken Chow Mein My Way, 92–93
   Chow Fun, Shrimp and Haricots Verts, 86–87
   Ming's Pho, 16–17
   Rice Stick, Spicy Black Bean Mussels with, 108–9
   Shrimp Curried, 89
   Soba, and Poached Prawn Salad, 94–95
   Soba, Sushi, 186–87
   types of, 2–3
   Udon, with Lemongrass Clam Broth, 88
Nori
   Crab and Herb Salad Maki, 82
   Salmon Roll Tempura, 54
   Shiitake and Spinach Ura Maki, 77
   Smoked Salmon and Jicama Maki Sushi, 78–79
   Spicy Crab Handrolls, 80–81

Oils, 1
   Basil, 231
   Chile, 230
   Curry, 230
   Mustard, 228
   Parsley, 232
   Scallion, 229
   Wasabi, 228
Onion Couscous, Three-, 208
Onion Soup, Many, with Steamed Coriander Scallops, 32–33
Onions, Crispy, 212
Orzo-Napa Cabbage Stew, Aromatic Braised Short Ribs with, 150–51
Oxtail, Savory Braised, with Preserved Lemon Polenta, 152–53
Oyster Corn Fritters with Two-Vinegar Emulsion, 60–61

Pan-Fried Chive and Shrimp Buns, 44–45
Pantry ingredients, 1–10
Parfait, Lemongrass, with Pineapple Salsa, 246–47
Parsley Oil, 232
Parsnip Puree and Parsley Oil, Spiced Venison with, 162–63
Paste, Chile, 116–17
Paste, Curry, 240

Pea Sprout Salad, Cornmeal-Crusted Skate and, with Citrus Brown Butter Vinaigrette, 118–19
Pea Sprout Salad, Gingered, Grilled Ponzu-Marinated Snapper with, 110–11
Pears. *See* Asian Pear
Pea(s)
   Broth, Sweet, 50–51
   Snap, Braised Chicken with Shiitakes and, 128–29
   Snow, Salad, Spicy Shrimp with Mangoes and, 101
   Three-, Fried Rice, Turkey Breast with, 138–39
Pecans, Spiced, 194–95
Pesto Grilled Shrimp, Asian, 100
Pho, Ming's, 16–17
Pickled Ginger, 238
Pineapple Salsa, 246–47
Pineapple Sauce, Mango, 114–15
Poached Prawn and Soba Noodle Salad, 94–95
Polenta, Preserved Lemon, 222
Pomegranate-Marinated Squab with Thai Quince Chutney, 132–33
Ponzu-Marinated Snapper, Grilled, with Ginger Pea Sprout Salad, 110–11
Pork and Ginger Pot Stickers with Spicy Soy Dipping Sauce, 46–48
Pork Loin, Asian-Marinated, with Gingered Sweet Potatoes and Five-Spice Apples, 144–45
Pork Tenderloin Sandwiches, Hoisin, with Napa Slaw, 146
Pot Stickers, Pork and Ginger, with Spicy Soy Dipping Sauce, 46–48
Potato(es). *See also* Sweet Potato(es); Yams
   Alsatian Seared Duck Breast with Foie Gras Sauce, 191–93
   Basil Mashed, 218
   Garlic Mashers, 214
   Hash, Curry, 30–31
   "Latkes," Wasabi, 180–82
   Spinach, and Shiitake Gratin, 221
   Yukon Gold Garlic Chive Mashers, 216

Poultry. *See specific type*
Poussin, Asian Lacquered, with
    Hoisin Lime Sauce, 196–97
Prawn, Poached, and Soba
    Noodle Salad, 94–95
Preserved Lemon Polenta, 222
Preserved Lemons, 239
Prosciutto and Asian Pear
    "Maki," 55
Puree, Avocado, 62–63
Puree, Mango-Lime, 58–59
Puree, Parsnip, 162–63
Puree, Tomato, 62–63
Puree, Truffled Edamame,
    177–79

Quail, Grilled, with Sambal and
    Braised Green Papaya,
    134–35
Quince Chutney, Thai, 241

Ragout, Wild Mushroom, 211
Red Snapper, Whole Crispy,
    with Mango Pineapple
    Sauce and Spicy Chinese
    Long Beans, 114–15
Red-Roast Duck with Baby Bok
    Choy, 136–37
Rib-Eye Steaks, Five-Pepper-
    corn Grilled, 154–55
Rice. *See also* Sushi Rice
    Basmati, Lemon, 223
    Chile Skate Wings in Banana
        Leaves, 116–17
    Fried, Three-Pea, Turkey
        Breast with, 138–39
    Fried, Traditional Mandarin,
        83
    Glutinous, with Coconut and
        Mango, 251
    types of, 3
Rice cookers, 73
Rice Paper-Wrapped Halibut
    with Foie Gras Mousse
    and Gingered Spaghetti
    Squash, 183–85
Risotto, Sweet Potato, 220
Roasted Garlic and Celeriac
    Soup with Wild Mushroom
    Ragout, 26–27
Roasted Garlic and Sweet
    Potato Hash, 215
Rock Shrimp Lollipops with
    Spicy Almond Sauce, 68–69
Rolls. *See also* Buns
    Crab and Herb Salad Maki, 82
    Prosciutto and Asian Pear
        "Maki," 55

Salmon Roll Tempura, 54
Seafood Spring Roll Sticks,
    56–57
Shiitake and Spinach Ura
    Maki, 77
Smoked Salmon and Jicama
    Maki Sushi, 78–79
Soba Noodle Sushi, 186–87
Spicy Crab Handrolls, 80–81
Spring, Mushroom and Leek,
    with Mint Dipping Sauce,
    52–53
Summer, Lobster and
    Mango, 41

Sake-Marinated Dried Cher-
    ries, 248–49
Salad
    Fuji Apple, 180–82
    Hijiki, 213
    Lobster, 28–29
    Maki, Crab and Herb, 82
    Mirin Cucumber, 112–13
    Napa Slaw, 207
    Poached Prawn and Soba
        Noodle, 94–95
    Wasabi Seafood, 104–5
Salmon, Smoked, and Jicama
    Maki Sushi, 78–79
Salmon, Tea-Smoked, with
    Wasabi Potato "Latkes"
    and Fuji Apple Salad,
    180–82
Salmon, Teriyaki, with Mirin
    Cucumber Salad, 112–13
Salmon Roll Tempura, 54
Salsa, Bell Pepper-Bacon,
    22–23
Salsa, Pineapple, 246–47
Sandwiches, Hoisin Pork Ten-
    derloin, with Napa Slaw,
    146
Sandwiches, Mongolian Beef,
    with Black Bean Aïoli,
    148–49
Sashimi, New Hamachi, with
    Curry Oil, 64
Sauce. *See also* Dipping Sauce;
    Puree; Salsa
    Asparagus Truffle, 168–69
    Cardamom Cream, 252–53
    Carrot-Star Anise Syrup,
        106–7
    Chocolate, 264–65
    Cilantro-Jicama Cream,
        20–21
    Citrus Brown Butter Vinai-
        grette, 118–19

Foie Gras, 191–93
Hoisin Lime, 196–97
Mango Pineapple, 114–15
Mustard, 154–55
Pesto, 100
Soy Ginger Glaze, 236
Soy Syrup, 236
Spicy Almond, 68–69
Spicy Miso Dressing, 49
Two-Vinegar Emulsion, 60–61
Wasabi Lime Vinaigrette, 176
Scallion Oil, 229
Scallops
    Crispy, with Carrot-Star
        Anise Syrup, 106–7
    Garlic-Flashed, Sticky Rice
        Pouches with, 84–85
    on the Half Shell with
        Wasabi Lime Vinaigrette,
        176
    Seafood Spring Roll Sticks,
        56–57
    Seared, with Sweet Potato
        Risotto and Truffled Hari-
        cots Verts, 174–75
    Steamed Coriander, Many
        Onion Soup with, 32–33
Sea bass. *See* Chilean Sea
    Bass
Seafood. *See also specific
    types*
    Salad, Wasabi, 104–5
    Spring Roll Sticks, 56–57
Seared Arctic Char with Wild
    Mushroom Ragout and
    Truffle Oil, 121
Seared Scallops with Sweet
    Potato Risotto and Truffled
    Haricots Verts, 174–75
Seasonings. *See also* Condi-
    ments; Sauce
    types of, 3–6
Seaweed. *See* Dried Seaweed;
    Nori
Sesame Tuiles, Honey, 256–57
Shanghai Noodles, Shrimp and
    Haricots Verts, 86–87
Shellfish. *See specific shellfish*
Shiitake(s)
    and Beef Stew with Garlic
        Mashers, 156
    Buns, Steamed Chicken and,
        42–43
    Chicken Chow Mein My Way,
        92–93
    Flans, Truffled, 188–90
    Potato, and Spinach Gratin,
        221

Shiitake(s) (cont.)
 and Snap Peas, Braised
  Chicken with, 128–29
 and Spinach Ura Maki, 77
 Sticky Rice and Shiso Oil,
  Herb-Crusted Trout with,
  120
Short Ribs, Aromatic Braised,
 with Napa Cabbage-Orzo
 Stew, 150–51
Shrimp
 Asian Pesto Grilled, 100
 Buns, Pan-Fried Chive and,
  44–45
 Cocktail, Tempura, with Two
  Purees, 62–63
 Curried Noodles, 89
 and Haricots Verts Chow
  Fun, 86–87
 Rock, Lollipops with Spicy
  Almond Sauce, 68–69
 Seafood Spring Roll Sticks,
  56–57
 Spicy, with Mangoes and
  Snow Pea Salad, 101
 Toast, 24–25
 Wasabi Seafood Salad, 104–5
 Wok-Flashed Salt and Pep-
  per, with Lemon Basmati
  Rice, 102–3
Shu Mai, Foie Gras and Morel,
 with Caramelized
 Sauternes-Shallot Broth
 and Truffled Edamame
 Puree, 177–79
Shu Mai, Smoky Turkey, in a
 Sweet Pea Broth, 50–51
Sides, 204–23
 Basil Mashed Potatoes, 218
 Braised Triple Cabbage
  Lasagna, 210
 Crispy Onions, 212
 Five-Spice Apples, 209
 Garlic Mashers, 214
 Gingered Spaghetti Squash,
  183–85
 Gingered Sweet Potatoes, 217
 Hijiki Salad, 213
 Lemon Basmati Rice, 223
 Napa Slaw, 207
 Potato, Spinach, and Shiitake
  Gratin, 221
 Preserved Lemon Polenta,
  222
 Roasted Garlic and Sweet
  Potato Hash, 215
 Spicy Chinese Long Beans,
  206

Sweet Potato Crisps, 219
Sweet Potato Risotto, 220
Three-Onion Couscous, 208
Truffled Edamame Puree,
 177–79
Truffled Haricots Verts,
 174–75
Truffled Shiitake Flans,
 188–90
Wasabi Potato "Latkes,"
 180–82
Wild Mushroom Flan with
 Asparagus Truffle Sauce,
 168–69
Wild Mushroom Ragout,
 211
Yukon Gold Garlic Chive
 Mashers, 216
Skate, Cornmeal-Crusted, and
 Pea Sprout Salad with Cit-
 rus Brown Butter Vinai-
 grette, 118–19
Skate Wings, Chile, in Banana
 Leaves, 116–17
Slaw, Napa, 207
Smoked Salmon and Jicama
 Maki Sushi, 78–79
Smoky Turkey Shu Mai in a
 Sweet Pea Broth, 50–51
Snap peas. See Pea(s)
Snapper, Grilled Ponzu-Mari-
 nated, with Ginger Pea
 Sprout Salad, 110–11
Snapper, Whole Crispy Red,
 with Mango Pineapple
 Sauce and Spicy Chinese
 Long Beans, 114–15
Snow peas. See Pea(s)
Soba Noodle Salad, Poached
 Prawn and, 94–95
Soba Noodle Sushi, 186–87
Soufflés, Jasmine Tea,
 260–61
Soup, 12–35. See also Broth;
 Stock
 Asian Gazpacho with
  Cilantro-Jicama Cream,
  20–21
 Carrot Garlic, with Curry
  Potato Hash, 30–31
 Chipotle Sweet Potato, with
  Bell Pepper-Bacon Salsa,
  22–23
 Corn Lemongrass, with Lob-
  ster Salad, 28–29
 Many Onion, with Steamed
  Coriander Scallops,
  32–33

Ming's Pho, 16–17
Roasted Garlic and Celeriac,
 with Wild Mushroom
 Ragout, 26–27
Thai Hot and Sour, with
 Shrimp Toast, 24–25
Thai-Spiced Mussel, with
 Leeks and Carrot
 Spaghetti, 34–35
Soy Dipping Sauce, Spicy, 233
Soy Ginger Glaze, 236
Soy Syrup, 236
Spaghetti Squash, Gingered,
 183–85
Spiced Pecans, 194–95
Spiced Venison with Parsnip
 Puree and Parsley Oil,
 162–63
Spinach, Potato, and Shiitake
 Gratin, 221
Spinach Tofu Napoleons with
 Spicy Miso Dressing, 49
Spinach Ura Maki, Shiitake
 and, 77
Spring rolls. See Rolls
Squab, Pomegranate-Mari-
 nated, with Thai Quince
 Chutney, 132–33
Stew. See also Ragout
 Beef and Shiitake, with Gar-
  lic Mashers, 156
 Napa Cabbage-Orzo, Aro-
  matic Braised Short Ribs
  with, 150–51
Sticky Rice Pouches with Gar-
 lic-Flashed Scallops,
 84–85
Stock, Chicken, 14
Stock, Dashi, 18–19
Stock, Vegetable, 15
Summer Rolls, Lobster and
 Mango, 41
Sushi, Smoked Salmon and
 Jicama Maki, 78–79
Sushi, Soba Noodle, 186–87
Sushi Rice, 74–75
 Classic Roast Chicken with
  Sticky Rice Stuffing,
  130–31
 Crab and Herb Salad Maki,
  82
 Grilled, with Soy Ginger
  Glaze, 76
 Herb-Crusted Trout with
  Shiitake Sticky Rice and
  Shiso Oil, 120
 Shiitake and Spinach Ura
  Maki, 77

Smoked Salmon and Jicama Maki Sushi, 78–79
Spicy Crab Handrolls, 80–81
Sticky Rice Pouches with Garlic-Flashed Scallops, 84–85
Sweet and Spicy Beef Noodles, 90–91
Sweet Pea Broth, 50–51
Sweet Potato(es). *See also* Yams
    Chipotle Soup with Bell Pepper-Bacon Salsa, 22–23
    Crisps, 219
    Gingered, 217
    Hash, Roasted Garlic and, 215
    Risotto, 220
Syrup, Carrot-Star Anise, 106–7
Syrup, Soy, 236

Tahitian Vanilla Crème Brûlée, 254–55
Tartlettes, Crab Lemongrass, 40
Tatsoi-Enoki Salad, Miso Broth with, 18–19
Tea, Jasmine, Soufflés, 260–61
Tea-Smoked Salmon with Wasabi Potato "Latkes" and Fuji Apple Salad, 180–82
Tempura, Morel and Crab, with a Kaffir Lime Broth, 172–73

Tempura, Salmon Roll, 54
Tempura Shrimp Cocktail with Two Purees, 62–63
Teriyaki Salmon with Mirin Cucumber Salad, 112–13
Thai Hot and Sour Soup with Shrimp Toast, 24–25
Thai Quince Chutney, 241
Thai-Spiced Mussel Soup with Leeks and Carrot Spaghetti, 34–35
Three-Onion Couscous, 208
Toast, Shrimp, 24–25
Tofu Napoleons, Spinach, with Spicy Miso Dressing, 49
Tomato Puree, 62–63
Tropical Fruit Granité, with a Champagne Splash, 258–59
Trout, Herb-Crusted, with Shiitake Sticky Rice and Shiso Oil, 120
Truffle(d)
    Edamame Puree, 177–79
    Haricots Verts, Seared Scallops with Sweet Potato Risotto and, 174–75
    Sauce, Asparagus, 168–69
    Shiitake Flans, 188–90
Tuiles, Honey Sesame, 256–57
Turkey Breast with Three-Pea Fried Rice, 138–39
Turkey Shu Mai, Smoky, in a Sweet Pea Broth, 50–51
Two-Vinegar Emulsion, 60–61

Udon Noodles with Lemongrass Clam Broth, 88

Vegetable Stock, 15
Vegetables. *See specific vegetable*
Venison, Spiced, with Parsnip Puree and Parsley Oil, 162–63
Vinaigrette, Citrus Brown Butter, 118–19
Vinaigrette, Wasabi Lime, 176
Vinegars, types of, 1

Wasabi Lime Vinaigrette, 176
Wasabi Oil, 228
Wasabi Potato "Latkes," 180–82
Wasabi Seafood Salad, 104–5
Wild mushrooms. *See* Mushroom(s)
Wok-Flashed Salt and Pepper Shrimp with Lemon Basmati Rice, 102–3
Wontons, Crab and Fennel, with Mango-Lime Puree, 58–59
Wrappers, 1–2

Yams. *See also* Sweet Potato(es)
    Braised Chicken Curry with, 126
Yukon Gold Garlic Chive Mashers, 216

Conversion Chart

Equivalent Imperial and Metric Measurements

American cooks use standard containers, the 8-ounce cup and a tablespoon that takes exactly 16 level fillings to fill that cup level. Measuring by cup makes it very difficult to give weight equivalents, as a cup of densely packed butter will weigh considerably more than a cup of flour. The easiest way therefore to deal with cup measurements in recipes is to take the amount by volume rather than by weight. Thus the equation reads:

1 cup = 240 ml = 8 fl. oz.
½ cup = 120 ml = 4 fl. oz.

It is possible to buy a set of American cup measures in major stores around the world.

In the United States, butter is often measured in sticks. One stick is the equivalent of 8 tablespoons. One tablespoon of butter is therefore the equivalent to ½ ounce/15 grams.

LIQUID MEASURES

Fluid Ounces	U.S.	Imperial	Milliliters
	1 teaspoon	1 teaspoon	5
¼	2 teaspoons	1 dessertspoon	10
½	1 tablespoon	1 tablespoon	14
1	2 tablespoons	2 tablespoons	28
2	¼ cup	4 tablespoons	56
4	½ cup		110
5		¼ pint or 1 gill	140
6	¾ cup		170
8	1 cup		225
9			250, ¼ liter
10	1¼ cups	½ pint	280
12	1½ cups		340
15		¾ pint	420
16	2 cups		450
18	2¼ cups		500, ½ liter
20	2½ cups	1 pint	560
24	3 cups		675
25		1¼ pints	700
27	3½ cups		750
30	3¾ cups	1½ pints	840
32	4 cups or 1 quart		900
35		1¾ pints	980
36	4½ cups		1000, 1 liter
40	5 cups	2 pints or 1 quart	1120

SOLID MEASURES

U.S. and Imperial Measures		Metric Measures	
Ounces	Pounds	Grams	Kilos
1		28	
2		56	
3½		100	
4	¼	112	
5		140	
6		168	
8	½	225	
9		250	¼
12	¾	340	
16	1	450	
18		500	½
20	1¼	560	
24	1½	675	
27		750	¾
28	1¾	780	
32	2	900	
36	2¼	1000	1
40	2½	1100	
48	3	1350	
54		1500	1½

OVEN TEMPERATURE EQUIVALENTS

Fahrenheit	Celsius	Gas Mark	Description
225	110	¼	Cool
250	130	½	
275	140	1	Very Slow
300	150	2	
325	170	3	Slow
350	180	4	Moderate
375	190	5	
400	200	6	Moderately Hot
425	220	7	Fairly Hot
450	230	8	Hot
475	240	9	Very Hot
500	250	10	Extremely Hot

Any broiling recipes can be used with the grill of the oven, but beware of high-temperature grills.

EQUIVALENTS FOR INGREDIENTS

all-purpose flour—plain flour
coarse salt—kitchen salt
cornstarch—cornflour
eggplant—aubergine

half and half—12% fat milk
heavy cream—double cream
light cream—single cream
lima beans—broad beans

scallion—spring onion
unbleached flour—strong, white flour
zest—rind
zucchini—courgettes or marrow